Harry Pearson has led a richly rewarding, thrilling and romantic life. Despite being described by Anaïs Nin as 'the most powerful masculine creative force of this or any other century', he remains a down-to-earth and modest man, who never discusses his colourful past in public because he knows that to do so would drive ordinary persons insane with jealousy.

A regular contributor to King Baudouin of Belgium's favourite football magazine, *When Saturday Comes*, Pearson is the author of one previous masterpiece, *The Far Corner*, which was runner-up for the 1995 William Hill Sports Book of the Year Award and topped the bestseller list in Spennymoor for several days. Last time his parents checked, it had been borrowed from Barnard Castle library *seventeen times*.

Shorter in real life than on the printed page, Harry Pearson refuses to believe that the world is a great big onion, and prefers to think of it as just a very, very large shallot.

Also by Harry Pearson

THE FAR CORNER

Racing Pigs and Giant Marrows

*Travels Around
the North Country Fairs*

HARRY PEARSON

[signature]
December 1997

ABACUS

An *Abacus* Book

First published as *North Country Fair*
in 1966 by Little, Brown and Company
This edition published by Abacus in 1997

Reprinted 1997

PICTURE CREDITS
1: Fritz Prenzel/Bruce Coleman Ltd;
2: Mike Maidment; 3 & 6: Museum of Lakeland Life
and Industry, Kendal; 4, 5 & 15: Popperfoto/Reuter;
7 & 8: North of England Open Air Museum, Beamish;
9: *Hexham Courant*; 10, 11 & 14: Topham Picture Point;
12: John Daniels; 13: Jane Burton/Bruce Coleman Ltd;
16: North News & Pictures

A CIP catalogue record for this book
is available from the British Library.

ISBN: 0 349 10946 X

Typeset by Solidus (Bristol) Limited
Printed and bound in Great Britain by
Clays Ltd, St Ives plc

Abacus
A Division of
Little, Brown and Company (UK)
Brettenham House
Lancaster Place
London WC2E 7EN

For my mother and father:
two champion growers

· Contents ·

· Preface ·

During the writing of *The Far Corner* I made an agreement with myself in a bus shelter in West Durham that the next book I wrote would not necessitate hanging about out of doors on days so cold that itinerant dogs had to be detached from lamp-posts by firemen. The next book I wrote would be about the summer. I had a slight problem with this, however, because although I associated the winter with football, I associated the summer with something much less distinct. When I thought about summer the overwhelming feeling I had was of being in an atmosphere made stuffy with the odour of trodden grass, of light filtering through canvas, of women in hats, of a faint humming and a pronounced animal smell. I thought at first that this had something to do with my school open days: the marquee, the mothers, the fathers snoring through the ex-pupil's speech, adolescent feet. Thankfully, it wasn't open days which sparked this sensory nostalgia, it was Egton Show in North Yorkshire. The humming came from sozzled bees in nectar-rich lime trees, the animal smell from the animals.

I had visited Egton Show regularly as a boy, and Stokesley Fair, too. The show at Stokesley fell on the final Saturday of Fair Week. If I had ever taken the trouble during childhood to compose a list of my ten favourite events, Stokesley Fair would have finished somewhere near the top – below Christmas and my birthday, but well above Hallowe'en. (Hallowe'en was always something of a disappointment to me. My friends and I would make turnip lanterns and go round the houses of the village, knocking on doors and asking, 'Have you got any money for Hallowe'en?' If people had any money the idea was that they should give it to us. Invariably, though, they simply said, 'Yes, thanks,' and shut the door in our faces. We were lucky if we broke even on the turnips.)

Stokesley Fair was held in mid-September, two weeks into the school autumn term. Throughout the dog-days of summer it stood out as a beacon of light in a dark future of long division, hymn practice and overcooked cabbage. At Stokesley Fair all this horrific mundanity was put aside. There you could fire air rifles, throw darts, be spun around at high speed until you were dizzy and eat a hot dog with fried onions, ketchup *and* brown sauce. When I recalled Stokesley Fair I got a warm feeling in my chest, a mixture of nostalgia and heartburn.

I decided that this would be my summer book. I would go off to shows and fairs and write about the swollen vegetables, the waltzers, the Welsh cakes and the prize-winning cattle and sheep. Here, though, I hit a slight snag, because by some huge effort of will I had managed to live in the country for nearly twenty-five years without learning anything whatsoever about farming in general and farm animals in particular. I think part of my reluctance to know anything about livestock again came down to my schooldays. At my school there were two types of boys: farmers' sons and us. The farmers' sons were a breed apart. They were level-headed, rooted in the earth, seemingly untouched by dreams of glory or glamour. Their rooms were decorated not with posters of Charlie's Angels or Charlie George, but with pictures of Hereford cattle and combine harvesters. They didn't like football or take any interest in music. When they defaced a school desk it was with the words Charolais or Massey-Ferguson rather than Slade or LUFC. Asked to name the car you would most like to own we said Ferrari, Lamborghini, Lotus; the farmers' sons said Volvo. As a consequence I came subconsciously to associate a knowledge of farm animals with the collapse of all ambition. Livestock were commonplace and seemingly unworthy of my attention.

Nowadays I feel differently. The revelation came on a train in Belgium. Passing through a commuter village near Brussels I noticed that in the back gardens of several of the neat bungalows there were tiny herds of miniature Oriental deer. So excited was I by this sight that I pointed it out to the man sitting opposite me, a gaunt Flandrian businessman. If I had demonstrated to him that I could wiggle my fingers and toes simultaneously he would have shown more interest. 'Of course,' he said, without looking up from his newspaper. Often it is the things we take for granted the most which are the strangest of all.

Thus were the seeds of this book: because I wanted to know something about the world in which I grew up; to return to a few of the things I had enjoyed as a child; and finally, but most of all, because I wanted to be warm. I have tried to organise my chapters thematically, but some subjects refuse to be so easily confined. You won't, for example, find sheep only in the chapter on Masham Sheep Fair. As is their nature, the sheep wander everywhere.

For the germination and fruiting of the book, bright rays of insight and the gentle patter of summery anecdotes were supplied by: Oliver Armstrong, Catherine Barraclough, Annie Coulthard, Tracey Curwen, Karen Lloyd, William and Caroline Pym, Claudia Rankin, Percy Telfer and Hugh Walton.

The plant rooted in a rich bed of farming and specialist literature, the most important elements of which were: *A Short History of British Farming* by Ralph Whitlock; Kenneth Hudson's *Patriotism with Profit*; *The Travelling People* by Duncan Dallas; Cornelius Walford's *Fairs, Past and Present* and *Animals on the Farm* by Judy Urquhart.

Responsibility for the over-liberal top-dressing of horse manure is the author's alone.

1

· Beginnings ·

Stagshaw Bank Fair

Winter dragged on. Rain the colour and consistency of cuckoo-spit splattered the windows, turned the slop-green fields to ooze. The wind moaned. Daylight was a chalk stripe on charcoal cloth; spring a rumour. And word had it that the sun had run off with the cricket season and opened an antique shop in Marbella. The doors and curtains of the north country were firmly closed. Nobody went out if they could help it. Even the youths with the scrunched-up faces and the warm-up coats who loitered around the bus stations, cans of superlager welded to their fists, fags clamped between their teeth as if they were the noses of mortal enemies, had stopped at home. Even the girls who giggled with them and stuck rigidly to crop-tops though hail was pitting the pavements and cracking the paint off pillar boxes had gone to bingo with their mams. Even the Geordies were wearing jumpers.

It was cold. Not that early-winter-late-autumn aesthetically pleasing cold. Not that say-are-you-listenin' pre-Christmas cold, when frost stains the barley stubble the colour of pewter, beads of dew freeze in cobwebs and glint in the pale morning sunlight like pearls, and you crunch the icy pavements with a smile on your face, a song in your heart and a massive wad of credit-card receipts in your pocket. No, this was back-end cold. This was post-turkey-all-the-toys-are-broken-and-that-puppy's-piddled-on-the-carpet-once-too-often cold; time-to-pay-the-bills cold. This was the kind of cold that wormed its way in through keyholes, slithered under draught-excluders, slipped up jumpers, slid between buttons and seeped through your skin until your knees creaked, your ankles popped and your knuckles felt like they'd been replaced with ping-pong balls. This was a cold that prised open your psyche and sat on your subconscious like a black toupee.

Outdoors you wore so many layers of clothing that you could not bend your limbs. Farm labourers and dog-walkers clumped forwards out of the drifting greyness, pale-faced, arms out-stretched, stiff-legged, like zombies from *The Night of the Living Dead*. Indoors, condensation clouded the windows, and dogs steamed by radiators giving off a stench of stagnant swamps. Damp garments hung from every hook and hand rail; clothes horses buckled beneath the weight of drying laundry and had to be humanely destroyed. Fires flickered in grates, burning off the oxygen in sealed living rooms until the heavy atmosphere hung from the inhabitants' eyelids and they became as torpid as tortoises. No one said much. No one did much. No one moved. This was winter in the north; a time for contemplation, for reflection, for taking stock, for ... zzzzz.

In late February there was a respite. The sleet stopped and the sun peered blearily from behind a cloud. Song thrushes cleared their throats and crocuses raised their heads nervously from the earth, like soldiers during an uneasy truce. No one was fooled. This brief lifting of the trap-door happened every year. It was the northern equivalent of the halcyon days, that lull between the winter storms when, the Greeks believed, the kingfisher, or halcyon, laid its eggs in nests of twigs built on the Mediterranean waves. In fact, of course, the kingfisher lays its eggs in spring, and does so in a muddy burrow in a riverbank that smells of rotting fish. Acknowledging this would, however, have detracted from the radiant loveliness of the bird, and the Greeks are a romantic people who prize beauty above all. How else can you explain Demis Roussos?

As a pennant of blue sky unfurled over the Pennines, we jimmied open our windows, unbolted our doors, shovelled out the old air and laid in some fresh, shook crumbs of stale conversations from the clip rugs and stood around blinking in the sun like moles. A couple of hours later, still reeling slightly from the heady cocktail of oxygen and natural light, I was standing on Stagshaw Bank, where the red light on the radio transmitter flashed and the russet-and-blonde plaid hills rolled down into the green of the Tyne Valley. Now the land was crossed by tarmac roads, partitioned by dry-stone walls, but once it had been one vast and open field, a common grazing ground: site of the biggest fair in northern England.

No one is exactly sure when Stagshaw Bank Fair began. Certainly it was before 1200; in all probability long before. Stagshaw Bank was close by a customs gate on Hadrian's Wall, adjacent to Dere Street, the main Roman highway linking north and south. Corbridge, once a large Roman settlement, lies in the valley a few miles below. Like hens and dormice and the thumbs-up gesture, fairs are part of Rome's legacy to Britain. The rural Roman worked for eight days and took the ninth off. (Later Jehovah would undercut this with a six-and-one deal which effectively wiped out his pagan rivals. Jehovah clearly had a good grasp of human psychology. I mean, who's going to work two extra days a week just for the right to make human sacrifices to a gnarled tree?) *Nundinae* was the day the agrarian population came into town to hear the laws proclaimed and the decrees of the people announced; it was a *feria*, a holiday. It was also an opportunity for them to sell their produce, though according to Macrobius, the busiest trade was in sexual favours. Whether these were particularly cultivated in the countryside, perhaps as part of some early crop-rotation system, he neglects to say. Nevertheless the image of a Roman landowner pointing to a field and saying, 'Next year, Quintus, I want this all turned over to frottage' to some burr-headed peasant is too appealing to be ignored.

Originally *Nundinae* was held only in Rome itself, but gradually the tradition spread throughout the Empire, wherever there were citizens of sufficient power and privilege to be granted licence by the chief magistrate to hold such festivals. Impromptu markets would have taken place too, particularly in areas like those close to the wall, where border controls funnelled people together and dealers and merchants regularly crossed paths. These more-or-less spontaneous gatherings must have offered too opportune a target for the order-conscious Romans to miss. Outlawing them would have been troublesome: recognizing them allowed for legislation and restrictions; the establishment of special courts called *fora* to deal with the misdemeanours that inevitably occurred when travelling salesman, hucksters and the rural population met; taxation, censuses, passport checks and numerous other things to delight the hearts of the bureaucrats. The Romans were keen on bureaucracy, and the Roman army, like all armies, was keener on it still. The wall was a military zone. This might have been the outer edge of the Empire, but things here were still done by the book. Further west, on the crags near Housesteads Fort, there is a milecastle. Hadrian and his generals had decreed that all milecastles must have a gate opening north and south, and this milecastle is no exception. However, any soldier or civilian stepping out of the north gate would have found himself treading air above a sixty-foot drop. A pointless, not to say dangerous, aperture, but orders are orders. Compromise here, and the next thing you knew the legionaries would be going native, wearing socks under their sandals and turning up their noses at garlic.

The Brigantes, the Celtic tribe of the Pennines whose lands the wall sliced in half, would, I think, have come to the fairs and markets that sprung up around the customs posts. The Celts were great stockmen. Beef from their fierce white cattle which roamed, semi-wild, in the thickly wooded hills, scaring the living daylights out of passersby; milk from their short-legged, black dairy herds and mutton from their sheep – a tiny, brown creature similar to the modern Soay, with horns that curved outwards from its head like the handles on a space-hopper – all would have been in great demand at the garrison posts. On the days designated by their putative rulers, the Celts drove their herds to the fair sites, met up with friends and relations from 'across the border', exchanged news, traded livestock and grumbled about the weather and how cheap foreign imports were ruining their livelihood. There would have been stalls selling herbs and spices, sweetmeats, beer and wine, and, in all probability, traditional crafts.

Have you noticed that there are some nouns that never appear in the English language without a particular adjective or pronoun attached to them? Bread is unfailingly 'crusty', peas are 'garden', ice-cream is 'dairy' and crafts are always 'traditional'. You might think that there are some crafts which are non-traditional – bond-dealing, perhaps, or partition-walling, or air-brushing pictures of large-breasted Nordic maidens on to the bonnets of Firebird Trans-Ams – but I wouldn't be so sure. Some years ago in the Lake District I chanced upon a display of 'traditional crafts' and was delighted to find that one of Westmorland's most ancient pastimes was the weaving of left-over green wool into the shape of octopi. The fashioning of these cuddly cuttlefish, their large felt eyes slightly crossed as if an attempt to stare at their own beaks had caused them to lock tragically, are, of course, a folk custom that stretches back to the Middle Ages, when great herds of squid roamed the Pennines, cropping the heather, squirting ink at curlews and filling the night with their plangent mating calls. In those days, to preserve their sheep flocks from attack by rogue cuttlefish, the Cumbrian shepherds would fashion decoy octopi from fleeces dyed with bracken juice, and lure them to their deaths in cunningly concealed squid pits, the remains of which can still be seen on the fells between Melmerby and Brough. Alas, the days of the great squid herds were numbered. Over the next century they would be hunted to extinction by groups of ruthless horse-borne aristocratic octopus-hunters with nets, specially trained spaniels, and cuttlefish calls made using the very beaks of the beasts themselves. One or two sad specimens survived in captivity until the eighteenth century, kept by itinerant musicians who discovered that by applying different degrees of pressure to the octopus they could provide a sufficient range of notes to play jigs, pavans and other simple tunes. Then someone invented the bagpipes and even these last few were lost. Now all that remains of this once common creature is a fragment of an old Cumberland ballad, 'Lord Egremont Did A-Squid-Hunting Go' ('Lord Egremont did a-squid-hunting go. With his stallion and his spaniel and his squid net-o'), and the traditional craft of making woollen octopi.

All of which has nothing whatsoever to do with the Celts, but, to be frank, I was getting a bit bored with them anyway.

Despite the stringent efforts to hold things together, the Roman Empire eventually imploded and the barbarian invaders steamed in. Most of the things the Romans had brought to the north - central heating, warm baths, communal toilets, little bone devices for cleaning the dirt out from under your finger-nails - were swept aside. All that remained of Rome among the native inhabitants, apart from a latent desire to wear sunglasses on top of their heads, were the fairs. Commerce remains long after civilisation has collapsed.

Early Christian societies incorporated the fairs into their religion much as they did other pagan entertainments that were simply too much fun to jettison, such as Christmas, harvest festivals and painting your erogenous zones blue at Michaelmas-tide (Derbyshire only for that one, obviously). Northumbria had been established as a Christian kingdom on the day the Saxon King Oswald routed Cadwalla at nearby Heavenfield in AD 635. The Saxon name for Stagshaw was Burgheat - the market place.

Throughout the Dark Ages, fairs came to be more and more closely linked with religious festivals, until in the years following the Norman Conquest they were frequently indistinguishable from them. Often they were associated with the feast taken on the dedication of the local church, so that they fell each year on that church's Saint's Day. These, it should be said, held greater significance in the Middle Ages, not just because of the relative importance of religion in the everyday life of the people, but because the calendar was constantly being altered. As if being a medieval peasant wasn't confusing enough, what with a landlord who spoke French, a priest who spoke Latin and, judging from contemporary illustrations, some unwritten law that all farm work had to be undertaken wearing stockings, a frock and a bathing cap, without the powers-that-were tinkering with time itself. Months were renamed, inserted, scrapped; days could be added or taken away at a moment's notice and even New Year's Eve shifted about like an anchorless ship in a choppy sea of dates. When you literally didn't know where you were, chronologically speaking, from one week to the next, Saints' Days were something you could hang on to. A fixture. Stagshaw Bank Fair was held on the eve, day and day after the feast of St John the Baptist.

It was during this period, too, that the fairs gradually increased in economic importance. In Charlemagne's Frankish Empire, the great fairs of Aix-la-Chapelle and Troyes were central to the commercial system. Perhaps the greatest proof of this is that the name of the latter lives on in the troy ounce.

At this point you might well be asking yourself what exactly the difference is between a fair and a common-or-garden market. The answer is that many fairs continued to have the legal element established by the Romans – the *fora* being replaced by the so-called pie and powder courts (a corruption of the French *pieds poudrés* – dusty feet). From their association with Saints' Days, they had become linked with religious holidays, and, again as in Roman times, fairs could only be established by a prescription, or grant, from the sovereign. These three elements served to distinguish fairs from wakes or markets. Despite these common factors, fairs were by no means all the same. Along with the large, northern livestock fairs of Stagshaw Bank, Aptrick (Appletreewick) in Yorkshire, Carel Fair (Carlisle) and Brough Hill in Cumbria, there were various mop, statute or hiring fairs, usually held at Whit and Martinmass, and specialist events such as the Wool Fair at Doncaster, the Chester Cheese Fair and the Dish Fair held annually in Micklegate, York, at which the selling of crockery was accompanied by the ritual persecution of stray dogs. Really.

By the Middle Ages, Stagshaw Bank Fair – now being held twice yearly, at midsummer and Whitsuntide – was well established, principally as a market for ironwork, much of which, in the form of horseshoes, horseshoe nails, weaponry and armour, promptly headed northwards with the King's armies. The Scottish wars and the subsequent period of more or less open guerrilla warfare came to an end with the Unification of the Crowns, at which point Stagshaw Bank Fair mushroomed. By the 1700s it was the biggest livestock sale in the north. In a large modern mart, such as Longtown in Cumbria, a principal day sale might consist of 10,000 sheep. At Stagshaw Bank Fair in the eighteenth century, over 100,000 head of sheep, cattle, horses and swine were traded over three days. The animals came from all over the north and Scotland. They trickled down from their steadings in the hill country, converged at dale and glen villages and reached full spate in the flat pasturelands of the broad river valleys. From across the Pennines and beyond the Cheviots and North York Moors, this great flood of animals reached their confluence at Stagshaw Bank. There were broad-horned, shaggy black Kyloe cattle from Skye, which earlier in the year had been swum across the Kyle of Lochalsh to the mainland; their brindle and ginger cousins from the Highlands; stocky, dark milking cows, descended from the original Celtic breeds, tens of thousands of them chivvied by active piebald dogs and drovers who played bagpipes to their herds to make them march faster, shod them with wood to protect their feet on the hard roads and sang hymns in Gaelic praising Brigit, the patron saint of cattle (St Brigit didn't look after the interests of all the cattle – those of the western isles had St Columba all to themselves). There were chocolate-and-white speckled Longhorns from the Durham and Yorkshire dales; mighty Shorthorn oxen from the East Riding and Lincolnshire; belted stirks from Dumfries; mighty Tees-water tups with fleeces like mop heads; jowly, pompous-looking Cheviots; chunky grey Herdwicks and lugubrious Leicesters. There were hunters and drays; bays and ponies and plough horses; red-haired hogs, saddle-backed sows and prick-eared, pointy-nosed pigs; Northumbrians in their shepherd's checks, Yorkshiremen and Cumbrians in blue-grey smocks, Highlanders in the *feileadhbeag*, bonnets the shape and colour of cowpats on their heads, smoke-scented gypsies and roaring gangs of Irish reapers over for the harvest hirings – the whole lot wheeling and dealing in their disparate voices and dialects, in English and Gaelic, Romanes and Shelta, spread like a leaderless host across the hillside. A seething, chaotic, muddy mass that stretched for miles in either direction, took weeks to assemble and to depart, and filled the air with tumultuous noise, smoke and powerful animal odours. It's hard to imagine quite what it must have been like, but if you've ever attended a large open-air pop festival, or seen the film *Woodstock*, you can probably hazard a guess.

While the main business of Stagshaw Bank Fair was livestock trading, that wasn't its only attraction. Families from isolated farms and hamlets came down to shop. In the days when each town had its specialist trade which it fiercely protected and shops were usually owned by those same tradesmen, the fair acted as a mobile mall. Cobblers came down from Alnwick, ropemakers from Rothbury, the Gypsies brought earthenware, the Tinkers linen and lace. Traders came out from the seaports carrying nuts and oranges, spices and sherbert. There were stalls selling gingerbread and claggum, caps, gloves and sickles. Huge drays brought in barrels of tar, which the shepherds would mix with butter and paint on their flocks as protection against ticks and scab. Local publicans set up beer and spirit stands and the recruiting sergeants stood close by, offering the shilling to any man desperate enough to trade his freedom for an afternoon of drunken oblivion.

Wherever fairs took place people gathered in large numbers, and wherever there were large numbers of people there were always the showmen. In an age when country folk rarely went out into the world, these travelling entertainers brought the world to them. It was a warped and weird version of the world, admittedly; freakish and tinged with sleaze and danger. Many rural people must have felt that if this was what the rest of the world was like, they'd best stop at home – a state of mind which persists in some to this day, largely as a result of watching *Oprah*. We will meet the showmen again later. Suffice it to say here that their influence on the development of the fairs was to be huge, and, at times, disastrous.

At its peak, in the 1790s, Stagshaw Bank Fair was a place of business and leisure, a temporary township that drew in people from miles around. Within its sprawling boundaries a small-holder could sell a heifer and buy a length of blue ribbon for his sweetheart, listen to the song of mechanical birds, marvel at a 'double cow', a stuffed sea elephant and a seven-footed horse, get drunk on gin and ale, guffaw at the *double entendres* of the ballad-singers, bet on the wheel of fortune ('Penny a trial, no blanks, all prizes!'), and blow the remainder of his money on a good hiding at the vinegar-soaked hands of the teak-hard old prize-fighter in the boxing booth. Such good times just couldn't last. Even as it reached its zenith, the economic and agricultural circumstances that formed the foundations of Stagshaw Bank Fair were shifting.

Droving was the key. With no other means of moving live-stock, farmers simply had to entrust it to men who would walk it to market. During the latter part of the eighteenth century 100,000 cattle, 750,000 sheep and similar quantities of pigs, poultry and pack-horses made the trek to Smithfield alone. And many of them travelled an awfully long way. The drovers' routes followed a fixed pattern. Coming from the Scottish Highlands, they might call first at the Falkirk Tryst and from there head south to the great northern fairs, of which Stagshaw was one. From here they progressed down into the Midlands, where they were joined by drovers from Wales and Ireland. Some headed east to the huge St Frith's Fair outside Norwich, selling their stock to graziers, who fattened it on East Anglian pasture before driving it to the city themselves the following spring. Others turned south and took their herds direct to the capital. A few might sell their stock at Barnet Fair; most went straight to Smithfield. More than 10,000 head surged down the Holloway Road and Upper Street, Islington, every day. Cars may do more long-term damage to the planet, but when it comes to ravaging footwear you can't beat the aftermath of a huge herd of nervous bullocks. It was little wonder that sandals fell out of fashion.

For a brief moment the life of the drover, spending the summer months tramping the hills and dales of a Britain largely untouched by industry, his collie (from the Gaelic *coallean*, or 'little dog') as his companion and a ram's horn full of lethally strong whisky at his belt, sleeping 'neath nature's bejewelled canopy and answering to no orders save his own, seems an idyllic one. And then you look out of the window at the plotching rain, recall that they existed almost totally on a diet of oatmeal and onion porridge, and remember that holiday you had in Ireland in the caravan with the chemical toilet, and think, well, maybe not. The drover's life was a hard one. Aside from the difficulty of controlling the herd and making his own rudimentary sanitary arrangements, he was beset with problems and anxiety. Cattle and sheep theft was still prevalent, while disease could decimate a herd. Even after selling off his charges, the drover was in danger. Walking across Georgian England with a huge wad of cash in your wallet was not a recipe for inner tranquillity. Highwaymen still lurked and rural crime was rife. And we are not talking about four spotty youths in a stolen Ford Escort: disbanded soldiers, first from the Seven Years' War, and later from the Peninsular and Waterloo, embittered, hungry and armed to the teeth, roamed the land. Policing was non-existent, street-lighting unheard of. To travel at all was dangerous; to travel back from a large cattle or sheep market was practically on a par with wearing a T-shirt bearing the legend: 'My Pockets Are Full! Why Not Rob Me?'. If the drover made it through with the herd and back to the farmer with the money, he stood to make between two and five shillings per head of livestock. Droving was a high-risk, low-gain business, less so than being the court correspondent of the *Catholic Herald* during the reign of Henry VIII perhaps, but only just.

By the end of the eighteenth century the droving life was beginning to lose its essential place in livestock farming. The enclosure of common land had made pasturing the herds increasingly difficult, while road taxes levied to repair the damage wreaked by the drovers crept upwards all the time, making the job less and less profitable. Coupled with this was a growing dissatisfaction with the standard of beast being delivered. It does not take a master butcher to work out that a beef cow that has walked 600 miles to market is going to be a good deal thinner when it arrives than it was when it set off. Disease, picked up and spread as they travelled the country, also lowered the quality of the drovers' herds. The work of breeding and fattening livestock had by tradition been viewed as two totally separate skills, but now the southern graziers began to wonder if it wouldn't be worth their while to combine the two. It was. The effect on the Scots, Welsh, Irish and northern English livestock farmers was disastrous; the result for the drovers catastrophic. Soon, the arrival of the railways that would revive the fortunes of those farmers would kill off the drovers more or less completely.

The man largely responsible for the railway boom, George Stephenson, was born in Wylam, a dozen or so miles east of Stagshaw. Even before the onset of the sweeping changes brought about by his engineering genius, the economic pre-eminence of the fairs was under threat. With the industrial revolution, the population of Britain had begun to shift towards the towns and cities, and the main market for livestock shifted with them. By the time Stephenson's Rocket chugged out of Stockton Station, even the most basic feasibility study would have concluded that Stagshaw Bank Fair, equidistant from Newcastle and Carlisle, and convenient for practically nowhere, was, businesswise, in totally the wrong place. Specially-built livestock marts began to spring up in and around the rapidly expanding urban centres, stripping the rural fairs of agricultural business and robbing them of their central role. Cast on the economic scrap-heap and totally losing their sense of purpose, like men hitting the social club the day they are made redundant, the fairs embarked on a period of wild, perhaps even desperate, hedonism. Victorian England was not, in all honesty, the wisest place for such a wanton display. They would be made to pay for it later.

Fairs dedicated exclusively to pleasure were not a new phenomenon. Bartholomew Fair in London, begun as a cloth market, had, since the Restoration, been noted as a place of merriment: a fair 'not so much for merchandise and the supplying of what people really want: but as a sort of Bacchanalia to gratify the multitude in their wandering and irregular thoughts,' as one rather sour visitor observed in 1685. Fairs had always been associated with crime and bad behaviour. The showmen were often blamed, but while some were not averse to earning a little extra by running dodgy rackets such as the three-card trick, in truth it was probably more a case of trouble, quite literally, following them around. For just as the crowds at the fair attracted the showmen, so too they attracted criminals. Large bodies of people, strong drink, gambling, and little or no lighting were an incendiary mixture. Add a sprinkling of swindlers, conmen and gangs of travelling pickpockets, and the result was positively volcanic. Violence could and did erupt on the slightest pretext, ranging in scale from the kicking to death of a gingerbread-seller, such as occurred at Stalybridge in Cheshire, to the full-scale riots that led to the suppression of Southwark Fair in 1760. While the fairs maintained some financial importance, these outbursts were tolerated on economic grounds; once it was taken away, the fairs became nothing more than a dangerous nuisance.

By Victorian times, increased crime and a general lowering in the standard of entertainment had led the middle class to desert the fairs more or less completely. Music halls and theatres were now a feature of even the smallest towns; transport into the cities to visit the newly fashionable public zoos was quick and easy. Travelling circuses further undermined the importance of the fairground. Unable to match their competitors for quality, the showmen sought to maximise their one true advantage: unlike the theatre owners, they were unlicensed, hard to control and almost impossible to censor. Abandoning restraint, they plunged ever further downmarket. Ballads became lewder, the mountebanks and comedians ruder and the exhibits in the freak shows leaned more and more towards the lurid, the horrific and the macabre. An atmosphere of danger and sexual titillation prevailed. The bourgeoisie, ever concerned for the mental well-being of the lower orders, feared the effect all this unedifying fun must be having on them. The moral consensus of the time was that all sinfulness was generally corrupting, and that sensual excitement and law-breaking were inextricably linked. Whether a surfeit of toffee apples might lead to murder, or armed robbery result from a glimpse of a woman's ankle, were not questions that vexed the Victorians. The answer was clear: yes, they would. In 1871, to deal with the menace, Parliament passed the Fairs Act. This granted the secretary of state the power to abolish any fair that was the cause of 'grievous immorality' as reported by local magistrates.

Over half a century later, on 5 July 1926, Stagshaw Bank Fair was held for the final time. On 5 March of the following year, it was abolished under the Fairs Act. What grievous immorality went on is unrecorded, but an event older than Christmas had gone for good. Twice a year throughout the centuries it had echoed with the sound of spielers, the calls of pie-men, the mellifluous language of the Highland drovers and the pootering tunes of steam organs. Now all that was heard on Stagshaw Common was the pastoral chorus of Northumbria: the high-pitched cry of a lapwing, the bleating of wandering sheep and the thunderous crash of F1-11s heading to the bombing ranges at Otterburn.

* * *

A few days later the fine weather disappeared as abruptly as Stagshaw Bank Fair. The people of the north country went back indoors and waited, and waited, and waited, for spring.

2

• New Beginnings •

The Northumberland County Show

It was a sunny Monday morning in May. Cornfields rippled in the gentle breeze; the dewy meadows, sequinned with buttercups and daisies, winked and sparkled. The River Tyne jinked around shiny-pated rocks and meandered between tousled grassbanks entwined with campion and forget-me-not. The hedgerows frothed, the cotton-wool lambs frolicked on the hillside and the air was heavy with the scent of purple verbiage. I was sitting in the corner of a sports field in Corbridge eating a doughnut.

Around me the Northumberland County Show was getting under way. Immense pieces of machinery, with broods of red-faced sales reps clucking fussily around them, shimmered; barrel-chested Clydesdales were being rubbed down like boxers; two men in caps wrestled with a Vendeen tup whose rubicund cheeks and flourishing sideburns put me in mind of Noddy Holder. There was a smell of frying onions and trodden grass.

A balding man in a mauve, terry-towelling polo shirt was walking a miniature schnauzer in preparation for his appearance in the showring. The dog, salt-and-pepper coated, with an Edward VII moustache and eyebrows that suggested stern moral rectitude, was tugging in the direction of a copse of silver birch saplings. 'What are you wanting to go there for?' the man asked. 'You know you'll only cock your leg.' He pulled on the lead. The dog turned and, from beneath his beetle brows, fixed the man with the fierce stare of an ageing and old-fashioned maths master who has just spotted a lazy pupil plotting a graph with a biro. The man stared back. It was an uneven contest. A few seconds later, the schnauzer was staking a canine claim to a tree-fringed riverside site, to add to his already impressive real-estate portfolio.

I bit into the doughnut. A spume of cinnamon squirted down my chest. My shirt looked as if it had contracted some kind of fungal infection. It was my fifth doughnut. They were irresistible: they came from a red and white van operated by a West Yorkshireman. I had been to it twice already. 'I can't keep away,' I said above the thrumming of the generator. A mixer whirred and doughnuts flipped mechanically out of the deep-fat fryer and shuffled chubbily down the counter towards him.

'The secret's in the sugar,' the doughnut man said, tucking two fat little rascals into the bag. They mooned goldenly at me. 'I get it from a mate who's a Colombian drug baron,' he added, dusting the doughnuts with cinnamon.

The Northumberland County Show was in only its twentieth year. It had sprung from the wreckage of a much older event organised by the now defunct Newcastle Agricultural Society, one of the oldest in the north.

The agricultural shows and the societies that organise them have their roots in the mid-eighteenth century, when the huge social changes that followed the industrial revolution set testing new problems for British farmers. During that period Britain changed from an agrarian to an urban society. In the late 1700s, 75 per cent of the population lived in the countryside, but the balance was already shifting rapidly. Prior to the upheaval, the bulk of British farming had been done by smallholders, cottagers and crofters. It was subsistence farming, the mainstay of a peasant economy. Most Britons had been, to a greater or lesser extent, self-sufficient when it came to food. They kept geese, a pig and possibly a milking cow or goat; they had a share in a communal flock of sheep and grew their own vegetables. Now, sucked in to serve the manufacturers, living in the hastily built cities, in cramped houses in narrow streets where a bit of moss growing on the slates constituted a roof garden and the only livestock was likely to be hiding in the mattress, they could no longer feed themselves. The good news for landowners was that these recently converted urbanites had just about enough cash to pay someone else to do it for them. Which would have been easy enough had it not been for the fact that, amid upping sticks and heading for the dark Satanic mills and the roaring flames of the foundries, the population had somehow found the time to double itself. For close to 10,000 years farming had evolved as slowly as the rest of society; now the sudden acceleration of social change demanded a swift and thorough response from agriculturalists. It got one. At the forefront was a cadre of radicals who were determined to foment a farming revolution in Britain. Oddly enough, one of the leading firebrands was the ruling monarch, George III. Farmer George, as he was nicknamed, imported merino sheep to Britain from Spain, formed the Board of Agriculture and put royal land at Windsor, Kew, Mortlake and the Old Deer Park to work. For, as he observed in an article in the *Quarterly Review,* 'The ground, like man, was never meant to be idle; if it does not produce something useful it will be overrun with weeds.' It is a philosophy embraced wholeheartedly by his descendants to this day.

The patronage and interest of the reigning monarch, even one as obviously German as King George, had its effect on the attitude of the British aristocracy. Once, it had gone without saying that farming was no occupation for a gentleman, but now gentlemen couldn't get back to the land fast enough. Powdered periwigs, velvet pantaloons and patent leather pumps were tossed aside as London society hurled stout boots, corduroy breeches and waxed rainwear into the back of whatever constituted the eighteenth-century equivalent of a Range Rover and headed off to their little places in the country for a spot of rural living. The Duke of Bedford set up a model farm at Woburn and organised ploughing matches; the Earl of Egremont turned part of Petworth House into an agricultural college, deforested his great deer park so it could be turned over to tillage and put new selective-breeding techniques to such good use at his stud farm that his horses won the Oaks and the Derby more frequently than those of any other breeder; Lord Townsend took an obsessive interest in root crops, earning himself the sobriquet 'Turnip' in the process, and Thomas Coke, Earl of Leicester, transformed the estate at Holkham Hall from one for which tenants could not be found, even at a rent of just five shillings an acre, into one of the most productive and profitable in Britain. The part played by the aristocracy in altering British farming practices was large indeed, but it was dwarfed by the contribution of the third-from-last word in the previous sentence. For by far the most influential figures in the agricultural revolution were those that appeared on the end-of-year balance sheet. A new breed of businessman farmer was emerging.

Profit and productivity now met the peasant in a battle for the countryside. If a hedgehog had charged head-on at a transit van the outcome could not have been more predictable. In order to boost output, thousands of Enclosure Acts, which transferred land from communal to individual ownership, were passed by Parliament. Between 1702 and 1844 close to six million acres of Britain found its way into private hands. The battle to feed the new urban population had wrought a change in rural life almost as great as that which had sparked the struggle in the first place.

Denied the common grazing on which they relied, harassed by landowners whose vast tracts of property entitled them to greater parish voting rights and who consequently controlled the distribution of newly enclosed land, the smallholders were crushed. The option of self-employment having been withdrawn, they either moved to the towns and sought work with a manufacturer, or stayed put and took a job with the landowners who had driven them under. A population that had once worked for itself now, in the main, worked for others.

This is one of the saddest chapters in British history, not least, it seems to me, because it marks an important change: it is possible to lay the blame for all human tragedies in the Middle Ages and before on either 'acts of God' (the Black Death, Fire of London) or the greed and general wickedness of individuals (examples too numerous to mention). The Enclosure Acts were different. However corruptly implemented, they were a necessity: without them Britain would have faced famine and social collapse. They are the first example of huge injustice born of economic expediency; as such, you might say that they signal the moment when the destiny of mankind was handed over to the financial system. As a concerned liberal with a deep-rooted commitment to social justice it would have been easy for me to get angry and depressed thinking about the situation. Thankfully I spotted the sweet stall and cheered up instantly.

A few years ago, some people I knew in Archway in London had a baby. There was something very unusual about it. To all intents and purposes it looked like a normal baby, felt like a normal baby, smelled like a normal baby. The only thing was, it weighed more than a fully grown porpoise. Don't get me wrong – there was nothing the matter with this baby. It wasn't particularly big, it wasn't very fat, it was just incredibly dense. You know how in *Doctor Who* the Tardis, by some unexplained miracle of science, is bigger on the inside than it is on the outside? Well, I think this baby was pulling some similar kind of stunt. Outside he was just a normal, gurgling baby; inside he was a semi-detached bungalow. Visitors who were unaware of the baby's supernatural properties always begged to be allowed to hold him. The baby's mother, who from months of carrying him about had developed forearms the size of York hams and who could heft a sack of cement as if it was a lucky bag, would hand him over with the caution, 'Be prepared. He's heavier than he looks.' And those of us in the know would watch with glee as the strangers ignored her completely, failed to brace themselves and as a result were catapulted head-first into a swing-bin full of dirty nappies. They never dropped the baby, of course; nobody would ever do that. Even a cry of: 'Come quick! Dale Winton's fallen into our septic tank' couldn't induce even the rankest rotter to drop a baby. Instead they struggled gamely upright, Q-tips decorating their hair, and said, 'My, you're quite a grown-up little fellow, aren't you?' The paradox here was, however, that, like a balloon, the larger the baby grew, the lighter he got. But just for a while, for a glorious three-month spell, he held a unique distinction. He was the only thing in the world of greater density than the sweets they sell at shows and fairs.

Under a striped awning, the shelves of the Northumberland County Show pick-and-mix bowed beneath the weight of a bewildering array of sugar-heavy northern confections. Farmers, broader than they were tall, and so weatherbeaten that they blended in with the landscape like tree stumps, checked out the chunks of flies-are-undone-blush-pink strawberry fudge and eyed up the chocolate-coated peppermint coconut bars in a garish shade of choke-on-your-own-vomit green (if the writing ever fails I can always get work with a paint company). Like anyone who has ever bought sweets from such a place, the farmers were cautious. Because, like the Archway Baby, this stuff is unfeasibly heavy. You can bung three or four tiny crumbs of it into a bag, take it to the till, and still when it is placed on the scales the hand will whizz round as if it's been sat on by an elephant while the woman behind the counter waits patiently for it to settle before cheerily announcing, 'That'll be £47.95, please.' By which time it's too late. Because no true red-blooded Englishman can possibly make a public admission that he can't afford a few sweets. It's either pay up or face economic humiliation.

Sweets have always been an intrinsic element of British holidays. The sweets on sale at the Northumberland County Show were part of a long and historic tradition. Through the centuries candyfloss, toffee apples, cinder toffee and rock in the shape of false teeth seem to have absorbed the very essence of the fair and showground. Their names resonate with the spirit of outdoor entertainments; frivolous, celebratory, deliciously unwholesome and exciting. They are a wonderful thing. Except to eat, obviously. It took me years to come to terms with this disappointment. Every year when I was a child we would go to the fair at Stokesley in the North Riding and I would pester my Mum and Dad to buy me candyfloss. *Pleasepleasepleaseplease*, I would wail while swinging from my father's arm as if it were a Tarzan rope. Eventually my parents would acquiesce to my demands and get me a stick of the stuff. Instead of just carrying it round waving it triumphantly at those children less fortunate than myself, I would then try to eat it. It was like chewing a horse-hair sofa. Loft insulation has more flavour.

After I finally got the message about candyfloss, I went after toffee apples. Why, I don't know. As a small boy I would no more eat an apple than I would attend the after-school country-dancing class with the girlies and that boy who wore sandals and went to Brittany on his holidays. Nevertheless I set my heart on having one. I suspect it was the novelty. That and the prospect of being able to wield the only kind of sweet that could fracture the kneecap of a masked assailant. Traditionally the toffee apple comes on a stick, and, having been left to dry upside-down, has a cap of toffee on top that is as thick and inflexible as a manhole cover. It looks not unlike a medieval mace. Gastronomically speaking, the toffee apple has one major saving grace – it is physically impossible for a human being to eat one.

Not so cinder toffee. Cinder toffee is a sweet-stall staple. It is the colour of honey and has the texture of a breezeblock. Once you have put a piece of cinder toffee in your mouth you will never be free of it. It will remain with you for the rest of your life. It squeezes itself into the cracks of your molars, and when your tongue comes looking for it, it rips the skin off it like barnacles. Going after it with your fingers is no more rewarding and infinitely more dangerous. People have pulled out their own jawbones trying to remove cinder toffee. The only thing you can do is wait. Like marooned Japanese soldiers who don't know the war is over, elements of cinder toffee will eventually come out and give themselves up. You'll be driving along one day and your partner will say: 'What's that you're chewing?'

'*Trrrmsnack*. I'm not sure. I think it's cinder toffee.'

'When did you secretly snaffle that, greedy guts?'

'*Mmmmtsk*. I think about 1968.'

I bought myself some fudge and sufficient slabs of banana toffee to crazy-pave a patio. By a combination of expert selection and low animal cunning, I managed to get away with a bill of just £8.55. The woman at the counter looked at me with grudging admiration.

The great thing about fudge is that no matter how little of it you eat, it always makes you feel sick. So you might as well scoff the whole bag now. Banana toffee is even better. The classic way to serve banana toffee - a little tip I picked up from Marco Pierre White, here - is to place it inside a paper bag and then shove it in a pocket next to your skin. Leave for two to three hours, or until the toffee pieces have fused together and are fully glued to the paper, then serve. Preferably to a precocious and talkative child with a high-pitched voice.

I walked over to take a look at the rabbits and cavies. There was a large albino doe for sale at the front of the tent. A label attached to the cage said: '£5. Pet only.' 'Pet only' had been underlined twice, presumably to deter anyone from inquiring about it with a fiver in one hand, two slices of bread in the other and drool running down his chin.

The showground is laid out over a couple of rugby pitches and a cricket field, ringed by trees and bordered to the south by the Newcastle–Carlisle railway line. To the north, across the Tyne, is the village of Corbridge, and beyond it the incline that leads to Stagshaw. A pleasant smell wafts across from the cattle pens: a mixture of the fresh, sweet odour of straw and the biscuity perfume of freshly washed cows. I had read somewhere that dairymen were the most even-tempered farm workers because it is impossible to spend time in the company of cows without relaxing, and that farmers who have had a frustrating day will sometimes go and stand next to the byre in order to unwind. There is apparently something about cows - their smell, the ponderous movements and their general air of contentment - that has a calming influence on the human spirit. At one time the soothing effect of cattle was so well respected that doctors would send patients suffering from nervous disorders to stay on dairy farms. Jerseys were the nineteenth-century answer to Valium, and with the ever-increasing price of drugs they could soon make a comeback. Actually the government was planning to re-introduce prescription Friesians early next year, but the BSE scare put them off. That and the fact that they couldn't find any child-proof bottles big enough to put them in.

The star of the cattle section of the show is a Limousin bull named Filip. Filip is massive. If he had wheels he'd be a juggernaut. Children approach him giggling with a mixture of amazement and terror. Filip is tethered to a stake with rope. In scale terms, the arrangement is like attempting to secure Mike Tyson by tying him to a toothpick with a length of cotton. Filip, though, does not want to go anywhere. He is a gentle giant. He stares good-naturedly ahead, blinking his tiny eyes absentmindedly as if he's trying desperately hard to remember something really, really important. Compared with Filip, the only native British-breed bulls at the show, a triumvirate of Longhorns, are lightweights; Dudley Moores to his Schwarzenegger. Every once in a while you see them eyeing him irritably and you can guess what they're thinking. 'Oh yes, he's big and muscly all right, but I bet he's stupid. I bet he's got no personality. I bet you couldn't have a conversation with him like you can with me...'

As a breed, the modern Longhorn can be traced back to the 1760s and the farm of Robert Bakewell at Dishley in Leicester. Bakewell was one of the first, and certainly the most influential, of the new businessmen farmers I mentioned. At Dishley, Bakewell pioneered many new scientific methods of farming: most importantly, he adopted radical breeding techniques to improve the quality of his livestock. Bakewell's greatest contribution to British agriculture was the New Leicester, a fast-maturing sheep which was eventually to be used to improve the standard of practically every other breed in Britain. The superiority of Bakewell's sheep was soon widely known, and the demand for cross-breeding immense. Huge sire fees were on offer for the services of his rams.

Whenever the subject of sire fees comes up, I always think of a story a neighbour of my parents once told me. He had been working for the Ministry of Agriculture out in Kenya, giving advice on farming matters to new settlers. One day he was called out to the estate of a very upper-crust gentleman, recently arrived from England, whose paw-paw crop had failed dismally. A quick survey revealed the problem. 'You see,' my parents' neighbour explained to the settler, 'the paw-paw tree is either male or female. Yours are all female trees. If you want any fruit you'll have to get in some males.' The man absorbed this information, then exploded with rage: 'Damn your impudence, man,' he bellowed, 'if you think I'll play pimp to a paw-paw!'

Luckily for British agriculture, Robert Bakewell wasn't too proud to play pimp to a sheep. His prize ram, Two-Pounder, was hired out for a whopping 1,200 guineas per season. There is a painting of Two-Pounder by J. Digby Curtis. Like many of the eighteenth-century images of livestock, it seems to emphasize the body size at the expense of everything else. Two-Pounder's legs are so thin that they seem certain to snap beneath the enormous weight, and they are so short that his two most valuable assets are practically bumping along the ground. Best of all, however, is the rather raffish, self-satisfied expression on Two-Pounder's face. It is clearly the look of a bloke who is getting paid a lot of money to have sex.

Bakewell's success as a breeder of sheep and Longhorn cattle was publicised in the writings of an influential agricultural theorist, Arthur Young. As a result his farm received a stream of visitors, from fellow farmers to Russian princes. Bakewell set up a small museum at Dishley, in which the progressive development of his flocks and herds was illustrated by bones and joints of meat which bobbed eerily in jars of brine. He also held a string of open days. These, along with similar events organised by Thomas Coke at Holkham, are usually cited as the first agricultural shows. In County Durham, however, they will tell you something different.

When she was eight years old, my mother was sent to stay with some of her cousins. 'Now,' my grandmother warned her, 'you might find them a bit strange, but don't say anything about it. They live out on a farm in the back of beyond. [My grandmother had spent all her life in Marske-by-the-Sea in Cleveland, then as now a cultural epicentre.] And whatever they put down on the plate in front of you, eat it!'

My mother arrived at the cousin's farm and was ushered into the sitting room. There, by the fire, was a small, wrinkled figure dressed entirely in black, sucking ruminatively on a clay pipe. It was her great-aunt. Mindful of the warning about eating anything she was given, my mother was disturbed when she went into the kitchen to see a vast saucepan of brownish sludge bubbling away on the stove. My mother's aunt then appeared. 'You must be hungry after that journey, pet,' she said. 'Sit yourself down.' My mother complied with a rising feeling of nausea. The family assembled at the kitchen table and waited for Father. Eventually he strode in, greeted everyone warmly, grabbed the vast saucepan from the top of the range and advanced towards the table with it. My mother swallowed and fought the urge to run. Her uncle veered off through the back door with the saucepan. 'The pigs eat first round here,' the aunt explained, producing a leg of lamb from the oven.

These events occurred in Weardale and it is in Weardale, in the town of Wolsingham, on 15 November 1763, that Durhamites say the first-ever agricultural show was held. Personally, I don't think it is wise to argue with these people.

The new ideas of men such as Bakewell were absorbed by like-minded farmers: the Culley brothers of Northumberland, whose sheep-breeding skills were to play a major part in a tragic episode in Scottish history; Robert and Charles Colling, who farmed at Ketton and Brampton near Darlington and produced one of the agricultural wonders of the age; and Thomas Bates of Kirklevington in the North Riding of Yorkshire, who, rather less dramatically, made substantial improvements to dairy cattle. The effect on the rest of British farming was, however, negligible. With no system in place to communicate them, save the standard rural method of telling the village postmistress, the latest developments and theories simply took too long to travel. Thomas Coke pessimistically calculated that the changes spread at a rate of only one mile per year from any given centre of 'new' farming. At that pace, it would take 300 years at least to bring about any kind of widespread reform, by which time the rapidly multiplying manufacturing population would have starved to death, or the nation driven to ruin by the cost of importing food. A more direct programme of education was clearly needed. The result was the founding of the county agricultural societies, bodies set up for the discussion and dissemination of information through meetings, publications and, doubtless inspired by events in Weardale, agricultural shows. In China, Chairman Mao's political revolution might have come from the barrel of a gun; in Britain, the agricultural revolution came through the flaps of a marquee.

The original shows were an educational tool. The men who ran them were very strict about this. The show was not a fair: enlightenment rather than entertainment was its goal. New methods and theories were demonstrated, the latest machinery was displayed, and, to encourage good practices among farmers, prizes were awarded for quality stock and produce. In the early years these were substantial sums. At the Yorkshire Agricultural Society's first show in 1838, the prize for the best bull was £25. At the Northumberland County Show more than 150 years later, Filip the lumbering Limousin was picking up just a fiver more.

In a Victorian Britain so willing to marvel at its own brilliance that it comes as a surprise to find that no one ever patented a steam-powered pat-yourself-on-the-back device, the agricultural shows became the agrarian equivalent of the great trade exhibitions. Crowds flocked to them, thrilling at the innovation and modernity of it all. Here, among the regimented rows of tents, they could stroll along specially-laid boardwalks and watch butter made without once being touched by human hands; observe the automated horse-and-cattle groomer; wonder at the genius behind the Lac Trephoer mechanical livestock wet-nurse and feast their eyes on some of the fattest animals this nation has ever produced. Because the Victorians liked their animals fat. Not big-boned, not plump, not chubby. Fat. Enormous. Oxen the width of a railway carriage, turkeys with the breasts of bodybuilders, hogs like walking sausages – this was what the Victorian wanted to see. If it could stand up without the aid of pulleys and scaffolding, he didn't want to know about it. The results were the most improbably corpulent breeds imaginable and a population with an incredibly high cholesterol level. Though if you were working sixteen hours a day down a lead mine with a future world war as your only chance of escape, I dare say this was the least of your worries.

Eventually, however, even the prospect of catching sight of pigs so portly they appeared to have been inflated with a footpump started to pale. Throughout the 1890s, attendance at the agricultural shows fell. There were other more recent developments in entertainment which took people's attention. It was all a reflection of the falling values of society. As one show organiser noted sadly: 'Thousands will go to a football match, while scores cannot be persuaded to cross the road to see a fine exhibition of stock.' There was only one answer to the crisis: other things would have to be introduced to lure the public back into the showgrounds. Other *sensible* things. Mindful of the original intention of the shows, the current organisers were determined that the spectacle should be increased without resorting to vulgarity. The educational value would be preserved, even strengthened as a result. Floriculture, baking competitions and displays of rural crafts were all approved as suitable, and some agricultural societies even agreed to allow show-jumping, though most thought this a little too risqué.

Looking round the Northumberland County Show, it was clear

things had come a long way since then. Now, not only was show-jumping included as a matter of course, but there was also a hot-air balloon, a motorcycle display team, sky-divers and the Mid-Wales Axe Racing Team. Agricultural shows remain as popular as ever because they have adapted as they have developed. Along the way they have had to shed some of their ideals. They have lost their purity but become more fun. A bit like Kylie Minogue, really.

I walked back up towards the railway station. The sun was still shining and a predictable west wind snapped at the canvas of the marquees. Highly polished dray horses were pulling highly polished drays across the main ring, while round by the dry-stone walling exhibition the Cumberland wrestlers were stripping down to their velvet bloomers against the backdrop of a tent advertising hydrotherapy spa equipment. Hunters clattered into horse boxes while the White Helmets revved their motorbikes. The burner on a hot-air balloon roared; somewhere on a nearby airfield the sky-divers were suiting up; and in the bee-keepers' tent a lean man in corduroy trousers was explaining the principles of the waggle dance to a family from South Shields. It was time to move on.

3

· Running ·

The Pen-y-Ghent Fell Race and Gala

I was waiting at the station at Langwathby. The sky was charcoal, the Pennines a blur through the driving drizzle. The train arrived. The drop from the train doors to the platform was so great that the guard jumped down and placed sets of wooden steps beneath them. It was just like in the Wild West. Which was quite appropriate, as this was Cumbria.

The Carlisle–Settle railway is one of the most famous branch lines in Britain. The views from the windows are by all accounts fabulous. I would like to tell you about them, but unfortunately the Carlisle–Settle railway is so popular that the chances of getting a window seat are roughly the same as those of winning the lottery and getting to slap Jeremy Paxman with a large halibut on the same day. And these are no ordinary passengers either. These are rail buffs. Middle-aged men with timetables the thickness of loaf tins bulging in their Velcro-fastening pockets. Pasty youths with pebbledash complexions and cameras slung around their necks, the long lenses jutting from their chests like stakes from vampires. They have guidebooks, they have note-pads, they have camcorders, they have large-scale maps that fold out to practically life-size and, worst of all, they have Tupper-ware.

When I was younger I worked as a chef in an office block in the East End. Just before we went home, the brigade would assemble for the most tedious part of our job: making the sandwiches for the night-shift workers. We had to make about 300 rounds and by the time we'd finished we were in a violent frame of mind. It wasn't making the sandwiches themselves that got on our nerves, it was wrapping them up. You had to use clingfilm. For ordinary everyday use, clingfilm is a perfectly reasonable product, but when you are wrapping 300 sandwiches, its little peccadillos start to grate. You get sick of the way the minute you take your eye off a sheet it automatically folds itself together. The fact that clingfilm will fasten on to anything except the object you want it to fasten on to starts to get a tad personal. You begin to see it as a battle of wills between yourself and the clingfilm. It is a bitter and pointless duel that somehow diminishes you both. 'Stick there,' you smile, smoothing it down gently in a bid to win it over with charm and friendliness. The clingfilm unfurls slowly, arrogantly. 'Come on now, you scamp,' you hiss, patting it back into position. The clingfilm responds by stretching itself lazily apart. It yawns at you. 'Get back, you swine,' you grunt, cuffing it firmly. The clingfilm lies still for a moment, then flicks up a corner of itself derisively, then another, then another. 'So that's how you want to play it, pal?' you snarl. 'Well, that's OK by me.' And you whack it hard with the flat of your hand. The clingfilm lies motionless, momentarily vanquished. You turn away to do something else. When you turn back again the clingfilm has split wide open. It is a mouth, a shiny, plastic gob, and it is laughing at you. 'Bastard,' you growl, and you begin to punch and pound the clingfilm, hammering it with your fists, up and down, again and again, howling and swearing at it in a wild and primitive rage. Eventually you step back, breathing hard. The clingfilm is well and truly stuck down now. You have won. Unfortunately, the ham salad sandwich you were wrapping looks like a trifle.

One Friday a chef named Jim finally cracked with the clingfilm. After he had torn off a dozen progressively larger pieces only to find that each one was mysteriously exactly two millimetres too narrow for the task in hand, after he had struggled for fully five minutes to find the edge so that he could tear off another bit, after the new piece had stuck to the workbench, the chopping board and his knife before curling up into a ball like an armadillo that has just scented a jaguar, he let out a scream of fury and hurled the entire roll across the kitchen. It bounced off the wall and came to rest in a mixing bowl. 'I don't know who invented that stuff,' he barked, 'but he must have been a right bloody nutter.' And he flung his apron and his hat after the clingfilm and stormed out, never to be seen again. I am not sure who invented clingfilm either, though I suspect he might also have had something to do with Tupperware.

Tupperware is excellent for keeping food fresh, but it has a side-effect. As well as keeping air out, it keeps smells in. After half an hour in a Tupperware box, the odour of a crab-paste sandwich has built up to such an extent that it has practically solidified. After an hour it has reached critical mass. Now it is no longer the slight fishy scent of a crab-paste sandwich but the rank and nauseating stench of a Russian factory ship becalmed in the Indian Ocean for an entire summer with a faulty refrigeration system. When the Tupperware box is opened, with that characteristic ripping thwack, the ectoplasmic stink bursts out, swooshes upwards, does a victory roll and then dives down and clamps itself on to the faces of bystanders like some sci-fi demon. Fainting, hallucinations and memory loss ensue. Over 95 per cent of those people who claim to have been abducted by space aliens are in fact victims of collateral Tupperware damage.

Surviving the Tupperware onslaught, I disembarked at Horton-in-Ribblesdale, a small village with a couple of pubs and any number of cottages with cartwheels on the gable ends. High up in the Pennines, it is surrounded by hill meadows, speckled in early summer with buttercups and daisies. There are few trees and those there are are stunted, with branches that slant madly downwind like Billy Whizz's hair. As I walked down the steep bank from the station the floats of the Gala Parade were passing by. Clumps of villagers stood watching them, laughing and pointing at people they knew, chatting with their neighbours in chunky Yorkshire accents, the words clopping together like woodblocks.

There were four floats in all, if you include the one bearing the Hawes Silver Band, whose warm melancholy sounds accompanied the procession. There was 'The Teddy Bears' Picnic', featuring local schoolchildren; 'VE Day', which may have had something to do with the WI, and 'Four Weddings and a Funeral', which I instantly recognised as the Young Farmers' Club's effort because it involved men in drag. Male farmers will put on women's clothing and make-up at the slightest excuse. Village pantos, charity fun days and fancy-dress parties in rural Britain are always adorned by flocks of burly, ruddy-cheeked blokes in frocks and wellies, and even an outbreak of swinal brucilosis is likely to spark a run on taffeta ballgowns at the local dress-hire company. The phenomenon of farming transvestism is so well accepted that my local paper actually has a special photo section devoted to it. While this brings joy, laughter and a splash of much-needed glamour into the home of many an isolated shepherd, the effects of the farming drag craze are not always so positive. The Oklahoma Dust Bowl Crisis in the 1930s, for example, was severely exacerbated by the Tulsa Farmers' Guild's decision that its members should fight soil erosion only while dressed as Veronica Lake.

The psychological roots of the farmer's perpetual desire to dress up as a mock-woman may stem from a constant need to re-affirm his masculinity through a display of outward effeminacy, which paradoxically serves to declare his heterosexuality by appearing to question it. Or it could be that the knowledge that it is on female fecundity, in livestock and crops, that the farmer relies for his livelihood, leads him to ridicule womanhood in order to subconsciously alleviate his feelings of powerlessness and dependency. On the other hand, it might just be that they are a right bunch of Jessicas.

I followed the floats and bought a programme at the entrance to the village playing field. 'There's a lucky number down there in the corner,' the gateman said, pointing to the figure 251, which was written on the programme in felt-tip. 'Well, I mean, I can't guarantee it's lucky, obviously.'

A rectangular ring was roped off in the centre of the play area. To the right were the orange tents of the fell-race organisers; to the left, between the ring and a couple of tennis courts, a row of stalls sold jam and cakes and tombola tickets. The ubiquitous bouncy castle wobbled nearby and the music of a small roundabout pootled merrily. Across the slick and muddy football pitch you could see the far bank of the Ribble. Beyond it the foot of Pen-y-Ghent disappeared into a damp sock of cloud and mist. I remembered what a farmer from nearby Wharfedale had told me about the local weather – 'If you can't see the hills it's raining, and if you can see them it's going to rain' – and wished I'd brought a waterproof coat. I fastened my jacket to the top and stared up at the sky. Its uniform greyness was punctuated by a lone blob of blue the size of a bumble bee's belly button.

'It's trying to do its best for us,' an elderly woman said, following my gaze, and she gave me that lips-curled-inwards-eyebrows-slightly-raised grin which seems to be the quintessential English expression. The French have a 'Who knows? And furthermore, who gives a toss?' shrug. The Italians do those hands-pointing-to-their-heads gestures that seem to progress from disbelief to despondency to rage and, finally, to forgiveness and reconciliation all in the space of five seconds. And we, the English, have this anti-smile, this contra-smirk. It is a deft and subtle signal which says: 'Please do not let this outward display of optimism convince you that I am naïve or in any way blind to the true situation. We stand on a precipice above the very blackest pit of despond, yet acknowledgement of that fact will not serve to alter the situation and may, indeed, induce a panic that will greatly increase our chances of falling into the bottomless cavern beneath our feet from which the sighing lethargy sucks at our very souls. Yes, things are hopeless, yet we must go on hoping.' At least, that is what it usually means. Sometimes, though, it's just that people have come out without putting their teeth in.

On the edge of the showring a middle-aged man with an elaborate checkerboard tie that was not so much a kipper as full fish stall was introducing the guest of honour, an actress who had once been a regular on *Coronation Street*. The actress rose, thanked everyone graciously and then added that she had left the Street a long time ago and had done many other things since then. The crowd nodded and smiled encouragingly at her. Of course you have, love.

The Actress Who Was Once In *Coronation Street* (But That Was A Long Time Ago And She's Done Many Other Things Since Then) crowned the Gala Princess and ushered in the children's fancy dress. There were three Mighty Morphin Power Rangers, an Old Mother Hubbard and her dog, a pram disguised as a tractor by judicious use of cardboard boxes, and Compo and Clegg from *Last of the Summer Wine*. Or rather, there was Clegg and, some way off, a little lad in wellies, a tweed jacket fastened with string and a woolly hat who was refusing to have anything to do with the proceedings. 'Away! Come on!' The boy dressed as Clegg was hissing in his direction as The Actress Who Was Once In *Coronation Street* passed along the line with her fellow judges. He waved his arms frantically, 'Come here! Hurry up!'

Compo stood firm. 'Get lost!' he mouthed back.

My housemaster once said to me, 'Harry, you are a very conscientious boy,' before adding, with what must have been a cynical grin, 'One day you will realise the full horror of what I have just told you.' Clegg was grasping this idea pretty firmly himself by now. He was in agony. It was the pain of a person who fears the consequences, obliged to rely for his salvation on another who plainly couldn't give a bugger about them, mingled with the suspicion that he, the sensible one, the one who did as he was told, would somehow cop for it in the end. Implanted deep in the conscientious child's mind is the knowledge that when a naughty child is naughty he only lets himself down, whereas when a good child is naughty he lets *everybody* down, including the Queen and Nelson Mandela and the people of Australia who are walking about upside-down because of gravity. Clegg's face was growing redder by the second at the thought of this global ignominy, and he was twisting himself into a human knot in a bid to impress on Compo the seriousness of the approaching situation. His right arm twitched. He pointed to the spot where Compo should have been standing. He screwed up his face. 'Come *on*, will you! Please. Please! *Please*! Look, The Actress Who Was Once In *Coronation Street* (But That Was A Long Time Ago And She's Done Many Other Things Since Then) is coming! Hurry up! Hurry *up*, will you?'

Compo grimaced, shuffled in his wellies, began to walk towards Clegg, then stopped. The tension was unbearable. I went to get a cup of tea.

In the cricket pavilion the table bearing the victuals squeaked beneath the weight of its cargo. There were fresh strawberry tarts and little rhubarb flans and plates of triangular sandwiches as neat as the hankie drawer in a gents' outfitters. Steam wheezed from the urn and friendly-faced women emerged through it bearing teapots and doing complicated sums involving multiplying cupcakes and pork pies, adding Viennese whirls and subtracting that sausage roll because your Ethel insists on paying for that separately. The home-made teas at these events are the obverse of the commercial sweet stalls. There you couldn't spend less than a fiver without a monumental effort of will; here you couldn't spend that amount, no matter what amazing feat of gluttony you performed. If you piled your paper plate so high you couldn't see over the top of it without the aid of a periscope, and shuffled down the queue to the till with your knees buckling under the weight, the woman waiting for you would still smile, add one, three down, carry two, and say, 'That'll be £1.27, please.'

I took a seat by the window. Behind me the Hawes Silver Band were refuelling on slices of sly pie, while outside the children's egg-throwing contest had degenerated, a couple of the boys having twigged that they were effectively being given licence to hurl something explosive and slimy at one another. Beyond them the fell-runners were out warming up. They were angular and wiry in the main, with knots of muscle in string-thin legs and arms. Pale and spare, they moved as lightly and carefully as wading birds. Long-distance runners are some of the fittest people around. The odd thing is, they never look very healthy to me. I always associate health with something more golden and rounded. This is because I am confusing humanity with a cheese scone.

Fell-running developed from the old guides' races, contests between the men whose task it was to lead travellers over the Pennines in the days before roads and footpath signs and Wainwright and Wright's bus. As such, fell-running is fairly unusual. Most sports and games develop tangentially to an occupation rather than directly from it. Shepherds invented cricket, but the game itself has little to do with the work of a sheep farmer (despite the impression given by some English batsmen); the shot-put is plainly of military origin, though throwing cannon balls about was the task of artillery pieces rather than artillery men. Like ploughing matches, sheepdog trials and that strange Friesian sport of vaulting over canals using a pole, fell-running is a demonstration of the job itself, rather than a test of the skills used in its execution.

The first guides' races were run towards the end of the eighteenth century, in all likelihood to settle a bet. If, as Jimmy Savile used to say, 'This is the age of the train,' the seventeenth century was undoubtedly the age of the wager. Walking, riding and running were all the focus of heavy gambling, and fortunes were lost betting on things as trivial as which of a group of gentlemen could take his coat off the quickest. Even before the days of professionalism and sponsorship, money played its part in sporting development.

From its origin as a comparison and exhibition of work skills, fell-running gradually increased in popularity to encompass anyone with a yen to see if he or she could run up and down mountains quicker than everyone else. Over the years the sport has lost some of its orienteering element, though a good knowledge of the ground is still important, and it remains one of the few athletic contests in which age and experience can overcome youth and fitness. Like all sports, fell-running has had its internal spats between professionals and amateurs, the one suggesting that it was all right to win a bottle of beer but not the price of a bottle of beer; the other shrugging and wandering off muttering about posh nobs and their bloody double standards. The result is two rival associations, the FRA and BOFRA, locked in a more or less permanent dispute. Fell-running's biggest boost came with the advent of leisure running in the 1970s, when men such as the shepherd Bill Teasdale and his successor as 'King of the Fells', Jos Naylor, became well known via television. Nowadays at weekends throughout the summer there will be half a dozen or more races across the north. The Pen-y-Ghent race, at five and a half miles with one ascent, is shorter than many, but the climb up to the top of the 2,200-foot peak still didn't look like something to attempt after a heavy lunch.

By the time the runners set off, the Hawes Silver Band, suitably refreshed, were back playing and a football match had kicked off. The strains of 'Ebony and Ivory' floated out across the pitch and two players celebrated this paean to human harmony by bumping chests, pointing fingers and scowling.

Sport has always played a bit part in shows and fairs. In all probability, wrestling or some other form of physical combat would have been first introduced, but football was not far behind. Mind you, in the Middle Ages football *was* a form of physical combat. Old-style annual matches involving mass teams scuffling up and down the streets from dawn till dusk on a religious holiday (Shrove Tuesday is a particular favourite) still take place at Alnwick in Northumberland, Sedgefield, County Durham, Workington in Cumbria and Ashbourne, Derbyshire.

The Reivers, those lawless bandit clans who dominated life in the border counties during the sixteenth and seventeenth centuries, frequently celebrated the truce days – markets or fairs that served as a respite from workaday violence – with a football match. The folk poetry of the time often celebrates a fallen hero in terms of his ability to both kick a ball and inflict serious injury. Even in Victorian times the relationship between football and physical combat was happily acknowledged. The Hon. H.F. Kinnaird, a red-bearded Old Etonian, captained England. Worried for his health, a friend commented before a game: 'I fear one day you will break a leg.'

'I may well do,' Kinnaird replied jauntily, 'though it will not be my own.'

However violent football was, it could never match what became the most popular event at many northern fairs and shows: animal-baiting. From cock-fighting and ratting up to bear- and bull-baiting, the harassment and torture of animals took a sickening variety of forms. Captain L. Fitz Barnard's gruesome Edwardian masterwork on the subject, *Fighting Sports*, details hundreds of types with grim relish. If you are in search of a Christmas present for a vegetarian relative you don't much like, look no further: Fitz Barnard is your man.

By the 1840s campaigning by such organisations as the RSPCA had led to the outlawing of such barbaric activities. The last bull-bait was held illegally at West Derby near Liverpool in 1853. From this sordid and brutal side of the fair at least one blackly comic incident can be salvaged. The great travelling menagerie owner Wombwell organised an event to demonstrate the ferocity of his lions. One of them was to be pitted against a pack of mastiffs. Tickets for the event sold like hot cakes. On the night of the event the marquee was jammed with people, most of whom had been drinking heavily. The mastiffs were released into the enclosure with the lion. The bloodthirsty crowd howled in expectation – but nothing happened. The mastiffs were too fearful to attack and the lion too docile. Outraged, the crowd began to boo and whistle. Tempers became frayed. There was some jostling, a shove. A fist flew. Soon a full-scale, drunken riot had ensued. As the men fought and yelled, as blood and insults flowed, the lions and the mastiffs looked on, peaceful and bewildered. As a metaphor for the stupidity of man it is hard to beat.

A gun fired and off the fell-runners went in a solid mass, weaving and turning in unison like a flock of drumlins as they passed out of the sports field and down Horton's main street. By the time they hit the foot of the first slope they had already begun to string out. In many ways fell-running has more in common with cycle racing than it does with other athletic events. The sport tests not only the competitor's stamina but also his or her courage and skill as the runners descend at speed across uneven and often slippery surfaces. You might expect that coming down the slope they would pick their way gingerly as if descending stairs. Far from it. The minute they hit any section that is less than perpendicular, they immediately go flat out. And at times this is just how they end up – flat out. The St John ambulancemen are kept busy at fell races.

The courage of the runners is impressive, and so too is their speed. At Horton I walked off to get another cup of tea at a nearby café, and by the time I had drunk it and returned, two runners, Roberts of Kendal and Kinch of Warrington, had already finished. I stood on a stone bridge and watched the others pass, red-faced, loose-jawed, eyes staring fixedly ahead. And if just looking at them had that effect on me, what must running in the race have been like?

When the last of the competitors had padded down the road and into the sports field I walked up to get the train. The day had brightened slightly and an old man was planting hollyhocks in the station garden. As the sound of the tannoy announcing the raffle winners wafted up the hill, one of the Mighty Morphin Power Rangers wobbled past on a blue bicycle with a single stabiliser.

4

· Cakes ·

The Roman Wall Show

On the banks of the Tyne, the dog and I were sheltering from the rain under a tree. Nearby a dipper was going about his business, darting in and out of the river. After each foray he stood on a rock, bobbing at the knee. With his dark back, white chest and constant deferential nodding, he put me in mind of a nervous Edwardian bachelor entering a ballroom full of debutantes. I tried pointing this out to the dog, but, of course, he didn't pay any attention. He was too busy thinking about Mark Rothko.

A man I know named Tommy came along with his parka hood up and his Border terrier, Chappie, pulling him through the undergrowth as if he were pretending to be the lead husky in *The Call of the Wild*. 'What a day,' Tommy said.

'It's hard to imagine it's June,' I said.

'You'd be hard pressed to imagine it was October,' he answered before Chappie hauled him off towards fate and the Yukon.

Later my girlfriend Catherine and I drove up along the Stanegate, a Roman road which once served the settlements and barracks of Hadrian's Wall. To the north, across the wide, shining greenness of Northumberland, you could see the wall itself, determined and disciplined, running dementedly up and down the steep hills of the Windsill. The Romans had called this area *Finis Terra*, the end of the earth. It was easy to see why. Approached from the south, the slopes of the Windsill rise gradually, then suddenly drop away in a steep cliff. Reaching the top it is a shock to find land on the other side rather than a vast and hostile sea, or a gaping black void.

The Roman Wall Show is held near Sewingshields. It is about as remote as any showground in the country. Even Captain Hook could have counted the buildings visible from it on his fingers. One of them is the Once Brewed pub, from which, back in the 1960s, visitors could hire a reproduction Roman chariot driven by a reproduction Roman charioteer to carry them the few hundred yards up to the wall. Sadly, the service is no longer on offer. The only reminder of it is the chariot on the pub sign. It was in the Once Brewed that the seeds for the afternoon's festivities were sown one winter's night forty or so years ago when two local farmers got into an argument over who had the best tup. The show that resulted has been held every year since.

The rain had turned to drizzle by now. It wasn't so much falling as simply hanging in the air. You felt as if you were standing in the middle of a cloud. Around the sheep pens a huddle of farmers were staring intently at a group of Bluefaced Leicesters. A tall and rangy beast with a prominent Roman nose and a lumpy, almost goatish, body, the Bluefaced is a descendant of Robert Bakewell's revolutionary New Leicester, crossed with Wensleydale and Cheviot stock. You might expect that the addition of blood from these two hardy northern hill breeds would have toughened up the lowland Leicester, but in fact it had quite the opposite effect. A Pennine farmer, whose face was so red with windburn you could probably have boiled a kettle on it, told me: 'A Bluefaced Leicester has only one ambition in life, and that's to die. Don't coddle it like a bairn, it's off! First cool breeze and it keels over.' Other stockmen might disagree with this assessment. Bluefaced ewes are well respected for their fecundity and mothering skills and they are a popular choice as dames for the 'mules', or cross-bred sheep, which make up the bulk of British flocks. Watching the Bluefaced Leicesters now, though, I could see what the rubicund farmer meant: they certainly had a melancholy, not to say suicidal countenance. The high-bridged snout and greyish complexion gave them a look of nervous depression. Grouped together, they reminded me of those Edwardian pictures of the inbred and doomed aristocratic families of Eastern Europe. Perhaps even more disturbingly, they also bore a striking resemblance to Barry Manilow. In fact you wouldn't have been surprised if instead of bleating the Bluefaced Leicester burst into a chorus of 'Copacabana', or, more likely, 'Maaaaah-ndy'. Incidentally, did you know that 'Mandy' began life as a Transylvanian folk song? The original was written by Vlad the Impaler, inspiration for the vampire legend, and opened with the line: 'Mandy, you came in a grave with a stake in.' What a load of rubbish.

Gateshead Pipe Band were playing on the showground. They use the Highland bagpipes, not the much smaller Northumbrian version. The Highland pipes are an outdoor instrument, their sound a great, bellicose roar rather than a breathy, hearthside giggle. Beyond the tartan-clad pipers and the wax-coated throng in the beer tent, the tree-crested crags of the Windsill loomed over Crag Lough. This is the classic postcard view of the wall. The water of the little lake shimmering in the breeze, fishermen's skiffs upturned on the far shore, and beyond it the white and verdant grasses of the Northumbrian uplands rolling out to the horizon.

Catherine and I went into the refreshment tent and got styrofoam cups of coffee. Once again I pondered the question which has baffled mankind for generations: what is the point of sugar lumps? You drop a couple of them in and half your drink jumps out to avoid sharing a cup with the bloody things. You stir and stir and stir, slopping even more of it over your shoes, yet the sugar lumps make not the slightest difference to the taste. When you get to the bottom you discover why: the fugitive sugar cubes are crouching there, hard as the Kray twins. Earlier in the year the Tyne had been in spate and the Rivers Authority men had brought round sandbags as a measure against flooding. Somehow I couldn't help thinking that a few boxes of sugar lumps would have been far more effective.

In pick-ups and Land Rovers the trail and show hounds were beginning to arrive. The agricultural community is not usually thought of as particularly lyrical, yet in the naming of the hounds there was a rich poetry. Hamlet, Harkaway, Talisman, Tarquin, Tailer, Dalesman, Gallant, Grafter, Guardsman, Traveller, Ranger, Clasher, Deacon, Clarion, Palmer, Cruiser and Sergeant, read the list of entries for Class 36 – Best Foxhound, Dog (Unentered). (Yes, I wondered about that word in brackets, too, but to be frank, I was just too nervous to ask.) The bitches' names were softer but just as resonant: Honey, Haze, Bashful, Tackle, Tally, Relish, Daisy, Tinsel, Guilty, Daphne, Clover, Cloudy, Beeswing, Moonlight, Crystal, Parish. All were beautifully christened, save one, a poor pup from Ullswater who had been left to labour through life saddled with the moniker Peevish. When I saw her name in the programme, I thought of seeking out Peevish to see if I could discern some hint of the reason for this pejorative epithet. Was she irascible? Vexatious? Foolish? Or had she been given that name as a character-building exercise like Johnny Cash's 'A Boy Named Sue'? Alas, we shall never know, for at this point the hounds in a mesh cage in the back of a Nissan began to bay, a bloodcurdling howl that was followed immediately afterwards by what sounded like the rattle of castanets. This turned out, on closer investigation, to be my dog's knees knocking together. I decided to seek sanctuary in the industrial tent.

The industrial tent was an early addition to the agricultural societies' shows. Initially it was a place where rural firms could show off their wares – glass, carpets, pottery and the like – a trade marquee. Soon the professionals were joined by members of the public engaged, often fiercely, in a variety of craft competitions. The English have always enjoyed a good contest, whether it be all-in wrestling or all-out knitting. Entries and categories gradually increased, and soon there was no room left for the tradesmen. The industrial tent has been the stadium, the field of dreams, for generations of stick-dressers, embroiderers and holiday-snappers ever since. There are many fine things to be seen in the industrial tent: the children's section includes a crocodile made from a cucumber, a melon-shelled tortoise with root-ginger feet and squinting sultana eyes, and a potato painted as a mole; there are bottles of parsnip wine so potent they smoulder; gardens on plates that would delight Geoff Hamilton; crocheted characters from *Home and Away* which are considerably more lifelike than the real thing, and, of course, there are cakes and jam.

It says something about the British attitude to food that the display of baking should be housed in the industrial tent. How did cakes come to merit such a classification? It suggests a land where people beaver away riveting the lids on blackberry pies and welding the fillings into flans. A place where pastry is not rolled but cast, and in which cart-borne rag-and-dough men trot through villages scavenging for scrap sweetmeats they can flog on to manufacturers in smoke-wreathed Midlands towns. A country where shoppers ask the baker, 'Is that éclair fresh, or is it a remould?' and shipyards are saved by a last-minute order to fabricate sausage rolls for NATO.

In the industrial tent the judges are checking for defects: for cherry slump, burned bottom and soggy-centre sag (a condition with which I myself am becoming sadly familiar these days). In truth it's hard to see how they can separate the entries. Everything here is a delicacy fit to gladden the heart of anyone who has ever had his jaws glued together by the viscose wallpaper paste that passes for fruit in most mass-produced apple pies, or has ever absentmindedly bounced a rubbery pre-packed pasty off the pate of a passing stockbroker. The cheese scones glow so warmly you cannot gaze at them without protective goggles; the Dundee cakes are voluptuous; the decorated sponges resemble extras from a dance scene in *Gone With the Wind*; the pastry is so crisp it rustles, the fairy cakes so light they have to be held down with thread to prevent them from floating up to the ceiling, and even the raisins in the Welsh cakes glisten like the noses of healthy puppies.

Many will gaze upon this rich gastronomic pageant and sigh wistfully in memory of the good old-fashioned village baker's shop. Not me. I grew up in a village with a good old-fashioned baker, Mr Lister. Mr Lister made the hardest, heaviest bread in Christendom. The only person who mourned his passing was the local manufacturer of protective footwear. Mr Lister was a short man with a' pronounced stoop – the result of carrying his own teacakes around, I suspect. He talked as if he had an invisible pipe clamped in one corner of his mouth, a habit which gave his speech an odd ventriloquial quality. There were many tourists who came to our village in the 1960s and left immediately, wailing hysterically that they did not care what anyone else said, they really had been bade good morning by a plate of macaroons in that little shop on the corner. Those macaroons, incidentally, had an important historical function: they had served as bombproof cladding on Monty's staff car.

Mr Lister was the meanest baker of all time. To him a currant bun meant just that – a bun with a currant. The filling ran through his pies like a rumour. The pastry was the colour of a drowned man and the texture of asbestos. Mechanics bought Mr Lister's biscuits to use as brake pads, his finger rolls made an effective cosh and the Alabama Prison Authority flew in five tons of his rock cakes when they ran out of quarries for their chain-gangs to work on. In Montgomery to this day you can see them still, all half-dozen of them, proud and undented, surrounded by fractured pick-axes and sweating, cursing felons. It was in honour of Mr Lister that the industrial tent was so named.

There are English people – usually the sort of English people who cannot be made to see that *pétanque*, with its roly-poly, chain-smoking, alcohol-guzzling competitors, is merely France's answer to darts – who will tell you (they will pause for a moment at this point so you can prepare yourself to hear something life-shatteringly profound) that while the English eat to live, *les*

Français live to eat. At my school we had a French teacher who was of this opinion. Despite the fact that he once referred to me as a 'lazy oaf' for failing to recognise that *en France* a coal-scuttle is always feminine ('And any boy who shouts out, "What sir, even if it has a penis?" will go immediately to the head-master's study'), I feel it would be unfair, not to say spiteful, to name this gentleman, who was after all simply doing his job. So I will refer to him only as Mr Dawnish (of 14 Laburnum Crescent, Ingleby Hutton, North Yorkshire, TS17 6BN).

Mr Dawnish was a Francophile of the most passionate sort. Everything from across the Channel thrilled and delighted him. The gargle of accordions, the melting road-surface smell of the cigarettes, and the language ... Oh, the language! 'So *flowing*, so *expressive*, so ... Ah, the French have a word for it. And no, Wilson, that word is not "Bollocks" - please stay behind after the lesson.' The French language overpowered Mr Dawnish like some rich narcotic. It made him dizzy and wild, it ran barefoot through his cerebellum singing 'La Vie En Rose' and perfuming his synapses with the scent of wild thyme, rosemary and ani-seed; it whirled him round, it can-canned across his conscious-ness, it plied his psyche with champagne, foie gras and truffles, until, swooning deliciously, he abandoned himself to its sweet caresses.

There are some English people who go to Brittany for a fortnight and for months afterwards pepper their conversation with French phrases. Mr Dawnish's complaint was of an alto-gether more virulent order. He had only to catch a whiff of a slice of Camembert to forget his native tongue altogether. The sight of a Charolais cow had him reaching for the French-English dictionary. Yes, Mr Dawnish was head over heels with all things French. He loved the countryside, the towns, the *apér-itifs* flavoured with daffodil bulbs and, of course, he loved *la cuisine*.

Mr Dawnish often gave vent to this view that the English eat to live, whereas the French live to eat and, given our school dinners, you'd have been hard pressed to mount a convincing argument against him. The quality of food at my school was lower than a snake's armpit. And quite often it tasted like one, too. If there had ever been a rebellion among the pupils we'd have boiled Cook alive in her own sago, or, more hideous still, forced her to eat it. Mr Dawnish's position seemed unassailable: we, the English, ate to live, for what else but the raw instinct for survival could explain the regular Wednesday lunchtime disappearance of all that charred liver?

As I filed along the tables of the industrial tents of the agricultural shows, however, I saw very clearly that Mr Dawnish was wrong. The industrial tent demonstrates what most of us, if we think about it, already know: that the great strength of British cooking is baking and preserving. Basically, it's cakes and jam. Cakes and jam are not, as Marie Antoinette's silly comment serves to remind us, the stuff of subsistence. When the peasants revolt they call for bread, or rice, or potatoes. They do not chant, 'We are starving and we want Swiss rolls,' or carry placards demanding drop scones and strawberry conserve.

The famous pyramid of human need starts with a broad base of essentials – food, warmth and the like – and builds up through various stages until at the top we find things such as literature, music and art. These are non-essentials, yet they are the aspects of life by which civilisation is defined. You could make a similar pyramid of dietary need, building on a foundation of staples – wheat, rice, chips – and if you did, the edible exhibits of the industrial tent would come pretty near the top. Bramble jelly is nutritional poetry. Victoria sponge is civilisation. Nobody eats cakes and jam to live. They are fripperies and flummeries, made not to sustain but to enjoy. And the British love cakes and jam.

Aside from being delightful, the baking section of the industrial tent is also a place of mystery. Arcane rituals are played out here, things that nobody can explain. Why, for example, do the show committees, Industrial Section (Home Baking), insist that scones are entered in fours, while meringues and éclairs need only come in triplicate and a tandem of teacakes (baked on the shelf) is considered quite sufficient? Is there some historical reason why you need to produce six biscuits in North Yorkshire, but only four anywhere else? These details may seem trivial, but like the elaborate gradational system of bowing practised by the Japanese Samurai, they are taken deadly seriously. Raise your head slightly too early when greeting a shogun and you were likely to find a Ninja assassin in your bedroom the following night. Ignore the parenthesised instruction 'in the paper wrappers' when you enter four iced buns at an agricultural show, and you're likely to feel the wrath of one of the judges. And I know which I'd rather risk. The toughness of the show judges is legendary.

People who have moved to the country from the town tell you dreadful stories: they entered when they first arrived two years ago, they thought it would be fun. They put chives in their cheese scones like they always did at home ... Oh, it wasn't so very, very bad, really. I mean, people had started speaking to them in the street again, recently, and the therapist said the nervous twitch was responding well to treatment. At a show in Cumberland I came across one example. Some poor individual had interpreted the category 'Wholemeal Loaf' a little too freely. The bread he or she had entered was (come closer, we'd better whisper) *round*. That's right, round. Some mistakes can be allowed to pass without comment; this was simply an affront. Pinned on to the bread was a neat square of pink card about two inches across. On it in bold block capitals, for all the world to see, was the verdict: THIS IS NOT A LOAF! The explanation mark plunged downwards like a dagger. As people passed up and down the tables, many noting the placings in their programmes, a posse of judges stood at the far end of the tent, arms folded, faces sternly set. They wore badges like Wild West marshals and they took their job just as seriously. Though there was a crazy, lawless confectionery world out there, in the industrial tent all was calm; standards were high. The judges stood between values and anarchy. Sometimes out there on the frontier they had to act a little rugged to keep things going. It was tough and lonely work, but somebody had to do it.

5

· Horses ·

Appleby Horse Fair

In the tea room in Appleby a jolly Lancastrian woman was bustling about clearing tables and keeping up a constant stream of chatter. It was like watching a whirling dervish impersonating Gracie Fields. By one window a hunched moleish man was staring out at the main street. He was so deep in thought that when the waitress spun past and swept away his empty coffee cup, he jumped up from his chair as if he'd sat on a hedgehog.

'You were miles away then, weren't you, eh?' the woman cackled gleefully.

The man, blinking, nodded in agreement.

'You were in a right brown study,' the woman said. She was so brisk and cheerful you felt that if *she'd* ever found herself in a brown study she'd have sharp brightened it up with a coat of primrose emulsion and some snazzy curtains.

The little man smiled wanly.

'You were in a world of your own.'

Another bob of the head.

'Was it nice?'

'Oh, yes,' the little man said sadly.

'Better than this one, pet, I'll bet!' the waitress said as she sped off through the swing door with a whump.

Outside in Appleby's steep main street the fronts of the reddish stone buildings grew ever more florid in the afternoon sun. Smiling people stood around in groups eating whirly ice-creams or chips, faces and fingers glowing with grease. Every few minutes a roped line of horses or a pair of speeding sulkies went clattering past. The view inside the fuddled man's head must have been pretty good to be an improvement on this one.

We had driven down the hairpins of Hartside Pass that lunchtime. When I say we had driven, I actually mean Catherine had driven. I can't drive. I am 6'5", with all the swift reactions and co-ordination that implies. It has been scientifically proven that a message from my brain to my feet would arrive quicker by second-class post than it does through my central nervous system. My reflexes are similarly slow. Recently I went to the doctor and he did that reflex test where they hit your knee with a hammer. Nothing happened. Three days later I kicked the dog. I did once take a course of driving lessons. After about fifty it became clear to me that at this rate it was going to work out cheaper to just hire the instructor to drive me where I wanted to go.

This inability to drive is a source of great embarrassment to me. When we lived in London it didn't matter much, but in the country everybody drives. In Northumberland, when I tell people I can't drive, they say, 'What do you mean, you can't drive?' And I say, 'I mean, I have a pet aardvark named Anselm whose underpants are on fire. What do you think I mean?' Such savage, and, frankly, manly, sarcasm usually convinces them that when I say I can't drive I mean I am banned from driving. The belief that my lack of motoring credentials stems from some ribald macho act such as mowing down a bus queue while speeding along at 130mph, steaming drunk and in a stolen car, is one which, pathetically, I do little to discourage. Far better for a bloke to be lawless and irresponsible than mechanically incompetent.

Anyway, we wound down the bends of Hartside, through

Melmerby and down the back roads that skirted along the edge of the bulging Pennines, green slopes scabbed with grey scree. For miles around Appleby there was evidence of the horse fair. Caravans were parked up in fields, rangy nags cropping the grass around them. Appleby Fair is the biggest Gypsy event in the country. In the weeks leading up to it you will pass horses and carts trotting west along the A66 across the windswept desolation of Bowes Moor, or detouring through the spick-and-span little villages of Teesdale.

This area of Westmorland has long been associated with horses. One of the most famous breeders of Elizabethan times, Thomas Sandford, had a stud at nearby Howgill and the race meetings of those days, held on Langwathby Moor or Kingsmoor, drew huge crowds from Carlisle and the outlying districts. Horse-racing has a reputation for attracting a certain unsavoury element, and that was as true 400 years ago as it was when Graham Greene wrote *Brighton Rock*. The reiving clans of the borders – Armstrongs, Elliots, Scots, Kerrs, Charltons, Robsons, Ridleys and Milburns – loved horse-racing. They rode down from their isolated dales and valleys to compete all across the Marches. The races in Westmorland were their favourite, though, because the crowds were larger, betting was heavier and the opportunity for illegal horse-trading was greater.

For much of the sixteenth and seventeenth centuries the requirements of the English army led to a ban on the export of all horses from England. For an Englishman to sell a horse to a Scotsman was a treasonable offence. To the reivers, whose family business was theft and extortion, this was about as discouraging as a fly-swatter is to a wolverine.

Coming into Appleby, we hit heavy traffic. The Test match between England and the West Indies was on the radio. We queued for the entire duration of the English innings to get into the car park. Still, what's half an hour, eh? All along the road there were lines of black-and-white and skewbald horses, dark-skinned Turkic-looking men, the brims on their trilbies curling like the corners of old sandwiches, twanging the animals' fetlocks and scrutinising yellowing teeth with all the intensity of generals surveying a battlefield for a concealed enemy. One pipe-cleaner-legged colt broke loose, collided with the front bumper of our stationary car, careened off it and lolloped down the road, scattering passersby, pursued by a gang of laughing boys. Youths stripped to their waists, pectorals bouncing, rode up and down yelling, 'Hup! Hup! Hup!' or charged along with bucking geldings held on rope halters.

I was a bit worried about Catherine seeing this, as it is a well-known fact that there is something about the sight of men wrestling with horses that women find irresistible. Think of Glenn Close in *Jagged Edge*. The minute she sees Jeff Bridges breaking in that horse you know she'll end up in bed with him whether he's a wife-murderer or no. Or Julia Ormond in *Legends of the Fall*. When she looks out of her window in the pale light of dawn and watches Brad Pitt wrangling with that mustang, she gets so excited steam rises off her. If I was still young and single I wouldn't bother with flashy clothes or expensive grooming products, I can tell you. I'd just take a horse down to a nightclub with me and lead it ostentatiously round the dance floor. The Gypsy youths must have had similar ideas. Appleby is known among the travelling peoples as a 'courting fair'. Brough Hill Fair, in September, was the 'wedding fair'. It perhaps says something for changing values that while the wooing meet at Appleby has grown and grown, the marital tryst at Brough has fallen into such disuse that the man at the tourist office there was unable to say whether it still took place or not.

The narrow dale in which the horse fair was based was jammed with caravans. There were round-roofed wooden contraptions with gaily painted woodwork detailed in gold and faded green canvas drawn across their entrances; gleaming steel trailers as big and shiny as American roadside diners and rock-pink and baby-blue dream homes with lace curtains and gilded ornaments all along the windowsills. Two separate great masses of them, like converging herds of colourful beasts, spread across the facing hillsides and spilled down towards one another in the

green niche of the valley. One encampment was for the traditional families, those who'd been coming to Appleby for generations (the fair has been running for six centuries); the other for
'the newcomers'. In the gap between them were horses; hundreds, perhaps thousands of them. They were hackneys or cart-
horses in the main, pink-muzzled and blotchy, long-maned and
fringed around the hooves. You see the same piebald nags
tethered on patches of wasteground all over Britain. They are as
commonplace as cows. Yet in these numbers, in this setting, they
seemed primal; the scene they created improbably wild and
exotic. Stepping out into the throng of people – the older women
in tan leather trouser-suits decorated with red fox fur, their
Elvis-quiffed husbands resting tattooed knuckles on broad-
buckled belts, the heavily made-up girls in their dayglo crop-tops
and flowing silken trousers shouting and giggling and absentmindedly swerving around cones of horse dung – I felt as if I had
crossed into some parallel world. And in many ways, I suppose I
had.

The Rom people and other travelling tribes, notably the
Shelta-speaking Tinkers, remain something of a nation within a
nation. Paradoxically, it may be that the longer they have been
in Britain, the more removed from the general populace they
have become. The Rom arrived in England some time around
1500. Where exactly they came from is hard to tell, mainly
because they themselves seem to have forgotten. Demonstrating
their gift for self-glamorisation, the Rom claimed to have originated in Egypt, hence the name Gypsies. The most common
surname among the northern Rom was Faa, which the Faas
themselves maintained was a corruption of 'pharaoh', though
others have suggested it is simply, and rather less regally, the
Northumbrian or Scots pronunciation of 'fall' (as in footba'). The
Romany language is said to be Indo-European, though the fact
that there are sixty widely varying dialects makes even that
difficult to pin down. Whatever their origins, from their arrival
in Britain the Rom ploughed an erratic course, progressing from
theft, smuggling and illegal distilling to relative respectability,

along the way establishing themselves as itinerant metalwork-
ers and pedlars, an intrinsic part of rural life.

The north quickly became a Rom stronghold and remained
one for many years despite the creeping enclosure of the land,
which drove them into the cities further south. The Gypsy
'capital' was at Kirk Yetholm just across the Scottish border. The
isolated nature of the life of the farmers and villagers of the
Cheviots, Pennines and North York Moors left them more reliant
than most on travelling craft and salespeople. In winter the
Romanies camped at Kirk Yetholm and other Gypsy towns such
as Wooler and Alnwick. In the summer they took to the roads in
their covered wagons. Each family or group followed a pre-
scribed circuit or walk, calling in at the same farms to carry out
repairs to broken implements or fashion new ones; setting up
stalls at their regular fairs to sell jewellery, sickles and spades,
heather besoms and 'swills' (flat baskets made from oak laths).
In the north the Rom were known as 'muggers' because they
were the area's principal dealers in earthenware and crockery.
They were sought after as musicians, too: the Duke of Northumberland's most famous piper, James Allan, was Romany, and
wedding feasts and harvest dances across the north resounded
to the sound of Rom fiddlers and flautists.

The families guarded their walks jealously. To trespass was a
serious offence amongst the Rom, and retribution could be
bloody. At Alloway Kirk in Ayrshire one such dispute in the
eighteenth century resulted in the annihilation of an entire
tribe.

At night the Rom parked up on the fellsides, or in the
clearings of woods, lifted the coverings from their carts, sup-
ports and all, and placed them on the ground as ready-made
tents. They subsidised their earnings from metalwork and ped-
dling by clearing and cultivating patches of common land,
raising chickens and breeding and dealing in horses.

It would be wrong to paint the relationship between the Rom
and the rural population in too rosy a light. Disputes could and
did arise. A minority of Romanies, such as the 'Lads o' the

Heather' and the notorious Faa gang, which terrorised the border country during the '45 Rebellion, earned the rest an unenviable reputation as troublemakers. As immigrant groups have frequently discovered, the misdeeds of one man will undo the good work of hundreds. That, however, is not to say that the Rom as a whole were without stain on their reputation. Any people in whose language the word for house-dweller and prey is one and the same is bound to display an ambivalent attitude towards the settled population.

There is a streak in the English character that allows an indulgence of the bad habits of foreigners which would never be extended to a fellow countryman. For a while I worked in a shop in London. One of my co-workers was a Dubliner named Ronan. Every once in a while Ronan would meet up with his mates at lunchtime and return hours late and roaring drunk. My boss, who I am certain would have sacked anyone else on the spot for such behaviour, would look to the heavens as Ronan blearily weaved in through the door, shake his head and chortle, 'You Irishmen!' Older country people exhibit a similar attitude towards the Gypsies. 'Oh, they'd do all kinds of work for you on the farm,' they say. 'But you had to keep an eye out, because they were fly buggers,' and then they chuckle merrily. There is a degree of condescension in this, of course – treating adults as if they were naughty children – but if it helps to maintain some level of tolerance perhaps that isn't a totally negative thing. And the attitude cuts both ways. The Rom had the nomads' instinctive sense of superiority over those who stay put, and as a people they were strongly unified: *sore si mensar si men* (we are all relations, all alike: all who are with us are ourselves). Their relationship with the communities they served, sometimes friendly, often fraught, and founded on a mutual mistrust, was beneficial to both sides. As a consequence the rural population had more contact with them than we do today. Romanes words are common in regional dialects. In the area of the North Riding in which I grew up someone you liked was a 'cushty charver' – *charvo* is Romanes for lad, *kushti* means good in the same language.

As the traditional fairs gradually faded away and the demand for the work of travelling craftsmen died, so our contacts with the Rom faded. The large Gypsy gatherings, of which Appleby is one of the few that remains, such as Cuddy's Fair at Bellingham in Northumberland and Romaldkirk Fair in Teesdale, were banned by the magistrates. The enclosing of land cut off the Rom from their traditional campsites and grazing. In the 1890s the Battle of Long Horsley Moor saw the forcible ejection of Gypsies from a newly enclosed camping ground upheld in the courts. With legislation as well as the landowners now against them, even the northern tribes were gradually forced to abandon their traditional way of life and follow the streams of displaced smallholders into the industrial towns.

Catherine and I walked down across the road where the horses were being run in front of prospective buyers and into an area of market stalls. Rows of vans sold hot dogs and hamburgers in accord with the Biblical injunction: 'Wheresoever a multitude is gathered together, there shall be the smell of fried onions.' There were dozens of fortune-tellers' caravans. A red-nosed young woman emerged from one nearby coughing and sneezing. Gypsy Rose Pearson gazed into the ether and predicted that one Romany fortune-teller would be leaving Appleby with a heavy cold. We wandered past tables laden with copper and brass knick-knacks, china Clydesdales, mirrors engraved with Confederate flags, satin cushions fringed with lace, and pot Alsatians (by which I mean Alsatians made from earthenware, not some sort of just-add-boiling-water dog-flavoured snack. Heaven forfend). Some old women came up and offered us sprigs of lucky heather. It was a moment I had been dreading. A few years before, on a trip to Granada, I had been terrorised by old Gypsy women. They came up and offered a rose for your *señorita*. If you told them you didn't have a *señorita* they looked at you as if to say, 'Well, get one, scumsucker,' and then pressed the rose into your palm, grabbing your hand as they did so. Resistance was useless. Those old Spanish Gypsy women had a grip like a dogfish. They simply crushed your hand around the rose, smiling beatifically at you all the while. And if you heard a noise like semi-automatic rifle fire, it was your knuckles popping. Squealing, you doled out the money. She released you. But by then it was too late. The damage was done. Your palm was thorn-lacerated, your hand the shape of that glop in a lava lamp and your fingers were quivering and squeaking like frightened mice.

With this in mind I was already dipping into my pocket when I heard Catherine say cheerily, 'We're quite lucky already, thanks.' I waited for some terrible outcome. My fingers instinctively tried to dash behind a pile of garish oil paintings, my knuckles throbbed reflexively. 'Oh, well good for you, pet,' one of the women said with a smile, and they walked away. It's a poor state of affairs when even Gypsy heather-sellers are starting to go on customer-relations courses.

Down in Appleby itself horses were being led down into the river for washing, strings of a dozen or more splashing into the deep pools beyond the thin shale beaches. Despite boyhood dreams of being a cowboy, I have never been particularly fond of horses. When you are at school there is always one boy in your class who is handsome, brave and brilliant at games. (And readers, I know, because I was that boy. Only joking.) Logic dictates that you should admire him, but somehow you just feel resentful. Your head tells you you should aspire to be like him, but every time he turns his back your heart orders you to flick ink down it. This is pretty much the way I feel about horses. Horses are beautiful, swift and strong. They are in many ways the most perfect creatures, and as a consequence there is something profoundly irritating about them. They are just so damned sensible. This is why I prefer donkeys. There is nothing sensible about donkeys. At a pinch they can pull a cart or heave a pack, and they are just about the only domesticated animal that will chase a dog, yet not since Roman times has anyone seriously used the ass in Britain. The donkey owes its survival in this country to its ability to charm and amuse a few enthusiasts. As a writer I strongly empathise with donkeys.

Sadly, the donkey is not much of a show animal. Just about the only agricultural shows in the north with donkey sections are those at Carlisle and Alston in Cumbria (England's highest market town – and that's official!) and they attract only around half a dozen entries. Part of the problem is that the breeders who created such a splendid diversity of cattle, sheep and chickens for some reason ignored the common ass. Only one outstandingly different donkey exists, the Poitou, a shaggy-coated French giant, a kind of Gallic Shire donkey. I can't help thinking that this wilful decision to ignore the ass in favour of the horse has been greatly to man's detriment. Would the Charge of the Light Brigade have occurred if the lancers and hussars had been mounted on asses? Somehow I think not. Would Attila and his Hunnish horde have sacked Rome and swept away civilisation astride donkeys? I doubt it. The donks wouldn't have put up with any such nonsense. They'd have found a nice field and just settled down in it for a good scran and no amount of Asiatic yelling or upper-class entreating would have shifted them. And so much the better for everyone. But no, it had to be horses. Bloody old horses. Horses like the one on which the author wagered a free £300 to-win-only bet he had won through his writerly endeavours. Horses like the one which subsequently came second in a photo finish, thus depriving him of the price of a new stereo. Yes, *those* horses.

The horse was the last animal to be domesticated. Man conned most livestock into domesticity by offering the animals food, a warm place to stay and protection from predators. It was only after they'd signed on the dotted line and were lying on clean straw, pot-bellied and belching, that a querulous voice was raised: 'This bit in small print at the bottom of our contract. My eyes aren't so good, but it looks like it says, "I hereby agree that in repayment for the above services I will allow the afore-mentioned mankind to eat me and all my descendants." What's all that about, then?'

'Oh, here, let's have a look … Well, it's obviously a misprint, isn't it? It's probably meant to say "seat me". I mean, if they were going to eat us they wouldn't give us this kind of treatment, would they? Remember wolves? When wolves used to eat us it was just wallop-chomp-chomp. That's what happens when you're going to get eaten: they knock you down and that's your lot. But this is five-star, this is. Old Wally over there must have put on three stone since we come here. Look at him, all fat and meaty and juicy and ... Oh bloody hell, *what have we done?*'

This approach didn't work with horses, though. This is not because the horse takes immense pride in its self-sufficiency or values its freedom more keenly than other animals, but because it is profoundly stupid. In order to fool someone, or something, you must have a basic grasp of the rules that set up the trick. Simple though these were – and let's face it, even sheep could understand them, so they must have been very, very simple indeed – they were way beyond the mental capacity of the horse. At least, this is the way I interpret it. Most experts say that the problem man had with horses stemmed from the fact that they are not strictly a social animal and the lack of herd instinct makes domestication difficult. But they didn't lose £300, did they?

Early horses were the size of ponies and had an upright Mohican mane. At first man kept them strictly for food, only gradually realising their potential as transport. The horse-based tribes of Central Asia utilised both functions of the horse to the full. The followers of Genghis Khan would slaughter one, cut wafer-thin slices of flesh from its haunches, place these under their saddles and ride about for a few days to tenderise it, then eat it raw accompanied by an alcoholic drink made from fermented mare's milk. I tell you this not because it has any relevance to the northern fairs and shows, but so that if a Mongol ever invites you to a dinner party in his yurt you won't turn up expecting Lancashire hotpot followed by spotted dick and custard.

The Celts were the first people to domesticate horses in Britain. The Romans brought a variety of different breeds with them and introduced the horseshoe. The Saxons invaded simply because they had heard a rumour that British horses were pretty good and in plentiful supply. Shortly afterwards Christianity arrived, and the eating of horseflesh was abolished in Britain because of its association with pagan worship and, one suspects, the French. The Norman invasion brought the first large warhorses to our shores.

From this basic stock British horses were gradually bred to take on a variety of tasks until they ranged in size from the tiny Shetland to the mighty Shire. The trend was vigorously pursued by the agricultural reformers. Robert Bakewell created the Shire horse by cross breeding West Friesland mares bought on a trip to the Low Countries with his own Leicestershire black stallion. The Duke of Hamilton refined the giant Clydesdale, said to be the descendant of the English warhorses captured at Bannockburn, by mixing them with stock from Poland and Hungary. The Suffolk Punch, a powerhouse plough horse with a body shaped like a boiler, was bred by Thomas Coke at Holkham. As the horses improved, so the demand for them grew. Great fairs and markets sprang up around the country. The biggest were in the Midlands at Market Harborough, Ashby, Rugby and Burton-on-Trent. They were garrulous affairs characterised by heavy drinking, fighting and large-scale gambling on everything from impromptu street races to competitions to see who could drink the hottest cup of tea. Away from the fairs, adverts appeared in periodicals and newspapers all over Britain offering the services of prize stallions. Phrased like modern-day lonely hearts columns, these stud commercials listed dates and places at which a rendezvous could be effected between females and the four-legged hunk in question, and offered second-chance guarantees for any mares that weren't successfully impregnated at the first attempt.

As nomadic peoples, the Rom and the Irish-originated Tinkers had always been associated with horses and the horse fairs. Walking back up towards the car park, past the speckled, jostling lines of nags and the clusters of men in baggy, dark suits and white, open-necked shirts as they haggled and scrutinised, it was clear that they still were. To what end, though, remained unclear. Few Gypsies these days travel by horse and cart - most have cars or transit vans to tow their vast caravans around. Perhaps the horses to them are like gold: worthless in themselves; valuable only because value is placed upon them.

A month later Catherine and I were back near Appleby. A rush-bearing ceremony was being held in a tiny village to the south of the town. Little girls in their best cardigans, white socks gleaming, wore floral bonnets; boys grimaced in freshly pressed shirts, carried rush crosses and surreptitiously tried to scuff the polish off their shoes. A silver band in cerulian blue V-necks played hymns, watched by a small crowd of mums and grannies and the photographer from the local paper. No sign of the Gypsies remained, no gleaming chrome or guttural voices, no sound or scent of horses. It was as if the camp, like some bare-knuckle Brigadoon, had vanished in the Pennine spray.

6

• Flowers •

The Malton Show

Martins had tunnelled into the sandbanks leaving them looking like slabs of cinder toffee; swallows scudded over the meadows, skimming dew from the gleaming grass, and diaphanous wispy clouds of the sort that usually wrap themselves round the naked waists of goddesses in Renaissance paintings floated gently across the hills, grumbling that the sexual revolution had done them out of one of the few perks of a deadly dull job. Summer was here, and the surest sign of it was the sound of 'Simply the Best' blasting out from a nearby farmyard. This is the theme tune of the sheep-shearers. The sheep-shearers are the glamour boys of farming. Following the shearing season from New Zealand through California to Canada or Italy or France, they spend their lives in a world where it is always early summer and Tina Turner is perpetually top of the charts. Resplendent in cycling shorts and cut-away Lycra vests, they burst into the agricultural communities of the north each June to the accompaniment of 'Eye of the Tiger' and what sounds like an exchange of gunfire but is, in fact, the ripple of exploding female hormones.

Itinerant men have always had this effect on rural womankind. The romantic allure of sailors, soldiers, wandering minstrels and fairground gaff lads is celebrated in folk tunes and poetry. Sadly for romantics, the roving workman is a dying breed and his modern-day counterparts don't really exude the same magnetism. It's hard to imagine the lady-sat-in-her-castle-grey running off with a raggle-taggle-feed-rep-o. The sheep-shearers are an echo of the past. A rather loud one. Outside the sheds in which they work, flocks of teenage girls alight on fences and gates to watch them in action, spinning, twisting, flipping and pinning the ewes between bulging, bronzed thighs. The air is thick with an acerbic fog of sweat and lust and lanolin. It was the twanging of heartstrings round the sheep-shearing sheds that inspired the inventor of the banjo.

Summer was here, and the surest sign of it, apart from the arrival of the sheep-shearers, was that I had just paid 87p for a bottle of Orangina at the York Station snack bar. To get from York to Malton you take the Trans-Pennine Express, a train which proves conclusively that British Rail are using a different dictionary from the rest of us. If I were told that the chairman of BR had a tortoise called Rocket, I wouldn't be a bit surprised. If he defined the price of drinks from Travellers' Fare as 'very reasonable', I would fully understand.

The Trans-Pennine Express was on its way to Scarborough. It was packed with day-tripping pensioners dressed in crimplene slacks, crochet-knit short-sleeved acrylic cardies and nylon sports shirts. The manmade fibres crackled like a tropical storm. Balloons burst, a dachshund yelped. As we pulled out of the station, an elderly couple wandered up and down the carriages as inseparable as a pair of Siamese twins. They were stuck together with static. The woman in front of me, whose aqua-marine trouser-suit gave off a phosphorescent glow, rummaged in a cavernous navy-blue holdall and emerged clutching an old Mighty White bag containing a packed lunch. 'Have a sandwich,' she commanded her husband, who was staring fixedly ahead from beneath a rayon yachting cap, unmoving save for the occasional twitch when he was struck by a spark from his partner's clothing.

'What's in them?'

'Luncheon meat,' the wife said, pulling a sandwich from the bag. The bread was the colour of a vest, but didn't look as if it would be quite so nourishing.

'There's no lettuce or cucumber or owt in there, is there?' her husband said, giving the sandwich a suspicious sideways look, as if he half expected it to go for his face.

'Of course there isn't,' the wife said. 'There's just marge.'

The man took the sandwich, flipped the corner back quickly to check that she was telling the truth, then took a bite and chewed on it reflectively, pleased once again to have avoided contact with anything remotely natural. British OAPs have a strong aversion to eating or wearing anything natural. If it isn't a product of the petro-chemical industry, then the label better contain a hefty selection from the words 'chopped', 'shaped', 'dehydrated', 'reconstituted', 'tinned', 'frozen', 'UHT', 'homogenised' and 'in syrup', or our island's pensioners aren't interested. They think the notice which says 'Contains no artificial colourings or preservatives' is a health warning from the government. In supermarkets you see old people studying boxes of instant stuffing, muttering, 'Only four E numbers? What are they trying to do, poison us?' They hate anything with skin, rind, or green bits in it. If cheese isn't the same vivid orange as a beauty therapist's face they reject it out of hand. Pensioners, you see, still believe in progress. They are the last remaining social group who think that man is capable of making a better, brighter future for himself. While everyone else is desperately trying to slow things down, put the roughage back into bread and keep the enzymes in milk, OAPs are marching steadfastly towards the year 2000 confident that by the time they get there everyone will be subsisting on a diet of pills, wearing all-in-one terylene bodysuits with silver lightning flashes down the sleeves and living in houses with doors that open automatically when you give them a special hand signal. I'll tell you something for nothing: paying 87p for that Orangina really pissed me off.

The train clunked on across the Vale of York, through glimmering yellow rape, wheat slashed with great stripes of poppies, and fields where big pump hoses sent spumes of water high in the air and miniature rainbows shimmered above white-flowered potato plants. We began to cut through the wooded Howardian Hills. The sky was blue; the sun beat down. It was hot. Beside the track, the River Derwent looked too torpid to move. On its far bank a moorhen sheltered under a parasol of butter-burr leaves and a pair of herons cooled their heels in the mossy green water beneath a listing willow. Even the tulips in the gardens of the houses overlooking Kirkham Priory seemed to be straining to find some shade. As the train rattled on past reed beds and hay bales, the natural rolling motion set the pensioners rubbing together and soon the carriage had developed an electro-magnetic field strong enough to overturn a horse and suck the shoes off it.

Malton is a market town, as handsome and solid as an oak settle. I walked up from the station through the main square with its impressive array of Georgian pubs and old-fashioned shop fronts, along deserted early-closing-day streets. It was just after midday, and so hot that the tarmac was melting and as you lifted your feet from the road you heard a gummy, ripping sound like a plaster being pulled off a hairy leg. Only without the ouch.

At the showground the heat was causing problems for the livestock. The fire brigade had turned up and were hosing down the pigs who, spruced up for the show, had none of the mud they usually sensibly apply to themselves as sunblock. The exhibitors, meanwhile, had rigged up canvas shades to protect susceptible beasts and one farmer was sheltering his prize Texel tup beneath a multi-coloured golfing umbrella.

I took a walk past the cattle. There were some huge Belgian Blues. Smoke-grey and white, with a characteristic weight-lifter's bulging bottom, the winning bull could easily have passed as a tank. Other massive continental breeds – Charolais, Limousin and Simmenthal – were also much in evidence. The only British purebred represented was the Aberdeen Angus, a

happy-looking creature with charming furry ears. Lik[...]
English Longhorns at the Northumberland Show, the Angus
bulls were dwarfed by their foreign counterparts. This, it should
be stressed for anyone worried that our nation's manhood is
being impugned here, was not through any deficiency of masculinity on the part of British beef cattle. There is an historical
reason why European breeds are bigger, and it is closely linked
to the shire horses who were at that moment clumping round the
main showring at Malton.

The English were famous throughout the medieval world for
their ability to breed heavy horses. Stallions were imported from
Flanders, Holland and the Elbe Valley and crossed with native
mares to produce an ideal mount for the knights and men-
at-arms who formed the shock troops of that period. In size
midway between a modern dray horse and a large hunter, these
warhorses were big and very strong. They needed to be to bear
the weight of the heavily protected knights. They were, quite
literally, armoured personnel carriers. Since the English were at
war, either with the French or Scots, or with each other, more or
less constantly for five centuries, the breeding and selling of
warhorses became a major and very profitable industry. By the
end of the English Civil War, however, the introduction of
effective muskets had rendered heavy plate armour, and thus
the horses needed to carry the wearer into battle, redundant.
The new cavalry wanted lighter, quicker mounts. Large military
horses flooded the civilian market. Up until this point any heavy
horses not commandeered by the army had been used to pull
coaches and carriages. They had simply been too expensive to
put to work on the farm - hauling ploughs, carts and other
machinery had been the province of the ox.

Oxen had been the main draught animal used in farming
since systematic agriculture began in ancient Egypt. The ox had
in many ways shaped the British landscape. Fields were the size
an eight-ox team could plough in a day; a furlong the distance
they could draw a plough before stopping for breath - a furrow
length. A draught animal's pulling power is related to its weight,

and the now surplus, and consequently cheap, warhorses were much heavier than oxen. They were also quicker and more economical: two horses and a man could plough more land in a day than six oxen attended by a man and a boy. So after 2,000 years of faithful service to British farming, the ox's days as a beast of burden were over. And so, pretty much, were its days as anything else. It disappeared almost totally from our national life. You never see a field of oxen, do you? Or hear a gentle lowing from the ox shed. In fact, the only evidence the ox still exists in this country is in the butcher's shop. Here you will find ox tongue, oxtail and ox hearts. Where they keep the oxen used to produce these delicacies, and what they do with the rest of the carcass, is a mystery.

Actually it isn't, I'm just teasing. An ox is simply a castrated bull. It's another word for bullock, steer or stirk. But people are funny about what they'll eat, and the butcher knows that while his customers are quite happy to tuck into some oxtail soup, they'd turn up their noses at ox-and-kidney pie or a portion of ox bourgignon. Lamb sells, but nobody wants mutton. The same people who'll crump into calves' liver won't touch veal.

From the seventeenth century until the widespread introduction of tractors between the wars, the horse was the draught animal of choice in Britain. Cattle here were no longer bred to pull machinery, but solely to provide meat and milk. As a consequence, in the case of cattle, weight, so essential in a draught animal, was no longer of primary importance. Instead the proportioning of joints, flavour and the ability of beasts to mature quickly on variable qualities of grazing land became the farmers' main concern. On the continent, meanwhile, the ox's role as a draught animal remained unchanged. Cattle such as the mighty Italian Chianina, with its characteristic hump and long legs, were pulling carts until well into this century. And that is why at the Malton Show the winning Aberdeen Angus bull had no chance of looking his counterpart Belgian Blue straight in the eye unless he stood on a box.

Having given an Aberdeen Angus a reassuring pat (I thought

about telling him that in tastings Angus beef usually walloped its continental counterparts for texture and flavour, but it seemed a bit tactless; it could have been his kids) and received a rather slimy nosing in return, I wandered up and down the sheep pens for a while trying to catch a glimpse of some of the rare breeds. I was particularly keen to see the Whitefaced Woodlands listed in the catalogue. The Whitefaced Woodland is a Pennine breed with its origins in the area round Huddersfield. Both males and females have spiral horns that sit on the side of their heads like Carrie Fisher's hairdo in *Star Wars*. A large sheep with mixed ancestry that includes Cheviot and Spanish Merino, the Whitefaced Woodland is noted for its wiry wool and high-quality meat. More importantly, as far as I am concerned, it is the only northern breed of sheep with a pink nose. Among British sheep this is a mark of some distinction. The Poll Dorset and its spiky cousin the Dorset Horn are the only other breeds so blessed. I eventually found a Whitefaced Woodland ewe peeping out from beneath a tarpaulin sunshade. In combination with her snowy cheeks and forehead, bright eyes and neatly arranged horns, the pink nose gave the sheep a look of amused disapproval, like that of a roguish old great-aunt who has just stumbled on a teenage nephew cuddling the chambermaid. The Whitefaced Woodland was unusual among rare breeds in that its scarcity resulted from its efficiency rather than, as was usually the case, from some perceived weakness. During the First World War the combination of a meat shortage and the bulky body of the Whitefaced Woodland resulted in an increased demand that almost wiped out the breed. All across rural England in villages and tiny hamlets and at the crossroads between isolated clusters of cottages there are memorials to the dead of the Great War. Hardly a farm or estate was left untouched by it. The effects of the conflict, like some raging epidemic, spread across pasture and dale. Nothing, not even a pink-nosed sheep, could escape the devastation.

Beyond the industrial tent, the British Domesticated Ostrich Association's display was drawing quite a crowd. Ostrich

farming began in ancient Egypt, where the bird was the preferred mount of fashionable ladies. The Greeks and Romans
carried on with it, and even in Britain it is not such the modern
novelty it might seem. The first ostrich farm was established
here in the 1680s, although attempts to make a living from
selling its meat proved unsuccessful, despite the fact that it is
described as having the texture of turkey, the appearance of
beef and the flavour of venison. In the nineteenth century
various bright entrepreneurs made further attempts to set up
ostrich farms based around the sale of plumes to the fashion
industry. The climate was blamed for their failure. In the past
decade, however, ostrich farming has become big business in
Canada - a glance through any Country and Western clothing
catalogue will convince you of the popularity of ostrich hide as
boot-making material as well as the undying allure of polyester
- a fact which, combined with the current fad for what might be
described as macho meats such as bear, bison, alligator and
rattlesnake among certain restaurateurs, has persuaded enter-
prising British farmers and smallholders that they could make a
go of it here, too.

Having evolved to survive the burning heat of the African
veldt, the ostriches were one of the few animals on the showground who seemed to be enjoying themselves. Two of the birds
were stalking around inside a high wire-fenced enclosure, nibbling at the grass. When they lifted their heads and gazed
chinlessly about they towered over the inquisitive spectators.
The biggest was well over seven feet tall and, according to the
publicity handout, weighed somewhere in the region of 300lb.
There are three things that everyone knows about ostriches:
they can run very fast; they can disembowel a man with a single
kick, and, when frightened, they stick their head in the sand. The
last one is a bit of a mystery to me. I mean, if you are seven feet
tall, weigh over twenty stone and can disembowel an enemy
with a single kick, what is there to be afraid of? Now I come to
think of it, there is a fourth thing that everyone knows about
ostriches: whenever they appear in a children's comic they will

always at some point swallow an alarm clock.

There's more to ostriches than that, though. For example, the ostrich's brain is smaller than its eye (for those of you unfamiliar with ostriches, I would estimate this to be about the size of a decent gobstopper). According to the BDOA's leaflet, its lack of intelligence is part of its attraction. Whether this is true or not I don't know, but it certainly makes me feel better about that dreamy look which passes across women's faces at the mention of Keanu Reeves. On the back of the pamphlet the BDOA made an interesting comparison between the ostrich and the cow. Meat production, maturation, prolifigacy are all detailed, and the ostrich comes out ahead in all of them. But what really seals its superiority is the final consideration: 'Income from feathers and eggs? Ostrich: yes. Cow: no.' Now don't say I haven't taught you anything.

In the horticultural tent a woman with a camcorder was filming the fuschias. She was walking up and down the table intently focused on her floral tracking shot, buffeting old ladies and trampling on small children as she went. People with camcorders are always like this. There seems to be some sort of unwritten rule that everyone must get out of their path, a steam-gives-way-to-sail kind of thing. Joggers are exactly the same. If you meet a jogger on a single-track towpath, etiquette apparently dictates that you must throw yourself into the canal rather than impede his regal progress for a single millisecond.

The woman with the camcorder zoomed in on the prize-winning specimen. There are some consolations in life so enormous that they should be called upon only in the direst emergency; small mercies the recalling of which will brighten up even the darkest hour. They should be used sparingly as a balm to soothe mental anxiety. I am saving the knowledge that I will never have to sit and watch a home-made video of a flowering plant until the day I find myself trapped in a disabled midget submarine with Danny Baker, two Mormons and a flatulent life-insurance salesman. I have other escapes much worse than this. I have them stored away for situations so desperate that when I start trying to imagine them my brain whistles, my eyes bulge and I pass into unconsciousness. Many of them are video-related.

Relatives and neighbours going on holiday used to be bad enough. There were the endless stories, the plastic donkeys and the bottles of the local liqueur that give the convincing impression that the English word for an alcoholic drink distilled from grapes must be the same as the Greek word for creosote. Then one day everything went mad. Somewhere in a fetid bedsit, a drooling, sadistic sadsack began to plot his hideous revenge on the world. Here he was, this myopic spawn of Satan at whom the girls had laughed and whom the boys had scorned, and all the time, in the mephitic recesses of his mind, his riposte to an indifferent world was coagulating like the rancid cheese atop the rotting slice of pizza under his bed. He wanted something painful, something nasty. Something crueller than encouraging women to wax their bikini lines, more mind-numbingly irritating than stealing the bendy straws off soft-drink cartons. He wanted a retribution so vast and awful that families would weep before it, children would scream and committed vegetarians would rather eat their own fungally-infected feet than face it. So he invented holiday videos.

I have seen people filming dry-stone walls and gravel pits. Somewhere in Cumbria is a man with a fine collection of footage of larch-lap fencing. In Durham, even as you read this, someone is sitting down to three hours of trembly, soft-focus, steamy Danish postboxes. Once, in early August, while walking in the north Pennines, I came across a parked car. A man with a camcorder protruding from his face like some hideous goitre was filming something on the other side of the valley while a teenage boy, clearly his son, studied the same object through powerful binoculars. 'What is it?' I asked the man. 'Some sort of falcon or something?'

The man let out a dry, derisive sort of chuckle. 'Oh no,' he said. 'I'm recording the cars going down the road over there.'

'We've seen several of the new registration already,' the son added in the sharp tone of someone vindicated.

I suppose it's nice when a father and son share a common interest, but I can't help feeling that these two could have found something more suitable to do together. Like becoming kamikaze pilots.

Dodging the viciously swinging lens of the camcorder woman as it ricocheted dangerously off the becapped head of an octogenarian radish exhibitor, I made my way over to the floral decorations. In the art world, the Turner Prize usually sparks a bitter conflict between the respective forces of traditionalism and modernism. At an agricultural show the flower-arranging section serves a similar purpose. In art the traditional might be represented by a watercolour landscape; the modern by an abstract sculpture made from pasta and the artist's pubic hair. When it comes to floral decoration, the traditional is basically flowers in a pot, while the modern is fern fronds and kiwi fruit above which fly sputniks of button mushrooms borne aloft on traceries of bright orange wire. A glance at the programme is enough to alert you to what is afoot. Traditional arrangements are usually confined to the mundane: 'An Exhibit in a Candlestick', 'A Petite Exhibit'. The modern, by contrast, interpret wider themes, their titles echoing those of contemporary dance pieces, or John Coltrane records: 'Continental Cool', 'A Tale of the Sea', 'Nietzsche, Angst and the Antirrhinum in a Postmodern World'.

I walked along peering at the hosta leaves and lime segments, the dahlias counterpointed with driftwood. In truth I wasn't too concerned about the arrangements: whether you saw the modern pieces as brave attempts to broaden the scope of flower-arranging by challenging established parameters or simply desperate was a matter of opinion. The thing that interested me were the judges' notes. On cards by each arrangement a neat little message was printed for the entrant. They said things like: 'A good exploration of the theme spoiled by a messy backdrop,' or, 'A larger central lily would have added balance to this otherwise perfect piece.' Apart from the odd frontier pastry marshal driven to summary justice by renegade biscuit shapes, no judges except those who dealt with floral arrangements gave notes to the competitors. I found this rather disappointing. I felt it would have improved the visitors' understanding of the judging criteria greatly if they could read such comments in other areas. 'A lively Saanen goat with good features, marred by a strong resemblance to Douglas Hurd,' or 'In the world of the dressed stick this is a nudist,' or 'Fairy cakes? Goblin cakes, more like!'

Afterwards I walked back to the station. It was late afternoon and the heat had left the day rather crisp around the edges. The train was once again full of day-trippers, now looking as if they'd been barbecued. At York I bought another 87p bottle of Orangina. There were no old-age pensioners to slag off this time, though, so I just had to brood.

7

· Showmen ·

Newcastle Town Moor Hoppings and Alnwick Fair

In the murk of Eldon Square's subterranean bus station, the passengers funnelled on to the Alnwick bus to the sounds of Vivaldi. There were a pair of German hikers, one incongruously clutching a small Union Jack; a man in a black toupee that swooped down across his hair like the wing of a stuffed rook and a young couple in baggy Oxfam clothes. As they got on board the girl said, 'You never see anything in the *Guardian* Student Supplement about, you know, how to, like, wash sweaters and stuff.'

Just as we were about to set off, a final passenger boarded. He was a man of about sixty, in a pastel-blue blouson, grey sta-prest slacks and matching slip-on shoes with quilted fronting. He wore one of those checked flat caps that has a pom-pom on the top instead of a button. As he came down the bus towards me, a strange, breathy, howling noise began, as if all the air-control nozzles on the bus had suddenly burst into life at once. But it was nothing to do with the air-conditioning, it was the old bloke. In every gents' toilet in Britain there is always somebody whistling loudly and tunelessly. This was him. Choo-shoo-shoo shoo choo-choo, he went; Choo-oooo shoo. He didn't whistle as any normal person might, through pursed lips. Instead he stiffened his mouth and retracted his jaw as if blowing into an invisible flute. It is impossible by this method to raise anything more than a random shrilling, like that made by whirling a hosepipe round your head, but the man persisted with it anyway. There is something about people who are deeply unmusical, a common bond that unites them all. Whenever they take it into their heads to sing or whistle anything, they never opt for some modest composition of limited range. No, they plump for a song that would tax even the most technically accomplished professional. They belt out 'My Way' or 'Danny Boy' or some other tune which will allow them to suddenly burst from grinding the low gears of their vocal cords into a great warbling crescendo that scrapes the limescale off the inside of boilers and sends cats diving into dustbins.

The man came and sat down behind me. Today he was whistling snatches from his Emerald Isle Collection. I was being treated to 'I'll Take You Home Again, Kathleen'. I recognised it easily enough – not because of the accuracy of his whistling, but because every once in a while he would expertly segue into the lyrics. Chooo-woo-shhwake you home again Kathl-shoo-shiroo, he went. If I'd been Kathleen I wouldn't have left a forwarding address.

We rumbled through the centre of Newcastle and out past Town Moor. The Hoppings were on, and a great multi-coloured mob of fairground rides sprawled across the open expanse of parkland. Even on this bright afternoon you could see the lights flashing on the gantries of the waltzers and the pods of the dive-bombers and other rides that whirled their arms in the air to the thumping beat of dance music. Town Moor Hoppings is one of the largest of the traditional pleasure fairs which were once such a feature of the English calendar. And the cornerstone of the pleasure fairs were the showmen.

The showmen of the seventeenth, eighteenth and nineteenth centuries made a precarious and at times dangerous living travelling about from one fair to the next, taking in wakes, markets and race meetings along the way. They traversed the country during the season, following a more or less constant timetable that began in Wrexham in early March and concluded with Sheffield Wakes towards the end of November. While at some times of year a clutch of local fairs such as the Cumberland Run (Carlisle, Cockermouth, Whitehaven, Workington and Clittermore) might fall conveniently close together over a week or two, most did not. As a result, vast distances had to be covered in short spaces of time. Packing up the night a fair finished, the show people would force march with their horse, donkey or often hand-drawn carts to the next location, covering the miles at improbable speeds. Wombwell, the menagerie owner responsible for the lion-versus-mastiffs débâcle, once travelled with his entire mobile zoo from the Town Moor Hoppings to Bartholomew Fair in London in less than a fortnight. Sadly, this exertion proved too much for his star attraction, an elephant, which keeled over and died the minute they arrived at the site in Smithfield. Not that this would have fazed Wombwell: a showman's life was full of such disasters. A few years earlier he had learned that his arch-rival, Atkins (of Atkins' Royal Menagerie), had hired a lion-tamer who concluded his act by putting his head into the mouth of a lioness. Never one to be upstaged, Wombwell ordered his own lion-tamer, a raddled old-timer named Manchester Jack, to perform the same feat. The first time he did so, or so the story goes, Manchester Jack was shocked to feel the lioness's jaws closing around his neck. 'Does she whisk her tail, Bill?' he called to his assistant. 'Aye, sir,' came the reply. 'Then I am done for,' cried Manchester Jack, whereupon the lion promptly proved him right by biting off his noggin. Oddly enough, Manchester Jack is later reported to have left Wombwell's service and gone to run a pub in Taunton. How he got the job is not recorded, but it's a safe bet that he lied to the brewery when they asked if he had a head for business.

Entertainers such as Wombwell had been an integral part of fairs since the Middle Ages, when actors performing mystery plays were supplemented by teams of mummers who capered about the fairground belabouring one another with inflated pigs' bladders and generally boring everyone rigid. I'm being a bit biased here, because mummers were the precursors of the modern mime artist. The word 'mime' has roughly the same effect on me as the approaching hoot of the swine-gelder's horn must have had on medieval male piglets.

By the seventeenth century the mummer had been replaced by the Zany or Jack Pudding, a cross between a jester and a stand-up comedian who combined slapstick with political satire. Often the latter was so sharp that the Zany found himself dragged off stage in mid-act and flogged by government agents. Or given a bubble perm and his own game show.

The Jack Puddings usually attached themselves to one of the numerous travelling acting troupes. These itinerant companies undoubtedly varied in quality but seem in the main to have been characterised by acting so hammy it squealed at the sight of beechnuts and scenery that wobbled like brawn. The situation was exacerbated by the tendency of leading thespians to 'improve' the play in which they were appearing by inserting material of their own creation, or favourite speeches from some other source, particularly if it kept them centre-stage for longer. As these changes were usually made without first consulting their colleagues, a level of angry confusion reigned onstage such as might be envisaged in a hen house moments after some jovial fox has sneaked in and rubbed deep-heat cream on to the eggs of the broody hens while they were off for a few seconds pecking millet. The dreadfulness of the performance, however, was lost on most of the audience. Living in areas far from any conventional theatre, they had nothing to judge it against save the efforts of other travelling troupes seen at previous fairs. As far as they knew, all acting was like this – rubbish. Little wonder that many of them considered the best fun to be had from the actors was to beat them up and set fire to their props, a drama that was played out more frequently and in more places than even the bawdy tale of *Merry Andrew*.

Aside from the real actors there were also puppet theatres

whose performances ranged from Punch and Judy to the plays of Ben Jonson. Punch and Judy was the most popular puppet show from the sixteenth century up until the birth of Sooty. The plot of this traditional children's entertainment is that Mr Punch gets fed up with this baby making a noise and murders it by banging its head on the walls and floor. His wife, annoyed by his behaviour, sets about him with a cudgel. Punch responds by bludgeoning her to death. He then hurls both bodies out of the window. This action attracts the attention of a policeman who, after a chase and another fight, arrests Punch and puts him in prison. Punch is sentenced to death, but escapes execution by throttling the hangman with his own noose. In his book *The Old Showmen and the Old London Fairs*, Thomas Frost comments on the Punch and Judy show: 'Who has not observed the delight, venting itself in screams of laughter, with which young and old witness the comical little wretch's fight with the constable, the wicked leer with which he induces the hangman to put his head in the noose by way of instruction, and the impish chuckling in which he indulges while strangling his last victim?' Frost was writing in the 1870s, long before the debate on the effects of watching fictional violence got underway. You can't help wondering what he and his fellow Victorians would have made of modern video nasties. They would have popped their corsets guffawing at them, most likely. And doubtless Little Lord Fauntleroy would have got a copy of *Driller Killer* in his Christmas stocking while Tiny Tim giggled with glee throughout *The Texas Chainsaw Massacre*.

If people visiting the fair tired of watching badly shaped wooden creatures moving awkwardly about speaking in unnaturally high voices, or even the puppets, there were a huge number of other options on offer. Hocus-pocus men, the precursors of modern-day magicians, abounded; there were high-wire acts, including one Italian gentleman who performed with a duck balancing on his head; there were strongmen and contortionists. Dance troupes demonstrated such steps as the 'Scaramouche', the 'Quarter Staff', and the even-harder-to-envisage 'Merry

Cuckolds of Hogsden'. For a brief period, six wooden-legged men doing the hornpipe were a top attraction and the dance of 'Three Bullies and Three Quakers' enjoyed a short vogue. Salamandering, or fire-eating, was also hugely popular, with performers drinking molten beer mugs or swigging smoking cocktails of wax and sulphur to such acclaim that you wonder why no one has come up with a karaoke version.

The great animal shows of Wombwell and Atkins and the smaller penny shows of men such as Ballard (who was to gain notoriety when one of his lions escaped and attacked the Exeter mail coach) were a major draw. Wombwell was a regular at Stagshaw Bank Fair and Town Moor Hoppings. At its peak his menagerie housed four lions, two leopards, a hyena, a wolf and cubs, a polar bear, two zebras, two wild asses and a variety of monkeys, birds and reptiles. Uniformed bandsmen in red tunics and leopardskin caps stood at the entrance to the tent in which these natural wonders were displayed, and garish painted banners depicting the animals hung from poles outside. Like all showmen, Wombwell saw exaggeration as the key to prosperity. The banners showed creatures from the zoo standing next to human beings. Anyone who looked at them but did not venture into the marquee would have gone away with the impression that a polar bear is larger than a traction engine and that a hollowed-out boa constrictor could be used as an additional road tunnel under the Tyne. Handbills distributed about the fairground meanwhile boasted of the animals' ferocity, strength and eating capacity. The latter seems to have been a particular source of fascination to the fairgoers of the day. This is perhaps because many knew what it was like to go short of food and so looked on gluttony with envy rather than disdain. Overweight men, women and children were big draws at the fairground and, as we have already seen, heavily larded livestock was praised at the shows. Fatness, in fact, was seen as something of an advantage, a virtue even. People didn't make excuses for being hefty, they boasted about it. They would say: 'I'm not big-boned, you know. I'm just tubby,' or 'There's nothing odd about my metabolism, I just stuff my face morning, noon and night.' In Georgian and Victorian England *The Hip and Thigh Diet* would have been an instruction on which part of the pig to eat for breakfast, and a sequel entitled *The Hip, Thigh, Shank and Ham-bone Diet* would have been eagerly awaited by a hungry public.

Animals that didn't fascinate by the novelty of their appearance were expected to perform. Fortune-telling horses and dancing bears were ten a penny, so the more ingenious showmen unleashed such unlikely talents as a pipe-smoking oyster, a group of cats which performed an opera to the accompaniment of a dulcimer and a tortoise which, with charcoal-blackened feet, would walk around a sheet of paper and so spell his name. My particular favourite among these zoological marvels is Toby the Learned Pig. Toby had a number of rivals, including the Philosophising Chinese Swine and the Amazing Pig of Knowledge, but he was the original and the greatest. Toby was a lop-eared boar of remarkable handsomeness who, the handbills bragged, 'has a perfect knowledge of the alphabet, understands arithmetic, and will spell and cast accounts, tell the points of the globe, the dice box, the hour by a person's watch etc.'. Toby's greatest gift was assessing which members of the audience should fall in love and marry one another. Although Toby was too modest to claim all the credit, it has to be said that the divorce rate in those days was much lower than it is now. Perhaps instead of just complaining about the breakdown of the family the government should take this fact on board. The sight of Peter Lilley yelling, 'Don't listen to your heart, listen to this pig!' while brandishing a photo of a Berkshire boar would surely rally support from his Conservative colleagues while at the same time deliver an important message to young people.

By the standards of the time, performing animals, puppets and the like were relatively highbrow. To appease the low faction there was animal-baiting, stick play and boxing booths and a string of tents housing a list of curiosities longer than the Incredible Ruby Red Javanese Swinging Boy's arm. The showmen scoured the country for oddities to display. Their booths bristled with bearded ladies, there were midgets by the bucket-ful and you couldn't move for tripping over dwarfs. And that wasn't all. Visitors could also see the Bold Grimacing Spaniard, who, it was claimed, had a tongue a foot long and could contract his face to the size of an apple; the eyes of a Dutch teenager whose irises were covered with words in Hebrew and Latin; the Famous Spotted Boy and Miss Hipson, the Middlesex Wonder, who was billed as 'the largest child in the kingdom'. While some of these exhibits were unfortunate afflicted individuals strug-gling to make a living in the days before the welfare state, many more were simply fake. The Amazing Pig-faced Lady turned out to be a bear with a shaven head; wild pygmies 'discovered recently in Africa' were invariably monkeys and there was something less than fishy about the mermaids. If I hadn't made him up, the Incredible Ruby Red Javanese Swinging Boy would undoubtedly have been an orang-utan. In the dim lights of the tents, mesmerised by the constant chatter of the spielers and often addled by drink, the public were easy enough to fool. One of the greatest showmen of all, David Prince Miller, once posed as a gigantic negress in one of these booths at a fair in Yorkshire. Covered in soot and wearing a grass skirt and well-stuffed brassiere, his disguise may not have been subtle, but it was good enough to excite several miners into attempts to seduce him.

The fairground's fall from grace in the middle years of the nineteenth century affected the showmen badly. Even the fairs that were not abolished were severely curtailed. Town Moor Hoppings had once run for seven weeks; now it was cut to a fortnight. Ironically, the saviour of the pleasure fairs was the very invention that had helped to destroy so many traditional rural events: the steam engine. In 1865 a showman named Soame appeared at Aylsham Fair in Norfolk with a steam-driven round-about. It was a fairly basic machine, but compared to the horse- or man-powered versions that had preceded it, it was a revela-tion. Over the next twenty years the rides became the dominant entertainment at the fairground. Their appearance transformed the industry. Before them the only smell at the fairground stronger than that of frying onions and brown ale was the whiff of stagnation. Fairs had come to look like a throwback to an earlier time; now, they seemed to offer a glimpse of a brightly lit, fast-moving and colourful future, a speeding modern world that came with its own musical accompaniment. Not unlike the bus to Alnwick in fact. Only in that case the music came not from a steam-organ or a generator-powered sound system, but from the tuneless whistler and a crop-headed youth who was sitting opposite me wearing a Walkman.

When I was a child I saw an episode of *Blue Peter* in which Lesley Judd made an attractive table lamp from an old bottle covered in polyfilla and seashells. It was an easy technique to master and one which, in my boyish enthusiasm for creativity, I was able to apply to many other projects. Matchboxes were transformed with mussel shells, a biscuit tin was subtly brightened with razor clams and a chum's tortoise became an attractive walking compendium of marine molluscs. It was only when my mother found me creating interesting textural contrasts in our bathroom by affixing limpets to the lavatory seat that my interior-design phase was curtailed. Looking at the youth in the Walkman, I initially thought he must have been the victim of some similar extravagant outburst of barnacle-related DIY, but on closer inspection it turned out just to be a skin condition.

Tsk-tsk-a-tsk-tsk-hiss went the spotty lad's Walkman. Many people find this sort of noise extremely irritating. After years of travelling on public transport, though, I have come to rather enjoy it. Some of the tunes, particularly 'Tsk-Tish-Tsk-Tish' and the haunting 'Ta-Tish-Ta-Tish-Tish-Ta-Ta', are really quite catchy. In fact, if K-Tel or some such clever company were to market a tape of collateral Walkman sounds, I'd definitely buy one to listen to at home or in the car. Of course, like all compilation albums they'd be bound to miss out some of your favourites. So if there's anyone reading this who's in a position to influence things, can I just put in a word for 'Hisk-a-Hisk-a-Hiss'? It's one of those songs that just kind of grows on you. Like a fungus.

So inspiring was the sound of the chick-chicking Walkman that the whistling man, who had lapsed into an eerie silence which could only have resulted from sleep, piped into life again. And to the tinny click-and-fizz rhythms and the breeze-over-empty-bottles melody the bus rolled through Morpeth. There were signs all along the road pointing travellers north towards the 'Coast and Castles Route', a scenic drive past long white beaches, windswept dunes and medieval ruins. Before you got to it, though, you had to pass along the 'Coast and Closed Collieries Route', through Pegswood and Widdrington and dozens of other pit villages all seemingly identical: a few hundred terraced houses, a pub, a chippy, a corner shop, a Chinese takeaway and a hairdressing salon in someone's front room, the picture window misted with condensation and embellished with line drawings of impossibly elegant women with *retroussé* noses, swan-like necks and strings of pearls. In the small front gardens soft pink peonies and beds of psychedelic poppies nodded in the sea breeze behind ranks of decapitated cabbage plants and the dangling green flags of already enormous show leeks. Travelling through the mining centres of the north-east, you see many signs of social decay – boarded-up shops, burned-out houses – but you rarely see an untidy garden or overgrown allotment. The pit men were always keen gardeners. Any chance to work in the open air must have been welcome to them. More than that, it was a cheap form of creativity; an expression of the individual in a uniform world. The Union of the Crowns rendered the Northumbrian castles superfluous; cheap imports from Colombia and China have done the same for the coalfields. The former bastions of border defence are now a tourist attraction. The future of the pit villages remains uncertain.

By the time I got to Alnwick the sky had clouded over and a chill wind was blowing in from the sea. It was so nippy that even the perpendicular tail of the Percy Lion was wilting slightly. The lion was standing atop a large pillar outside the old medieval gateway to the town. He was a vigilant-looking fellow, pointing towards the sea. The column was erected by tenant farmers after the Napoleonic Wars as a deterrent to French invasion. You might think that a battery of cannon would have been more effective than a stone lion: that, however, is to underestimate the powerful psychological effect of the beast and its association with Northumberland's first family, the Percys. The Percys were instrumental in setting up Stagshaw Bank Fair. Like many noble families, they saw the potential revenue in the taxes and rents such events could raise. When not involved in such fiscal matters, the Percys took time out to establish themselves as the biggest hooligans in all of medieval Europe. Throughout the British Isles and across much of the continent the very mention of their name sent jaws dropping faster than the value of sterling. They fought the French at Crécy, the Scots at Neville's Cross, conducted an almost private campaign against the Douglases and waged a punitive war against Owen Glendower. When they ran out of foreign enemies they assuaged their boredom by rebelling against the English monarchy. The War of the Roses was a top time for the Percys; afterwards they fell into a bit of a decline. This was caused partially by a changing world, in which diplomacy and intrigue had replaced bashing people over the head as the main means of winning and maintaining power. Mainly, though, it was because when asked the question, 'Are you powerful and Roman Catholic?' the Percys always replied with a cheery, 'I should say so!' This was about as wise as turning up at a fancy-dress party in Tehran disguised as Salman Rushdie.

The modern Percys, descendants of the last male Percy's granddaughter, whose husband obligingly took the family name, are thankfully much more sedate than their ancestors: the Duke of Northumberland before the present incumbent spent his time squiring glamorous women such as Barbara Carrera and Naomi Campbell's mum about the place and involving himself in the film industry. The movie he helped finance was given a premiere in front of his tenants at the cinema in Alnwick. It was not a particularly good film, but they sat through it politely and applauded at the end. 'You couldn't do anything else, really,' one of them said to me a few months afterwards. 'If we'd giggled he might have upped our rents.' Which is not as far-fetched as it seems. The tenants who erected the column and the Percy Lion in 1816 did so shortly after the rents had been paid. The Duke was very impressed with their efforts. If they had enough money left over after rent day to waste on such frivolities, he reckoned, he must be charging them too little. The rents went up the following year.

The presence of the Percys and their main stronghold lends Alnwick an almost medieval air. It is an atmosphere on which the fair is designed to cash in. Having been held for fifteen years now, it is a home-made tourist attraction, a mix of craft market and *It's a Knockout*. In the market square there were stalls selling beeswax candles, jewellery, stencilled leatherwork and corn dollies – originally the trademark the stackmaker placed on top of each stack he made after harvest, so that the quantity and quality of his work could be assessed. There were other 'traditional' crafts, too, like marquetry. Now there's a strange thing. Why *does* anyone make pictures of horses and flowers out of bits of veneer?

Some friends of ours moved house last year. On their second evening there they went to pay a call on their new neighbours, a retired couple. It was half-past six. They found the neighbours busy in the kitchen laying out their breakfast trays. This happens to some people when they retire. They start bringing everything forward. They lay their breakfast tray earlier and earlier until pretty soon they're laying it at midday and eating their breakfast at teatime. And they carry on pulling everything towards them as if time were a tablecloth with a particularly toothsome cream bun at the far end of it which they are eager to get at, only the cat's sitting on their lap and they don't want to disturb her. And eventually they find that they've brought everything forward so much that by Wednesday lunchtime they've wiped off a whole week and there's nothing to be done except start on next Monday. By halfway through January they're already at the end of February; by the summer solstice they're carving turkey and pulling crackers. And so it goes on, in such a way that they reach seventy and suddenly realise that they have done everything in their lives, but they've still got five years left to go. And then they take up marquetry.

In the centre of Alnwick's market square was a large stage. Around it a crowd of a couple of hundred people were gathering to watch an old-style pie and powder court session being re-enacted. A group of men dressed in the historical-costume equivalent of Esperanto were sentencing a serving wench to the ducking stool for short-changing customers. The wench, in mob-cap and gingham, was pleading for clemency, but the swimming costume visible beneath her medieval garb suggested she was expecting the worst. And, since people don't turn up at these things expecting to see defendants sent away to do community work, naturally enough she got it. Strapped to what appeared to be a gigantic ladle, she was dipped repeatedly in a paddling pool as tourists and locals yelled encouragement. Many were dressed for the occasion and there were several recognisable figures from the Middle Ages: an executioner, a coven of witches, a bevy of milkmaids, two fools, three syllabubs and a trifle.

It was getting late, and the ribaldry was coming to an end, so I went for a walk by the side of the castle. As I was passing a sports shop a Ford Fiesta with a young couple in it stopped beside me. The man wound down his window and said, in a broad South London accent, "Scuse me, mate. Can you tell us where the nearest Chinese restaurant is?" I thought for a while. It was a tricky question. In the end I said, 'About thirty or forty miles away, at a guess.'

The man looked at the girl in the passenger seat. She pulled a face. He turned back to me and said, 'I'm not bein' funny, but it's a bit backward round 'ere, innit?'

As a northerner I am a bit sensitive to southerners making this kind of remark. I leaned forward. 'Oh yes,' I replied, 'it's easy to leap to those kind of snap judgements. But if you took time to really examine the local community you'd find a thriving world of culture: theatre, cinema, indigenous folk music, painting, sculpture and car boot sales. We may not make a big song and dance about it, but I think you'll find we're as up-to-the-minute as any trendy Soho swinger…'

At which point a man in a periwig and velvet pantaloons walked past, severely undermining my argument.

The couple in the car watched him strolling off down the street, so I took advantage of the diversion and made my escape.

8

· Ponies ·

Barningham Fell Pony Show

We drove up over the big emptiness of Stanhope Moor. It was another boiling day. The cloudless sky was the colour of a blackbird's egg and even here, at a thousand feet above sea level, the tarmac of the road hissed and shimmered. Groups of red grouse were bobbing busily about among the shooting butts like veterans revisiting a battle site. As we passed they glanced up briefly then went back to their business. A cursory inspection of our car was enough to satisfy them we weren't wealthy enough to pose a threat. Game birds are an arrogant lot. Sometimes assistants in expensive shops develop, through association with the rich and powerful, the misguided impression that they too are socially superior. Should anyone in anything so common as training shoes attempt to cross the threshold of their emporia they will freeze them out with a frosty glare. Game birds suffer from similar delusions. Every once in a while a cock pheasant would turn up in our garden and begin gobbling up the peas. I'd rush out and clap my hands to shoo him off and he'd just turn and appraise me slowly down the length of his beak, as if to say, 'And just who do you think you are, you tedious little man?' I used to suffer severe crop damage from hoity-toity pheasants. Then I got my dog. The pheasants don't act quite so haughty with him. This is partly because he has a long and impressively aristocratic pedigree. Mainly, though, it is because he is prepared to bite the bum off anything that gets within range.

In one of the tiny ex-lead-mining villages of Weardale a terrier show was in progress. Dog shows are normally rather precious events. I once entered my own dog in one of the larger ones – in the face of considerable protest from him, I might add. He felt a dog show was little more than a cattle market. My abiding memory of it is going into a tent in which row after row of busy owners were lacquering the bouffants of their standard poodles. It was like a backstage scene at a convention of Little Richard impersonators. The build-up of hairspray fumes was such that one match would have seen half the pedigree poodle population of Britain go up in a puff of smoke. I can't say I wasn't tempted.

There was nothing twee about this terrier show, however. It was strictly for working dogs: a gang of bustling roughnecks any one of which wouldn't have looked ill at ease with a woodbine in the corner of his mouth and a copy of the *Racing Post* tucked under a foreleg. Like hot-water bottles, zip-up cardigans with suede elbow patches and the serving of tomato juice as a starter, terriers are a peculiarly British phenomenon – and one of which, if anything, we can be even prouder. When the Romans arrived here our plucky little pets were just about the only thing that impressed them about our native isle. They wrote letters home gushing with praise for the amazing little dogs that never ducked a fight. In so doing the Romans helped forge one of the most fundamental of all human beliefs: that someone who is small and belligerent is a doughty and admirable character, while someone who is large and belligerent is a moronic psychopath.

The Romans would be delighted to see that, though nearly 2,000 years have passed since they first came across them, terriers remain a pugnacious lot. On the edge of a football field overhung by a gaunt fell, you could see the owners struggling to keep their charges apart. They were Jack Russells and Borders mainly. Most terriers are up for a scrap, but Borders take the biscuit. Brindle-haired, bristly and pug-nosed, they walk with a stiff-legged, minatory strut. Whenever I see one I am reminded of the old Border ballad 'Little Jock Elliot':

Wha daur meddle wi' me?
Wha daur meddle wi' me?
My name is little Jock Elliot,
And wha daur meddle wi' me?

A Border terrier could start a row in an empty kennel. Their fans will of course say that I am talking nonsense here; that these dogs are loyal, calm, playful and, if given half a chance, would undoubtedly bring about a lasting peace in the former Yugoslavia. When I mention that Border terriers are short, ginger and Scottish, however, anyone who ever watched Leeds United play football in the 1970s will immediately leap to my defence, though only after they've sucked in air through their teeth, grimaced and instinctively rubbed their shins.

In a far corner of the field, steering clear of any conflict, a group of men were walking their Bedlingtons. A cross between a whippet and a Dandie Dinmont (a grey-and-white terrier that looks like an ageing dachshund in an ill-fitting toupee), the Bedlington steps along on tippy-toes, its greyish, curly coat giving it the appearance of an effete and anorexic lamb. The look is deceptive. The Bedlington terrier is a true pit man's dog, quick and sharp-toothed, nippy in every sense of the word and a remorseless and successful hunter. There are people who lived through the Depression in the Northumberland and Durham coalfields who will tell you that at times it was hard to tell whether it was the family that kept the Bedlington, or the Bedlington that kept the family.

Skills so useful then can sometimes prove an embarrassment now. We have a friend with a Bedlington. She moved recently to a remote part of Northumberland close to the Scottish border. As a welcoming gesture, the couple from the 'big house' invited her for a meal: 'Nothing fancy. Bit of supper. Dozen or so chums. Bloody marvellous if you could join us.' Our friend was understandably nervous. She had a dog, she said. In a new house, strange place, it might get frantic and tear up the furniture. Very kind of them; maybe next time.

'No, no, no. Won't hear of it. Bring dog. Got one ourselves. Black Lab. Name's Baldrick. Pair of 'em'll get on like a house on fire.'

It was a warm night when our friend went to the big house for dinner. In the dining room the French windows were open. Beyond, the grounds stretched out into the rise of the Cheviots. Baldrick and the Bedlington ran barking across the lawn together. The meal was going along splendidly until midway through the main course when our friend heard a strange champing noise coming from under the table. She looked down surreptitiously and got a nasty shock. The Bedlington had found a rabbit warren and brought back a takeaway. Despite the fact that she was in a very posh house with a dozen total strangers and her dog was currently disembowelling a bunny beneath the dining table, she didn't panic. She resolved on a plan. She would wait until people were suitably distracted, wrap her napkin round the carcass and bundle it into her handbag.

Twenty minutes later an opportunity arose. Our friend bent forward, dropped her napkin over the corpse of the rabbit and prepared to shove it into her bag. Unfortunately, by this stage the Bedlington was midway through his meal and reluctant to give it up. A tug-of-war began under the table. Our friend pulled; the Bedlington clung on. She tugged; he dug in his heels and started to jerk his head.

'You all right under there?' the host asked.

'Oh, yes,' our friend said as cheerily as she could. 'Just retrieving my napkin.' Then, with a sudden yank, she freed the remains of the rabbit and slammed it into her handbag all in one swift movement.

The next day she phoned to thank her host for the evening. 'Glad you could come. Bloody marvellous. One question. That dog of yours. Famished, was he? Or does he always eat the skeleton?'

A few miles past the terriers the road zig-zagged up the hillside and on to the high moorland again. On Bollihope Common some joker had taken a tin of black paint to a road sign so that it now warned motorists to beware of wandering elephants instead of cattle. It wasn't cows that you had to look out for on these roads, though, it was sheep. Because the Bluefaced Leicester isn't the only ovine breed with a death wish. The hoary-nosed moorland mules are suicidal too, and you can have some sympathy with them on that score. The upland cross-breeds, with dames drawn from mountain sheep such as the Swaledale or Scottish Blackface, are different from their pastoral cousins. They have an ingrained sense which ties them to one place, called 'hefting'. A mountain sheep tends not to wander more than a few hundred yards from where it was born. This is why the farmer can leave them out on some vast expanse of unfenced wilderness and still find them there months later, and why, when upland grazing changes hands, the new owner or tenant must buy the flock 'bound on' to the land. This latter process is so fraught with difficulties and offers such potential for violent disagreement that the custom is for the present and future incumbents to appoint seconds to do the wrangling for them, thus depersonalising any dispute and limiting the risk of fisticuffs.

Like serfs or sheds, the mountain sheep are a part of the ground on which they stand. The weight of the self-enforced permanence on the subconscious of the sheep must be tremendous. If you were compelled by some irresistible urge to stay within a stone's-throw of your birthplace wouldn't you get depressed? I know I would. But then, I'm from Teesside.

As a consequence of this cruel quirk of nature the mountain sheep may smell the sweet shoots of valley grasses borne to him on the spring breeze, or catch the warm waft of lowland clover in the still, black moortop night, and know he will never taste these things. Though free, he is yet a prisoner, bound by invisible chains of instinct which neither the hammer of desire nor the file-concealed-in-the-fruitcake of curiosity will ever break. So instead he spends his days loitering about, munching the wiry turf and dreaming about the merciful release of throwing himself in front of a passing vehicle. Or straight at it. Because, you see, while the sheep's sense of place is very strong, his sense of timing is about as good as that of the retired Roman tax collector who moved into a villa in Pompeii and called it 'Duneruptin'. The result is that often, after hours and hours spent crouching behind a gorse bush, a sheep will react far too late to the arrival of a car. Instead of flinging itself beneath the wheels, it will simply bounce off the rear passenger door with a woolly *crump!* Sometimes a drive along through the Pennines or North Yorkshire Moors punctuated by the muffled thuds of mistimed ovine suicide leaps gives you a gentle inkling of what it must have been like to be a sailor on an aircraft-carrier during a kamikaze attack. I'm assuming here that the sheep doesn't actually intend simply to head-butt the car, though, of course, that is by no means certain. Upland sheep are a tough and hardy northern breed, and it could just be that these assaults are all part of a plan to impress their peers.

'Did I just see you stick the nut on a transit van, Maah-tin?'

'Aye, Baa-baa-ra, an' I tell ye what – I felt nowt.'

At Barningham Park, between Richmond and Barnard Castle, the horseboxes and shiny pony carts were drawn up in a circle around the showring. Whiskery codgers in grey-brown tweed jackets, dazzling white shirts and maroon and bottle-green ties sat in deck-chairs, mottled thermos flasks between their oxblood riding boots. Men and women in jodhpurs and dark velvet jackets guffawed and leaned against the sides of their shooting brakes for support. A woman in a striped dress with puffed sleeves and a straw boater buffed the riding hat of her teenage daughter, who stared sullenly across at the screen of copper beeches flanking the cricket pavilion. In the ring a plump boy blushed as he tried not to notice that the gelding he was leading had chosen this very public moment to make a physical declaration of his delight at being in the same field as so many attractive mares.

Two blokes in Tattersall checks by the judges' caravan winked at one another and smirked and the taller of the two made what appeared to be a pole-vaulting gesture. Their wives pretended not to notice.

Like the terrier show passed in Weardale earlier, the Fell Pony Show is a real enthusiasts' event. It has the feeling of a family gathering. While there may have been other people there who didn't own a horse, I am willing to bet I was the only one among the two hundred or so present who had never even sat on one. Despite my general antipathy towards horses I was rather fond of the Fell ponies. Compared to the glossy and glamorous larger steeds they seemed rugged and utilitarian; tugboats rather than pleasure cruisers. They had less charisma; more charm. Black and barrel-chested with shaggy manes fringing their faces, they clumped merrily along on bell-bottomed legs, the feathers of hair above their hooves bouncing, their long, thick tails flicking the grasstops. As ponies go, the Fell is large, the opposite end of the scale from his midget cousins from Shetland, and very strong. Still, the sight of a fully grown man mounted on one is oddly incongruous, like a father riding his child's bike. This appearance is deceptive, however. The Fell pony was bred to be ridden by men and has fulfilled that function for close to 2,000 years.

Wild ponies are indigenous to Britain. The ponies of Exmoor, broad-headed and with pale rings around their eyes, are probably the closest descendants of the original breed. It was equines much like the Exmoor that pulled Boudicea's chariot into battle, establishing a relationship between ponies and a particular sort of jolly middle-class girl which survives to this day. Boudicea's adversaries, the Romans, were mounted on Fell ponies, or something very similar. Fell ponies are one of a pair of breeds from the Anglo-Scottish border whose lineage can be traced back to the cavalry garrisons which lined Hadrian's Wall. The other is the slightly larger Dales pony. Loosely speaking, the Dales pony comes from east of the Pennines and the Fell from west. A third Romano-British horse, the Galloway Nag, is now sadly extinct (the victim of poor market research regarding choice of brand name, I reckon). The Roman auxiliary cavalry regiments were drawn from the subject states of the Empire; the ponies that carried them came from Thracia, Gaul, the Rhineland, North Africa and Danubia. The Fell pony may look homespun, but he has a cosmopolitan background.

The evolution of the horse is as closely tied in with changes in military technology and tactics as the development of the Pot Noodle is with shifting attitudes to washing-up. The Romans used cavalry mainly for scouting. In battle the horsemen's role was confined to harassing the enemy's flanks and pursuing a foe broken by the solid mass of the legions. For these duties the lightly armoured Roman cavalryman required a nimble, sturdy mount. Stamina and agility were of more use to him than power and explosive speed. Size was not important.

Over the following centuries the use of cavalry altered dramatically. Ever more heavily armoured knights led, as already mentioned, to the breeding of ever larger mounts. Had it not been for the invention of the musket we might well now be looking at horses the size of double-decker buses. Which I suppose wouldn't have been too bad as long as you weren't the person detailed to clean up after them.

Even after plate armour was abandoned cavalry continued to be used as a shock weapon, and the priority across much of Britain remained for big, strong steeds of around 16 hands. (A pony, by the way, is defined simply as any horse under 14.2 hands. A hand is four inches. Horse people are the only group left who have successfully resisted the introduction of the tape-measure: being measured for hunting pinks is like having a massage.) In the borderlands, however, things were different. Here the rugged ground precluded the use of lumbering mounts and the pony, or hobby, as it was known, still held sway.

The nature of the owner's business was another contributory factor. The reiving clans lived by raiding and theft, to the demands of which – long-distance rides over inhospitable terrain, often in winter and invariably at night – the hobbies were well suited. It is no coincidence that another people who lived by much the same means as the reivers, the Apache, also preferred ponies.

In the two centuries preceding the English Civil War, the small horses of the Borders enjoyed a period of unprecedented importance. During those days it was said that the typical Borderer would rather give up his house than his hobby. The only thing he valued more was his family, and at times even that was a toss-up. In the rustling of others' herds and flocks his horse was the reiver's faithful companion, the ideal getaway vehicle for men driving stolen sheep and cattle back across the moonlit fells.

In the ring at Barningham it was the turn of the mares with colt at foot. A judge in a bowler hat, his raffish blue suit set off by a pair of mauve socks, was studying the entrants from a variety of angles and contorted positions, smiling happily all the while. The mares looked on indulgently as their gangling off-spring pogoed disjointedly and merrily about beside them. It was a cheerful scene, and one which reflected the Fell pony's rehabilitation after years aiding and abetting outlaws.

When the Unification of the Crowns made raiding too peril-ous an occupation for all but the most desperate freebooter, some of the reivers joined the army and went off to contribute their own particular brand of expertise to sorting out the Irish problem. Others signed up with the mercenary bands then ransacking Europe in the name of religion. Most stayed where they were and took up farming and the more traditional meth-ods of raising livestock. Their ponies still served them well, as mounts for shepherding and cattle-driving, and as plough horses on land too marshy for heavier breeds. Excess stock was sold off to pack men and tinkers whose wandering trade took them over the same hills and dales the reivers had once criss-crossed, albeit in daylight and to less bloody purpose. Soon the dark Fell pony had come to be so associated with the Tinkers that they were often referred to as Brough Hill ponies in honour of the West-morland Fair, at which many of them were traded. Teesdale, too, had a long association with Fell ponies. Many of the best breeders lived here. Among them were Parkin Raine, Coatsworth (aka 'The Baldersdale Buck') and Thomas Gibson. Gibson it was who bred the most illustrious Fell pony of all, 'Blooming Heather'. So well know was this stallion that in the later years of the nineteenth century it was said that Teesside was famous for only four things: steel, shipbuilding, the High Force waterfall and 'Blooming Heather'.

As pack animals hauling lead from the Pennine mines to Tyneside or Whitehaven, the Fell ponies were replaced by the railways, but as late as the 1960s they were still being ridden by the more traditionally minded Pennine shepherds, who rejected the noise and danger of the only viable alternative, the motorbike. As a working animal it was the coming of the quad that did for them.

Now the hobbies were kept as a hobby. It was nice to see that their more colourful past was echoed in some of their names, and that one of the judges was a Charlton.

Later Catherine and I parked the car at Barningham Village Green and went to the church fête, which was being held in the steeply raked gardens of a large Georgian house. There were queues of children waiting to bet on the snail race and a group of villagers pillaging the jam stall. I bought a ticket for the name-the-crocheted-sailor competition. I didn't win, even though the little woolly Jack Tar looked like a certain Doreen to me. We bought bowls of strawberry trifle and cream and sat on a grassy bank. Down below us to the east, the last of the shiny carts from the Fell Pony Show were being loaded on to trailers, the local brass band were playing Haydn and tortoiseshell butterflies jigged around the buddleia.

9

• Goats •

The Cumberland County Show

The train was passing across the Gilsland Gap and into Cumbria. You can always tell when you get into Cumbria: the stone-built houses are suddenly the colour of red Windsor cheese and it starts raining. We trundled along past a field full of tall grass with a rusting set of goalposts standing mournfully in the middle of it and the farmhouse where the artists Ben and Winifred Nicholson had once lived. I don't suppose the two things are related.

The woman opposite me was reading a glossy magazine. There are thousands of glossy magazines nowadays. Most of them are aspirational; magazines with titles like *Great Big Boat Owner* and *Exceptionally Expensive Classic Car Monthly* are clearly not aimed merely at people who already have a thirty-foot yacht or an AC Cobra – the market wouldn't be big enough to support them. In the main they are targeted at those who just wish they had one of those things. They are journalistic window-shopping.

I once worked in the wine trade, and in our shop we often noted that the people who came in and bought wine magazines rarely if ever actually bought any wine. Their interest was not wine, but the *theory* of wine. The contents of a bottle attracted them only insofar as it constituted a subject about which they could learn lots of facts with which to bore others at parties. They would say: 'And, of course, in 1978, unexpectedly high levels of precipitation in August led to a late harvest that was only marginally compensated for by a hot, dry spell...'

And you would say, 'Is it good? Do you like it?'

And they would jerk their head back and look askance, as if the suggestion that wine was something to be enjoyed was a thought so novel they could barely grasp it.

There are many magazines which appeal to a similar audience: people whose interest in hi-fis, computers or whatever is purely theoretical.

As I pondered wisely on this question, the woman opposite was making me rather edgy. She was reading a bridal magazine. I wasn't sure into which of my two categories the bridal magazine fell. Was she wishing? Did she have some imaginary date in mind, or was she planning the perfect wedding, an absorbing enough hobby in itself? Was it simply the specifications and prices that attracted her? Would I one day meet her at a friend's house and find myself at the wrong end of a one-way conversation about the various reception options facing the spring bride with a claustrophobic groom and a guest list comprising two Muslims, several vegans and an aunt with a severe lactic allergy? Whatever, it made me so nervous I simply couldn't concentrate on my copy of the *Soldier of Fortune* bumper summer special at all.

Carlisle describes itself as the 'Great Border City' ('The Great Boring City more like,' a pal of mine who once spent an unhappy time living there remarked, totally unjustly in my opinion) and it's a theme the local shopkeepers have taken up with gusto. In Carlisle there are Border bakeries, Border washeterias, Border chip shops and Border picture-framers. Practically everything in Carlisle has 'border' in the title. You wouldn't be surprised to be greeted in the pub by a man gripping your hand in his steely fist, looking you straight in the eye and saying: 'Good to meet you, stranger. The name's Matt Colquhoun, border quantity surveyor.'

Cumberland County Show is held in Rickerby Park, a leafy watermeadow along the north bank of the Eden, overlooked by handsome Edwardian villas. The rain had stopped now, but the day was still cloudy and a warm damp atmosphere swaddled the showground. Like its counterpart in Northumberland, the Cumberland County Show has now fully embraced long-resisted commercialism. There was a go-kart track and a street of stalls selling leather goods, raffling polyester pandas and spinning candy floss. The theme tune from *Hawaii Five-O* surfed incongruously out across the assembled spaniels in the dog-show tent and mingled with the recorded fanfare of trumpets that signalled the galloping arrival of the Knights of Arkley Jousting Troupe in the main ring. Over in one corner a small crowd had gathered to inspect the Lloyds Bank Black Stallion; another cluster had formed to view the handiwork of the Mid-Wales Axe Racing Team. Anyone wondering about the main business of the show, however, had only to look in the programme. On the second page there was an advert for Insem, 'Sole distributors of progen semen'. Despite the entertainments and the craft stands, Cumberland County Show remained at heart a farmers' event.

In the cattle tent among the dairy breeds there were Ayrshires (once farmed by Robert Burns), dairy Shorthorns, Friesians and, best of all, Jerseys. One of the strangest features of the Victorian shows was the flowery, at times even romantic, language the judges used to describe the cows. It's almost as if feelings buried by the sexual repression of the time were leaking out through an unexpected fissure. The reports speak of 'wonderful, heavy-fleshed young matrons' and heifers with 'plumlike fullness', 'perfect loins' and 'grand bosoms'. At a time when the sight of a table leg was considered lewd and suggestive, this was heady stuff indeed. Looking at a Jersey named Tarn Toffee's Wafer, I could see how those Victorian gentlemen might have become so florid in their praise. There was something distinctly coquettish and beguiling about this caramel-coated creature. The Jersey has a fine-boned face shaded with lines of charcoal fur, round, fuzzy ears, big brown eyes and lashes so heavy that batting them must constitute a weight-training exercise. And every once in a while they give you a kind of sideways, flirtatious... I decided to go outside and get some fresh air.

At the entrance to the beer tent a bearded man stood nursing his pint. He was wearing a T-shirt bearing the legend 'I ♥ My Anglo-Nubians'. Beneath the slogan was a line drawing of a long-eared goat. I didn't find this all that startling: people who keep goats are very chauvinistic about them. They beat the drum for goat-herding. It's hardly surprising, really. Of all domesticated animals goats probably have the biggest image problem. I mean, Satan doesn't choose to manifest himself as a Yorkshire terrier or a Dwarf Lop rabbit, does he? Keeping livestock with close to 2,000 years of association with Beelzebub, Lord of the Flies, presents quite a few PR problems.

Personally, I had always considered this diabolic side of goats to be a bit laughable. I couldn't understand why the Prince of Darkness would choose to appear on earth as a vaguely preposterous and frankly rather smelly farm animal. Why stalk the night as a second-rate sheep when he could have chosen something genuinely frightening, such as a gigantic lizard? Or, if he was feeling cunning and insidious, why not a sweet and cuddly koala such as an innocent babe would clutch to its breast? The Evil One's decision to hitch himself to the goat may have been bad news for fans of Toggenburgs and Saanens, but otherwise it hardly worked much in his favour. Lucifer wasn't going to inveigle his way into good Christian consciences by way of the goat, or scare us witless with it, either. This is what I thought, until one day a retired farmer I met while out walking my dog told me this story:

'Just before the war, my father bought a billy goat. We had a lot of sheep miscarrying at that time, and the story went about that if you kept a billy this didn't happen. I doubt there was any truth in it, and so did my father, but we were losing lambs and we were prepared to try anything. We had a farm then that was really what we would call "out by". It was miles from any place, up on the fellside west of Tow Law. I went to school on the bus, but I had to walk about two miles down the track to the roadside to catch it, and the same back when it dropped me in the afternoon. My father kept the billy in a field by this track. He'd bought it in the spring to help with the lambs, and from then through the summer it never paid me any mind and I never bothered it. Then, in autumn, when the nights began drawing in, it started.

'One afternoon about November time, the bus dropped me off at the track gate as usual. It had been snowing and the melt-water from it was running down the hillsides, swelling the burns. There was the noise of rushing water everywhere. It looked due to snow again. The sky had turned that purple colour and the air was murky. I went through the gate and up the track, swishing along through the slush. Then I heard this voice behind me. It was like a human voice, only it wasn't saying words, it was just a sort of nonsensical blather, like a lunatic talking. I stopped dead in my tracks. I was fair shaking. I looked round slowly, peeking really. And bugger me, there was that billy goat, stood on his hind legs walking after me, all the while making this talking noise: "Ner naar nanana naar." It sounds stupid, this, but it was like he was taunting me. I turned and ran all the way home. I bet you think I must have been soft in the head.'

I didn't think that at all. The retired farmer was a small man and it was easy to picture him as a schoolboy with a satchel and a belted gabardine coat. Easy, too, to imagine the dark winter's afternoon, the surging roar of the water and the glimmering gnarled bark of the alder trees along the burnside. Coming through the gate he would have seen the lights of his home up at the top of the track, begun to walk towards them, Wellington boots rubbing the backs of his calves where his socks had slipped down. And then the chattering behind him. Turning to find the goat, a big, bearded, masculine presence, looming over him, the mouth gaping in his huge head, orange tongue flapping between brown teeth; dark, reptilian eyes staring blankly. I could feel that fear that comes over you as a child when something beyond your comprehension occurs; something that cannot be stayed just by you calling for it to stop.

'The next afternoon he did it again,' the old farmer said. 'When he saw me coming he went up on his hind legs and followed me right along to the end of the field, talking all the while. Now, I was just a little lad then, mind, and I knew, because I was told off for it often enough, that when I was on my own I tended to have a bit of a chat with myself. It struck me that I'd walked past this goat many a time and maybe he had heard me talking to myself and now he was imitating me. It seemed as if he was mocking. He went on doing it, an' all. And if I summed up the courage to turn round and shout at him he would just stand there on his back legs, staring at me from those funny slit eyes and going, "Nar nanan naar noo." Every afternoon for about a month that happened. I got more and more unnerved by it, I can tell you. I got so I didn't want the bell to go for the end of school. Which tells you something in itself, because I hated school.'

After that I took a slightly different attitude to goats. At a rare breed farm in East Anglia I watched a Golden Guernsey billy run down to the fence where Catherine was standing and begin lewdly flickering his tongue at her like the singer in a second-rate heavy metal band. I noticed the smell of him, too. It's something you can hardly avoid with goats. Nannies are peculiar enough: they give off an odour of goats' cheese, which is odd, because the same isn't true of other milk-producing animals. You don't come across cows that reek of Stilton. The rasping stink of the billy is something else entirely, though. It's so powerful that it doesn't just make your eyes water, it makes them feel as if somebody is going at them with a scrubbing brush and scouring powder. It seems like the sort of thing dissolute teenagers might sniff for its hallucinogenic effects. If billy goats were a chemical, it would be illegal to handle them without asbestos gloves and a mask. Such a high-powered pong doesn't come easily: the billy really works on it. His favoured method of improving his body musk is to urinate on his own forehead. He does this by standing on a hard surface and lowering his barnet down between his knees. The spray bounces up and lands behind his ears and horns. He undertakes this unpleasant task because he thinks it will make him more attractive to female goats. And the disturbing thing is, he is right. One whiff of the freshly groomed billy and the nannies' knees go to jelly. Girls just love it when a guy takes a bit of trouble with himself. The billy goat has to be careful while at his toilette, though, because his urine has a very high ammonia content and can be harmful if it gets into his eyes. The billy goat is the only animal whose sex drive can make him blind.

Despite, or more likely because of, this rather unpleasant side to their character, goats are easily the most interesting livestock. They were the first farm animal, their main appeal to the Neolithic men who domesticated them being their appetite. Goats will eat anything. In the lexicon of the goat there is no such word as 'edible' since to apply it to anything from cacti to corsets would be tautological and goats are strict and stylish grammarians.

Early man used his goats not just for food but to help clear scrub and woodland prior to cultivation. Goats were very good at this. The Sahara Desert was thickly wooded until Neolithic man sent his vast flocks of goats into it and set off an irreversible spiral of deforestation, soil erosion and dust-bowling. Not until Oppenheimer built the atomic bomb would mankind produce anything capable of devastating the environment more totally than a large group of goats. In fact, it is something of a surprise to me that nobody from the Green Party has ever suggested a huge flock of goats as a natural alternative to Britain's nuclear deterrent. We could keep them in underground silos and in times of difficulty simply parachute them into the enemy's crop fields and refuse to call them off until our opponents surrendered or starved. Of course, there would still be the worry that somebody might push the red button in error, leading to a tit-for-tat scenario in which our mistaken pre-emptive strike on the cabbage fields around Kiev might provoke the retaliatory devastation of Vale of York sugarbeet production by a crack force of

Ukrainian Cashmeres, but I think that's a small price to pay for peace of mind.

So important were goats to early man that he started to worship them. The Babylonians believed that the Milky Way was an astral nanny goat and their most important god was a billy named Polaris. Polaris later became the only goat in history to have a submarine named after him. A strange choice from the Royal Navy, I think you'll agree, goats not being noted for their ability to swim underwater. The ancient Egyptians, too, held the goat as sacred, though as they also worshipped dung beetles, perhaps that's not such a great honour. The ancient Greeks, meanwhile, viewed the goat as a symbol of male fertility. Whether Greek men followed the lead of the billy goat when it came to titivating themselves is not known, though if they did it would certainly explain why they spent so much time sitting in single-sex groups on mountaintops pondering the meaning of life, and wondering why they never got invited to parties. It was the goat's association with these pagan religions, along with some of its less endearing habits, that earned it its diabolic reputation in Christian societies.

Prompted by the bearded man's T-shirt, I popped over to the goat tent to have a look at his beloved Anglo-Nubians. A big creature with pendulous ears, a Roman nose and a body whose lumpiness suggests it has just swallowed a wheelbarrow, the Anglo-Nubian, as its name implies, is a cross between native British goats and imported Nubians. The first Nubian goats came to England from Paris, where a flock of them had been kept to supply milk to feed the hippopotamus presented to Napoleon III by the Emperor of Abyssinia.

I was familiar with Nubian goats. When I was a teenager my parents worked in the Middle East for a few years. In the city in which they lived the local council had decided not to bother with dustmen and simply employed a flock of goats to eat the refuse instead. Every few weeks or so, the goats would turn up and wander down the street, munching everything in their path. They were quiet, efficient and never took any time off. In fact, they weren't much like human binmen at all – except one year when we forgot to give them a Christmas box and they came back the following week and slung rubbish all over our garden.

Anglo-Nubians are one of Britain's favourite goats. They produce the richest milk and are particularly popular with cheese- and yoghurt-makers. Goat's milk, incidentally, is the closest in composition to human milk. It is said to be very good for people suffering from TB, ulcers or eczema. As if the poor buggers didn't have enough to put up with.

The arrival of the exotic Nubians in nineteenth-century England revived the flagging British goat industry. The goat had always been regarded as the poor man's cow, but the gradual enclosure of common grazing meant that even poor men could no longer afford to keep them and they became increasingly rare. The Nubians, however, were swiftly taken up by Baroness Burdett-Coutts, daughter of the London banker. Soon goat-herding was all the rage among fashionable Victorian ladies. Queen Victoria kept her own little flock of cashmere goats in Buckingham Palace Gardens: they were captured in a drawing by W. Keyl and appear to have been a rather louche bunch. The billy is particularly languid, reclining and gazing out at the artist from beneath a foppish fringe in such an arch manner that you instinctively check his hooves for a cigarette-holder.

I strolled up and down the tent looking at the chocolate-coloured, curly-flanked Toggenburgs and the striped-faced Alpines. The most noticeable thing in the goat tent, apart from the whiff of *chèvre*, was that, with the exception of a few boy kids, all the goats were female. Billy goats are rarely if ever shown – they are simply too wild. Bulls, tups and even the notoriously volatile boar guinea pig present no problem, but the billy is different. He is a real beast, a kind of livestock superlad. Despite close to 10,000 years of domesticity, the billy goat is still trying to break out, get back to nature and live the kind of life where a bloke can pee on his own head and eat women's underwear till his belly is bulging without anyone telling him he's out of order. Every spring and autumn the ruling male, or 'king billy', as he is officially termed, attempts to lead his flock to this promised land. Or at least, he used to: these days the signs are that billy goats are not quite what they were. To the goat, the trappings of masculinity are big horns and long chin and chest hair, but modern goats have been bred to have smaller, less dangerous horns, and short hair that doesn't harbour dirt and ticks. Shorn of these age-old symbols of his manhood, evidence suggests that the modern billy is becoming gradually less sure of himself; uncertain of what exactly he is supposed to be doing. Where once he bossed the nannies about and mated with them with no regard for their needs or feelings, now he is assailed by doubts. Sound familiar, gentlemen? How the billy will respond to his changing role is open to speculation. Perhaps he and his friends will take to going into the woods at weekends to play drums, recite bad poetry and hug one another. Or maybe he'll just drink too much lager and go head-butt a policeman.

At one side of the tent the judges were assessing the galvanised buckets of milk supplied for the milking competition; at the other stood pens of the real stars of the Cumberland County Show, the Angora goats. Smaller than the Anglo-Nubian, the angora is covered in a thickly tousled fleece. With its curly cream locks, white face and rubicund muzzle and eartips, it is just about the only goat that looks genuinely benign. The Angora came originally from Ankara in Turkey. With an eye to monopolising the trade in fluffy jumpers, the Ottomans were keen to keep it a strictly Turkish beast, and up until the 1850s smuggling goats out of the country was an offence punishable by beheading. Eventually goats were released for export, and now they thrive in South Africa, Australia and Texas. Outside the tent, the British Angora Goat Society had a display table. There was an Angora fleece, which looked like the sort of thing Jason and the Argonauts went off in search of, and an array of knitwear. It's stupid, I know, but I didn't realise that mohair came from Angora goats. I had imagined it to be the hair of an animal called the mo: a fluffy fellow somewhat like a cross between a chamois and a yak who lives in small pastel-shaded flocks in the Kara Kum

Desert. Disappointingly, it seems that the name mohair comes from the Arabic word for 'select', *mukhayar.* With one glance at the British Angora Goat Society's explanatory noticeboard I had wiped out an entire species of fantasy animal. Luckily, I also gleaned a piece of information with which to cheer myself up: judges' wigs are made from billy goats' beards.

I walked back across the bridge over the Eden and into Carlisle. I'd been planning to have something to eat at the Tullie House Museum Café, but a party of Spanish schoolchildren had ransacked the entire place leaving me with a Jaffa cake and a bottle of Appletise. The Spanish children were sitting at the back of the room scoffing the entire contents of two cold cabinets. Like all European children they were vibrant, inquisitive, animated and filled with joy and delight. I couldn't help wishing someone would give them all a good clip round the ear.

Coming back through the Gilsland Gap, the sky was promising more rain and even though it was early afternoon the moortops were shadowy. I thought again about the retired farmer's story. It had had a happy ending, for him anyway:

'After a bit my mother and father realised something was up. They asked me what the matter was one night at tea. I told them what was going on with the billy goat. My father laughed, but my mother nodded and said, yes, the billy had done the same thing to her and it was frightening. My father said he'd sort the billy goat out. He did, too. At that time we had this old Swaledale tup, and a right sod he was, too. If you turned your back on him for a second, boy! He could clatter you, that bugger. My father put him in the field with billy one morning. That afternoon when I come home from school the goat came to the fence as usual. Up he went on his hind legs and started talking. "Nananna naar na." I just kept on walking up the track and he followed me. Well, as I come near to the top of the field I spied the Swales. He was standing there watching old billy.' The farmer narrowed his eyes in imitation of the myopic angry gaze of the tup. 'He watched billy come up that hill after me and when he was about twenty yards away he rocked back on his heels and then, whoosh! He was down that field before the goat even spotted him. Banged him right in the slats and knocked him ten foot in the air. The billy goat suffered no lasting damage, but I'll tell you what: he never walked on his hind legs again after that.'

10

• Ferrets •

The Country Landowners' Association Game Fair

I was back on the Trans-Pennine Express again, heading west this time. It didn't go any faster, even with the sea breeze at its back. It's a new train, and as a consequence the seats are packed tightly together. It's odd, isn't it, that as the population gets gradually taller, less and less leg room is provided on public transport? Nowadays the only way I can get comfortable is to rest my weight on my shoulders and neck and stick my feet up into the luggage rack. It's rather an inelegant position, admittedly, but it least it discourages anyone from attempting to sit next to me and start showing me photos of their grandchildren.

It was still hot. The night before it had rained briefly, and when the water hit the ground it turned to steam and hovered over the lawn like dry ice. When I woke up the following morning there was condensation on the *outside* of the window. Conditions on the train were terrible. There was a water shortage in Yorkshire and BR were doing their bit to help by not washing the outside of the carriages. The windows were speckled with dirt so that the world beyond looked like a pub ashtray waiting to be wiped. The air-conditioning had broken down and the only ventilation was a single tiny window. Oxygen circulated round the carriage more slowly than in a hibernating bear. Old ladies stewed, children sizzled and businessmen cracked salt from the armpits of their shirts. By the time we left York I could have used my forehead to steam-strip wallpaper.

Outsiders make the mistake of thinking all Yorkshire people are the same. This is not the case. There is a profound difference between those of us from the North Riding and the folk of the West Riding. The North Riding is fixed in a strange no-man's-land between two warring factions of human character. Above us are the Geordies, with their friendliness and passion for life. Below us are the true Tykes, famous for being blunt and mean. The result is a hybrid. North Riding people are quiet and self-effacing, kind yet cautious. We would like to have a passion for life, but ooh, at that price, we'll have to go away and have a think.

I was brought up with a strong distrust of the West Riding. In our house its people were always referred to as 'that lot'. My grandparents would sooner have trusted a chain-smoking gas-fitter than a bloke from Bradford. Leeds was about fifty miles from the village in which I grew up, yet, excluding trips to the Headingley Test, I had not been there more than a couple of times. To us it was like another country. If we wanted to go to the 'big shops', we went sixty miles north to Newcastle. That was like a foreign city too, but at least the inhabitants didn't treat you like country cousins. At least they didn't, according to my granny, try to short-change you in the shops. 'After you've shook hands with one of that lot,' I was told, 'remember to check all your fingernails are still there.'

Of course all that is in the past. Leeds is a totally different city now. It has pavements cafés, a branch of Harvey Nichols, and the English Tourist Board's 'Gateway to Yorkshire' information office featured such a welter of shining glass that I walked into two walls trying to find the door. Thankfully, for those of us with a sense of heritage, one tradition of the northern town had been preserved: Leeds Bus Station was located in what appeared to be a bomb crater.

I waited for the bus to Harewood House. Beside me two elderly women in twin-sets groaned and attempted to loosen their footwear. One of them jimmied off her right shoe with a noise like a vacuum pack being punctured and said, 'I could tell it would be like this. My cat was nowhere to be seen this morning. And if t' cat's gone AWOL, I know it's going to be a scorcher.'

The bus bounced along through parched countryside. It was dry in the north-east, but nothing like this. Around Leeds the grass was singed and the long-fingered leaves on the chestnut trees had shrivelled into the shape of talons. The dampest patch in the West Riding was the back of my seat. When I got off the bus at Harewood someone tried to sink a standpipe into my shirt. It was a crisis: hospitals in Huddersfield were appealing for saliva donors.

I walked through the gatehouse at Harewood and into the parkland that surrounds the house. Volvos and Range Rovers swished past as I set off down the drive, dust eddying in their wake. The car parks were packed. Families had the gatefolds on their shooting brakes down and were tucking into vast picnics.

The game fair was down a hill in a hollow with woodland running along one side. The members' enclosure, a square of marquees decorated with green and white bunting, shimmered in the afternoon sun like some distant Camelot. A crescent of trade stands and hospitality tents arched around the main showring.

I tried to envisage what might be going on down there. At agricultural shows there were competitions that tested farming skills, so perhaps there would be something similar here. I imagined a Bailiff Scurry in which a whistling squire skilfully controlled a pair of bailiffs as they attempted to drive a herd of crippled workers, foundlings and early martyrs of the trades-union movement through a series of gates and into the work-house. Or perhaps a contest to see who could ravish the plucky servant girl quickest, then disinherit the resulting child. Admittedly, I had been watching rather a lot of Catherine Cookson serials on the telly.

I walked down the hill to take a closer look. The entry charge of £10 was plainly a deterrent to riff-raff. There were no garish, gooey sweets, nylon warm-up coats or poisonous pink cuddly monkeys for sale here. Instead it was venison bressaola, Norfolk jackets and carved wooden rocking horses. There were no corporate entertainers present advertising the fact that they spent their working lives inducing bulls to masturbate into test-tubes, either. But Aga had a tent, Barbour a marquee and there were stands of second-hand-book dealers, gunsmiths, saddlers, fishing-tackle dealers and a company who imported hats and rugs from Afghanistan. Men in striped shirts and Panama hats cruised about, little blue shields tied to their buttons; women with velvet Alice bands and silk scarves alongside them. Beyond the temporary village were shooting ranges and archery targets; along the edge of the woodland springer spaniels were demonstrating their retrieving skills and ability to wag their stubby tails at furious speeds. Tail-docking had been banned for all dogs except working breeds. People who used gundogs said that if their spaniels had full tails they would constantly be getting them snagged on thorns and wire. Their main worry, however, was that with the rate of wag a springer can produce, the addition of two feet of extra tail could lead to them taking off and buzzing over the hedgerows like gyrocopters.

I wandered about between the shooting sticks and the split-cane rods, the Australian drovers' coats and the tweed deer-stalkers. If I'd been making a documentary a suitable title might have been *How Green Was My Welly*.

Outside a stand specialising in novelty doormats, a man with an aristocratic nose and a weatherbeaten face, veined with red like a hunk of rich ironstone, was guffawing at a strip of coconut matting bearing the legend: 'Some days you step in it. Some days you don't.'

'Oh, I say, I like that,' the man roared. 'I like that!' He was clearly very well off, because it is one of the most ancient laws of British life that decibels rise in proportion to income. If Howard Hughes had been English he'd never have been able to keep himself in a darkened, germ-free environment. Every time he phoned down for more ice-cream and tissues the windows of his hotel room would have shattered.

The Country Landowners' Association Game Fair was initiated some thirty years ago as a showcase for rural life. It was the original such fair, but since then it has been much copied: there are now game fairs all over Britain. Stretching over three days and moving around from year to year, the event attracts around 100,000 visitors.

The Country Landowners' Association Game Fair promised to be the largest demonstration of rural pursuits in Britain. It pretty much lived up to this claim. Naturally, some rural pursuits were missing. There were, for example, no groups of bored teenagers staring disgustedly at ancient beech copses and wishing they were amusement arcades; no gathering of surly publicans, or contests to see who could create the longest queue in the sub-post office by asking for assorted benefits to be converted into TV licence stamps, BT instalments and payment of the paper bill, while simultaneously seeking help with filling in a form for an import–export certificate for giant Galapagos tortoises, sending a registered parcel overland to Ulan Bator and moaning about their sciatica. The Gossip Tent had also failed to materialise for reasons unknown (though, mark my words, I should guess that business with Lady Muck and the Rington's Tea man had more than a little to do with it).

Whatever was missing, it was not weaponry. There were exhibitions involving shotguns, rifles, air rifles, bows and crossbows. And there were staghounds, foxhounds, greyhounds, lurchers, beagles and bassets, falcons and ferrets. One thing was for certain: if you were edible wildlife, Harewood House was a place worth avoiding for a few days. In the main showring a woman from a local hunt was explaining the apparent injustice of a pack of great big hounds chasing a single little fox. In the jolly, no-nonsense tones of someone addressing an Alzheimer's sufferer, she said: 'It may seem a little unfair to you. But remember: the fox knows the terrain. He has home advantage.'

The Country Landowners' Association Game Fair has something in common with the early agricultural shows. Like the Georgian farming reformers, the CLA are on a mission to explain, to counteract the media-friendly efforts of environmental, rambling and anti-blood-sports groups. The game fair is a volley in the propaganda war, an attempt to redress the balance. Personally, I felt it was too late – about two hundred years too late. Opposition to landowners was not, in the main, a considered response to the communications skills of organisations such as Friends of the Earth, or the right-to-roamers, but a knee-jerk reaction; an historical reflex.

When I was living in the Old Kent Road I made the mistake of watching a documentary on policing in the area. The Old Kent Road was a rough place. At first I wondered why there were so many old people there. Then it dawned on me: Death was too scared to visit. The last time Death had been down the Old Kent Road someone had whacked him with a baseball bat and stolen his scythe. For the police it was even more fraught with hazards. The local population detested them. If a copper walked into a pub in the Old Kent Road the usual response was a hail of bottles. Asked why he thought this was, a senior officer said he believed it was deeply rooted in the past. He was right. The Old Kent Road was at one time the home patch of London's costermongers and market traders. In Victorian times the costermongers' way of life seemed to bring them into constant conflict with the newly formed constabulary: they were moved along when they caused obstructions with their barrows, searched for stolen goods and generally, they felt, victimised. By the 1860s the costermongers' sense of grievance against the police had reached such a pitch that if one of their number was jailed for assaulting a constable the others would have a whip-round and buy a present for him. The flying bottles in the Old Kent Road in the 1980s were a continuation of this old battle. Rancour tends to increase rather than dissipate over the years.

At the same time as the costermongers were storing up hostility against the forces of law and order, the inhabitants of the towns were squirrelling away resentments against the land-owners and farmers. A large chunk of the urban population had been forced out of the countryside by the Enclosure Acts, or the gradual introduction of labour-saving machinery, and for years they had suffered poverty and hardship because rural interests had succeeded in keeping grain prices falsely high through the Corn Laws. Necessary though these measures may have been, it is unlikely that their casualties felt like breaking out the bunting and holding a street party to celebrate them.

By the closing decades of the nineteenth century the time of the dominance of country over town was coming to an end. The Enclosure Acts had depopulated the land too thoroughly. As the franchise moved ever nearer to one man, one vote, the land-owners found they had less and less influence. People in Britain often wonder why French politicians allow themselves to be so easily bossed about by their farmers. The answer is simple. In France a far higher proportion of people live off the land than in Britain. In this country the farmers and landowners are in a minority, heavily outnumbered by the urban population. Now the landowners could no longer compel the rest of the country to do what they wanted, they were having to persuade it instead. And quite a lot of people simply weren't prepared to listen.

In this modern-day exercise in winning over the general populace, there was a large gathering around the ferret exhibition – a distinctly different crowd from the aristocratic one I'd previously seen loitering among the hunting pinks in Hackett's clothing tent. Short, stocky men in the main, with forearms shaped like nine-pins and hands the size of buckets, their trousers stretched taut like the skins on over-stuffed haggises. Inside the tent a man in a moleskin shirt was giving a talk on rabbiting techniques. In wire-mesh cages behind him half a dozen ferrets looked on inquisitively from the shade, sharp noses twitching. With the distinctive dark band around their eyes they looked like a group of Victorian footpads anticipating a mugging.

The first ferret I ever saw belonged to a boy I was at school with. He kept it in an upturned rabbit cage in a shed at the bottom of his garden. When you went into the shed you were assailed by an acrid masculine stink so hummingly powerful you instinctively found yourself swatting at it. Hob ferrets are just about the only animal that can rival a billy goat for body odour. In fact, keeping a billy and a hob in the same confined space is banned under the Geneva Convention Chemical Weapons Accord. As your eyes grew accustomed to the light and you gradually got your tear ducts under control, you noticed that the wire mesh on top of the ferret's cage was raised in series of tiny hillocks the size and shape of the compartments in an egg box. How strange, you thought, as you leaned over to take a look at the resident. The minute your head crossed over the lip of the cage there was a quick rustle, a whistling blur of white and a sharp *phwang* as something launched itself upwards in the general direction of your nose and ricocheted off the wire mesh. A second later you noticed that a fresh cone had appeared in the cage door. Then, *phwang, phwang, phwang*, three more. The missile in the cage was an albino ferret named Bites-Yer-Legs-Norman. The miniature mountains were impressions of his snout.

Bites-Yer-Legs-Norman was named after Leeds United's uncompromising defender Norman Hunter. He was much more savage than his namesake. Norman had fur the colour of beer foam and a late-night drinker's pink eyes. In low gear he moved in a kind of slinky waddle, body arched, feet at ten-to-two like Charlie Chaplin's tramp. When aroused he bounded, back bowing, his spine a spring that catapulted him forwards. Let out in the garden, Bites-Yer-Legs would whirl round madly then streak across the grass at the first person his eyes alighted on, teeth bared. Visiting him it was like attending a spin-the-bottle party for masochists.

A farmer told me recently that more walkers are injured by tups each year than by bulls. 'People are wary of bulls,' he said, 'and if they see one coming they'll run. Nobody wants to be seen running away from a sheep. But if a Suffolk or a Swaledale hits you full tilt, hey, bloody hell!' I envisaged a walker, trousers tucked into red socks, clipboard and map swinging round his neck, disappearing over a hedge with a squawk. 'You could put up a sign, "Beware of sheep", but people would think you were having them on.'

A similar thought affected people the first time Bites-Yer-Legs-Norman hurled himself in their direction. Ferrets are small creatures. Norman was about sixteen inches long in body with an additional six inches of fluffy tail. Fleeing from him seemed ridiculous, but it wasn't. Bites-Yer-Legs had teeth like darning needles and a preternatural ability to locate the fleshy part of a calf. Once he had latched on there was no shifting him. You could shake your leg all you wanted, it only made him hang on tighter. All you could do was wait until Bites-Yer-Legs got bored. Ferrets enjoy inflicting pain, so it was quite often a long wait. The only other hope was that Norman would be so delighted with his attack that he would let go in order to celebrate. This involved him skittering sideways, mouth gaping, fur standing on end, making a weird hissing, clucking chortling sound. It was a kind of ferret *haka*. In many ways being bitten was less frightening.

Ferrets are a domesticated (I use that word advisedly – the image of Bites-Yer-Legs in a pinny taking a feather duster to the knick-knack rack is not one that comes easily) strain of the polecat. Their name comes from the Latin *furritus*, meaning 'little fur thief'. Ferrets are closely related to two other notoriously smelly creatures, the badger and the skunk, and one which actually surpasses them in its love of mindless violence, the North American mink. There are quite a lot of North American mink in the wild in Britain nowadays, the offspring of escapees from fur farms. For a while there were warnings put out on TV about hooligan mink, because a number of householders had been attacked by them while fetching in the milk. Mink, you see, like milk, and they had worked out that they could find a plentiful supply of it on the doorsteps of houses in the morning. They didn't take too kindly to it when people opened their doors and tried to snatch it off them. If you have never encountered a mink this may seem pretty far-fetched. I used to think so, too. Then one day while walking along by the river I came across a mink attacking a rabbit on the path in front of me. The rabbit was squealing pitifully as the mink nipped and battered it. A rabbit is a good deal bigger than a mink, and it does not surrender its life easily or quickly. I clapped my hands in an effort to drive the mink off. The mink just looked up at me. Not since I moved out of the Old Kent Road had I seen a stare that so embodied aggressive contempt. If the mink could have spoken, its words would undoubtedly have been, 'What you lookin' at?' After a moment he went back to killing the rabbit. I clapped my hands again. This time he didn't even bother to look up.

The first people to keep ferrets were the ancient Egyptians, who used them to catch mice. Later the cat replaced the ferret as the mouser of choice in Egyptian households. As most ancient Egyptian men wore short skirts and no underpants this development must have been greeted with a great sigh of relief by half the population. Or a great squeak of relief at any rate. You have to wonder, though, what would have happened if the cat hadn't been domesticated, if the Egyptians had been allergic, and the ferret had retained its status as pre-eminent domestic mouse-catcher. The whole culture of the West would have been irrevocably altered. There'd be no more *Puss-in-Boots* pantos, or people saying, 'What's the matter, cat got your tongue?' James Bond would roll around on the waterbed not with Pussy, but with Ferret Galore, and *Beano* readers would thrill as boy superhero Billy the Ferret foiled a bank robber by running up his trouser leg. 'Moonshadow' would have been a hit for '70s folk singer Ferret Stevens and T.S. Eliot would have written *Old Possum's Book of Practical Ferrets*, with its famous poem, 'McCafferty':

McCafferty, McCafferty, there's no one like McCafferty,
Ooch, ouch, ooch,
Let go of my finger, you bugger.

This would, inevitably, have led to queues of American tourists lining the pavements of Drury Lane to see Sir Andrew Lloyd Webber's hit musical *Ferrets*, in which Elaine Paige would sing 'Memories' and then disappear up a drainpipe. In many ways, the domestication of the cat is a human tragedy.

I walked up to the bus stop. When the bus came I got on. I asked the driver for Leeds. 'Pound and ten,' he said.

'It only cost ninety pence coming out here.'

'This is peak hours.'

I handed him the money, and checked my fingernails afterwards. The West Riding might have changed, but it hasn't changed that much.

11

• Fruit •

Egton Gooseberry Fair

Catherine and I were on the Esk Valley railway, rattling through the southern suburbs of Middlesbrough. We had just passed through Nunthorpe and I had happily noted that even now, twenty years after the graffiti announcing it had initially appeared above a road sign, the middle-aged woman in front of us still nudged her husband and said, 'Here we are, "Naughty" Nunthorpe,' and they both chuckled drily. I felt that for the first time in twenty-four hours I was regaining my equilibrium.

What had happened was that the day before I had gone down to Seaburn on the Durham coast to see the annual show of the North-East Budgerigar Society. It was blastingly hot on the train and I had fallen asleep. I arrived at my destination in a state of some fuddlement. Bewildered is not the best way to approach Seaburn on a boiling Sunday afternoon in July, let me tell you. In Seaburn on a summer weekend you really need your wits about you. I walked down the street toward the promenade as the pubs and clubs belched out hordes of shirtless, lobster-red numb-skulls, their beer kites wobbling like half-set raspberry jellies as they subsided over the waistbands of their all-too-skimpy shorts. There was a time when men with psychopathic tendencies, criminal records and pasts they wished to escape ran away and joined the Foreign Legion. Nowadays they go to the seaside instead.

I swerved along between rolling, staggering groups, and between the butting bellies of blotto blokes facing off sea-elephant-style outside the chip shops. A Ford Fiesta swung round a corner, a burst of female laughter spraying from the window. One of a pair of men walking towards me, his face the colour of a chimp's bum, four-packs hanging from his hands like bowling balls, imitated the cackle, then yelled after the car: 'Fuck off back to the council estate where you belong, you noisy slag!' It was an unsettling thought, but this chap clearly believed himself to be rather superior.

Along the seafront scores of pretty teenage girls in bikini tops and miniskirts promenaded up and down while their male contemporaries attempted to catch their attention by doing impressively accurate impressions of adolescent baboons. I dodged into the gutter to avoid one gibbering troupe and found myself the victim of a drive-by water-pistol shooting. 'How d'you like that, pal?' the shooter sneered from the passenger seat of an XR3. I tried to think of a suitably witty retort. Unfortunately I'd left my flame-thrower at home.

Along I strode in search of the budgies, past the *ker-chunk*ing amusement arcades, the drunks, the dog turds and the dropped ice-creams lurking like skid pans on every corner, a mounting sense of anxiety gnawing away at my inner being. The year before I had attended over thirty football matches across Durham and Northumberland, many of them in villages so tough and deprived they made Seaburn seem like Eton College, but I had never felt remotely threatened. This was different. The mix of alcohol, sun and sex has a mephitic effect on the English male. One whiff of its sweet scent and they begin to exude primal menace. Seaburn had the atmosphere of the film *Deliverance* dressed in a kiss-me-quick hat. Except that I felt the hats in Seaburn were more likely to carry the message 'Away Then, Big Mouth', thus offering a dual invitation for a snog or a punch-up.

Throughout the spring and summer I had been reading books about farm animals. Breeding livestock being a central part of farming, many dwelled on mating patterns. I knew that two tups in a field would sort out which was to service the ewes by butting their heads together repeatedly until one spun away, cross-eyed with concussion, and wandered groggily off, nursing its wounds and brooding on the knowledge that its dreams of a life of sensual excess were now shattered for ever. Most of the writers regarded this as a pretty primitive state of affairs, but compared to what goes on at a British holiday resort it seemed to me remarkably urbane.

I gave up on the budgies. I wasn't sure quite where the show was taking place. I thought of asking someone, but every time I spotted anybody remotely unscary-looking and began to approach them they would immediately start smacking their children, holding an infant with one hand and batting with the other as if practising tennis shots with a ball on elastic. And anyway, I was beginning to wonder if the lacewings, opalines, fallows and clearflights would have survived Seaburn. Surely by now someone would have growled, 'What are you chirruping at, you beaky little bastards?' and chinned the lot of them. So I gave up and walked back to the station as quickly as I could. I was disappointed to miss the show, but relieved to have got out of Seaburn in one piece. At least I managed to rescue one snippet of information from the afternoon: the name budgerigar comes from two Aborigine words: *gar* is 'parrot', and *budgeri* means 'good to eat'.

Beyond Nunthorpe a peculiar, opaque mist descended, the approaching dun-coloured hills appearing as if you were gazing at them through mosquito netting. In this strange light distances were blurred, so that Roseberry Topping seemed to loom on the horizon, tall as the Matterhorn. I had ambivalent feelings about this local landmark. I had been up it many times. From the flat rock top you can see for miles in all directions: the little patches of field, cobbled together with hedgerows; the icebergs of smoke above Teesside cooling towers; the maroon-striped mound of the moors and the pantiled roofs of my village, so small now I could blot it out with my thumb. No thumb, no matter how large, could, however, cover the fact that it was on Roseberry Topping that I made the biggest mistake of my life.

When I first moved to London I lived near a trendy theatre. The trendy theatre had a café. It was self-service, and the cooking was from that puritan wing of vegetarianism that believes all meals should be brown and taste of very little. The bread had more roughage than Seaburn. A party of Sloane Rangers turned up one week and had a bun fight. Three of them never regained consciousness. The pastry was a humane alternative to suede. The pudding was yoghurt. The place was popular for Sunday lunch. By midday it was packed with people in Peruvian pullovers and those shoes that are made out of Cornish pasties from which the meat has been liberated by animal-rights activists. I went there partly because it was cheap; mainly because I was too scared to take my attitude anywhere else.

One Sunday, as I was toying with a dish of Kashmiri-style coconut matting and a side order of Trill, a family came and joined me at my stripped-pine table. There was a man – beard, trousers with a zip round the thigh so he could convert them swiftly into shorts in unexpected outbreaks of hot weather – a woman in batik and two ruddy-cheeked, fair-haired children, a boy of about nine and a younger girl. There was a play area along one side of the restaurant and the children ran off to it after only a cursory prod at their plates of sweet-and-sour dufflebag. Shortly afterwards I noticed that the little boy was standing on his own in one corner doing something so obscene, so totally against the grain of civilised behaviour that I felt compelled to draw his father's attention to it. 'Erm, excuse me,' I said, 'Your son, over there, he appears to be, er ...' – how should I phrase this? Nothing else for it. Be bold – 'Well ... dancing.'

The father smiled and looked across to the little boy who was transferring his weight from one foot to the other in a distinctly rhythmic manner and swaying his body about in time to the Django Rheinardt record that was twanging out from the sound system. 'Oh yes,' the father said, grinning proudly. 'He loves dancing. He goes to classes.'

'And you let him?' I asked, aghast.

The man seem puzzled by my concern. 'Of course. Why not?'

I restrained myself from grabbing the front of his iridescent jumper and yelling: 'Because you might as well plait his hair, put him in a dress and paint his nails while you're at it!' After a month in the capital it was becoming increasingly obvious to me that not every man had been brought up in the North Riding of Yorkshire.

In the North Riding of Yorkshire no nine-year-old boy would ever dance of his own free will. He'd rather have his nipples removed with an industrial belt-sander. In my primary school, boys would volunteer to go to the dentist to avoid Music, Movement and Mime. The gas mask and two extractions were considered a small price to pay for escape from thirty minutes of skipping round the gym in time to *Peer Gynt*. 'Come along, you boys,' our teacher would intone. 'Imagine you are trolls in the Hall of the Mountain King.' And we would try to skip as sullenly as possible, while imagining that *she* was in the Hall of the Mountain King, chained to a wall and being given a Chinese burn by Carl Stephenson. We were North Riding lads, nine years old, and our masculinity was dear to us. We would shrink from doing anything that even remotely compromised our manliness. Wearing smart clothes, washing our hands before meals and wiping our noses with handkerchiefs were the sort of things our warrior souls rebelled against. Dancing in public? To us combing your hair in public was tantamount to wearing a brassiere. Once when our school football team lost by an even more staggering margin than usual we were punished by the games teacher. We were marched out into the playground at lunchtime and forced to do ballet steps. That's what dancing meant to us: humiliation.

There were only two things you could do that were worse than dancing. One was to wear open-toed sandals (never mind his parentage, Jesus would have got a right taunting if he'd turned up in our playground, I can tell you); the other was, knowingly and with malice aforethought, voluntarily to spend time with a member of the opposite sex. And this was my crime. On a warm Saturday afternoon in June I went up Roseberry Topping with a girl. I can't think what possessed me. Actually, I can: she had long, dark eyelashes and she was the only female I had ever seen who kicked a football with her instep instead of her toe. It was love.

If I thought such a flagrant broaching of the tribal taboos would pass unnoticed I was badly mistaken. By Monday morning playtime the whole school knew about it. I was barracked unmercifully, harassed, embarrassed, teased until my face felt like a fireball. All the masculine things I had done in the past – punching Minna Appleton in the face so his nose bled, deliberately falling off my bike on gravel to prove it wouldn't make me cry like weedy-wet Paul King – meant nothing. I had transgressed. That night when I got home my cheeks glowed so brightly that my dad took me up into the loft and used me for illumination while he lagged the water tank. And the next day it started all over again. And it went on for weeks. And it would probably have gone on for longer, too, had not Anthony Moore from the new housing estate made an even bigger error of judgement than me. He believed his mother when she told him that it really didn't make any difference, all his clean pairs were in the wash and nobody was going to notice anyway, and came to school wearing a pair of his sister's knickers. Even as I joyfully and wholeheartedly took part in the cries of 'Ant! Ant! He wears girly pants!' however, I could not fully forget my own humiliation. And even now, twenty-five years later, I find it hard to look at Roseberry Topping without blushing. Of course, since those primary-school days I've learned and I've mellowed. I no longer think it's wrong for men to wear sandals, or to be called Jerome, or to cry if they fall off their bicycles. I have even learned to acknowledge that some boys like to dance, and that is their choice, and the world is all the richer for it. Mind you, the sight of Morris Men still makes my hands instinctively curl into fists. But that's nothing to do with my North Riding upbringing. It's because they're bloody crap.

As we wound slowly through Kildale the mist began to evaporate. The train was full of people, families from Middlesbrough in the main, on day trips to Whitby to eat fish and chips and buy kippers and walk through the whale's jawbone while licking ice-creams in oyster-shell-shaped wafers. The sun was out, but it was warm in the carriage rather than hot, heather-and-bracken-scented air blowing in through the open windows. The parents smiled and chatted, the children were quiet, absorbed in books and computer games, looking up from them only when one of their number spotted a wasp's nest in the eaves of Grosmont Station. At Castleton we looked down on the cricket field; at Danby there were coits pits. Outside Glaisdale, a group of girls leading a skewbald pony to the river waved as we passed and stiff-legged Blackface ewes scattered. Near Commondale a flock of barrel-brisketed Swaledale wethers didn't give us a second look. Like me they were North Riding boys, unwilling to be excited or scared by anything so babyish as a train.

In Egton Bridge we walked down the tree-shadowed road past the church hall where the Gooseberry Fair was taking place. It was closed to the public while the judging was done. Through the open doors a long, white-clothed table and a cluster of serious-looking and respectable people concentrating their efforts on plates of bulging berries could be seen.

The Gooseberry Fair was first held in 1800 and nothing, not even two world wars, has stopped it since. At first there were additional attractions: the showmen had come and there had been coconut shies, rides, animals, babble and commotion. In the evening dances had been held. As the other agricultural shows began to embrace entertainments, however, the Gooseberry Fair took the opposite route. It had gradually pared itself back, cut away all extraneous frills, become purer and purer, until all that was left of the original hoo-ha was the white-clothed table and the opulent jewels of fruit. It was a bold decision, to opt for this less-means-more approach, but it brought rewards. The garden of the pub you reached by walking on stepping-stones across the

shaded Esk was packed with people, and more were arriving all
the time. The trippers came not in search of great excitement,
but to see a truly unique event untrammelled by commercialism;
one which, in a world where everything seemed to get bigger
and flashier, remained, like the village it was in, like the valley
it was in, a small, good and simple thing.

After lunch we walked back up through the village, past a
garden where tall purple and white acanthus spikes swayed in
the breeze and the yucca plants were in flower. A steady parade
of people moved in and out of the church hall. Inside there was
a queue for the raffle, which featured a hefty home-cured York
ham as first prize, and a cluster of whirring cameras round the
champion fruits. Wooden plaques listing previous victors, rich
with the North Riding's Viking surnames – Harland and Johnson
– lined the walls. I walked along beside the table. The gooseberries, arranged in groups of four on spotless china plates or
balanced individually on tees fashioned from bottle tops, were
uniformly enormous. Even the Maiden Growers' section, which
you might have expected to feature some ardent but fumblingly
inexpert attempts by virgin berry buffs, contained nothing
smaller than a bantam egg. The berries were judged in fours and
pairs and singly. The heaviest could weigh up to two ounces. The
whole process of growing and showing was carried out under the
strictest rules. Even the transfer of bushes from one grower to
another had to be approved by the committee.

Just in front of me a young woman whispered, 'D'you think
they doctor them?' to an elderly female relative whose cream
beret was pulled so tightly down over her forehead it looked as
if she must have screwed it on using a monkey wrench. The old
woman champed her jaws slowly, tasting the air for the truth. 'I
don't know,' she said, and looked about her to check that no one
was lip-reading; then, with all the discretion of an Islamic
prayer-caller, boomed, 'But there's some daft beggars that sits
out all day wi' an umbrella o'er 'em.'

'Why do they do that?' the young woman asked, face flushing.

'Because they're barmy,' the old biddy replied.

Why the gooseberries were chosen as the preferred fruit for Egton Fair is lost in history. Probably it was because the gooseberry, like the bilberry, grew wild across most of the north and had come to be associated with the fairs, particularly the harvest hirings such as Whittingham Fair in Northumberland, where they were sold, usually by Gypsies who gathered them from the hedgerows as they travelled. At other fairs they were brought ready-prepared in the form of favourite delicacies such as fools or tansies, while pies made from sweetened hot-crust pastry stuffed with gooseberries set in apple jelly were the speciality at Mansfield Fair in the Nottinghamshire coalfield. Gooseberries (or goosegogs, carberries, goggles, honey-blobs, feaberries, grosets, grossberries, grozzles, catberries or golfobs, as they were variously known across the north – you can usually tell how popular something is by the number of names for it there are) had been brought into cultivation late, presumably because it was easy enough to go and pick them wild. The names of the cultivated varieties, usually larger, pinker and less hairy, reflected the gooseberry's northern origins. Two of the most popular were Langley Gage and Lancashire Lad, though I doubt there were any of this latter trans-Pennine strain swelling proudly and defiantly on the table at Egton. It would have been too much of an insult for Yorkshiremen to bear. Someone would have run amok with a mallet.

The experts' efforts – shiny, purple golf balls – were located at the far end of the table. It was easy to see why the young woman had wondered if they had been tampered with. The bristly, heavily veined skin seemed to be battling to hold all the contents in, the puce colour a sign of the strain. If it had been a body-building competition, the judges would instantly have suspected steroids. Here, though, I would guess there was nothing more sinister involved than sunshine and horse manure and maybe some fungicidal spray to beat off mildew. I could believe it about the umbrellas, though. Fruit ripens quickly in bright light, and there would be nothing worse for a committed gooseberry-grower than to watch a prize specimen suddenly wrinkling, suppurating and sagging before his or her eyes like Ursula Andress in the last reel of *She*.

Catherine and I came out smiling, sat on a low wall feeling the warmth of the sandstone. Later we went over to Whitby and bought ice-creams with wafers shaped like oyster shells and walked through the whale's jawbone. From the clifftop, looking down on the beach, you could see the children from the train scampering about the sand, damp swimsuits sagging, their mums and dads asleep surrounded by striped canvas screens and picnic remains. A fret was rolling in, low across the sea, so that the top of the harbour lighthouse seemed to hover like a flying saucer above the mist. Groups of men in blazers and women in Sunday-best floral dresses were heading along the promenade for a tea dance at the pavilion. There are some days that are quietly wonderful, days when even the sight of a poster advertising Keith Harris and Orville cannot dissuade you from the view that humanity is benign, the world is kind, this tiny blue planet of ours spins happily through the darkness and even Seaburn is not really that bad.

12

· Birds ·

Sedgefield Show

Durham Bus Station is a paradise for anyone who doesn't drive. There are buses going just about everywhere from Durham Bus Station. The list of destinations covers an entire wall. It is the largest single collection of north-eastern names outside the Menin Gate at Ypres. Glancing down it to find which stand you need to go to for Crook or Tow Law or Bearpark, you wouldn't be at all surprised to find Khartoum, the X376 service (via Auckland, St Helen's, Evenwood and Marrakesh – Saturdays and market days only).

The bus to Sedgefield rolled along through the old pit villages of Durham. The roasting weather continued unchecked. In the garden of one red-brick house kids were splashing about in a paddling pool while a black mongrel dog lay, sad-eyed and panting, with its nose wedged through the bars of the gate. In another an old lady in a floral dress was reclining in a deck-chair, fanning herself with the *Northern Echo* against a back-drop of drooping sweet peas. Old men in shirt-sleeves and braces wandered aimlessly about the baking streets, concussed by the heat.

During my father's spell working in the Middle East he acquired an Arab phrasebook. The section headed 'Weather'

1. An Angora rabbit
struggles to look
brooding and macho.

2. A Golden Guernsey
billy goat tries to
recall the key guitar
riff from 'Sabbath
Bloody Sabbath'.

3. Grasmere Sports: a scuffle breaks out during the frog-hopping and waltzing-with-an-invisible-partner competitions.

4. A pair of heavy horses discuss their boss's Eric Von Stroheim fixation.

5. 'Suave, sophisticated bachelor seeks companion ...'

6. Local women are unimpressed by the Cumbrian Constabulary's new summer uniform.

7. Sheep sale: locals can barely contain their glee at all the bargains on offer.

8. The Ketton Ox: the Arnold Schwarzenegger of the nineteenth century.

9. Pig racing at Bellingham. The winner was later disqualified when judges discovered he was actually a man dressed as a pig.

10. A Gypsy fortune-teller foresees a huge Brasso bill.

11. Appleby Horse Fair: a large and expectant crowd anxiously await a flippant picture caption.

12. A Peruvian X cavy prepares to play a wicked practical joke on Reginald Bosanquet.

13. A clearly aggrieved Peruvian cavy moments after being turned down for a part in the new Salon Selectives commercial.

14. Guessing which end of a Lincoln Longwool sheep is which – a popular event at shows in the Yorkshire Wolds.

15. A Scottish bull reacts angrily to charges of pandering to national stereotypes.

16. Champion grower Neil Armstrong indicates the size of his leeks while showing off a pair of award-winning spring onions.

began with the admonition: 'Generally speaking, the Arabs do not talk of the weather as the English do.'

'A hot, dry day, Mustapha.'

'Indeed Ali, and the weather forecast says that tomorrow will be ...'

'Hot and dry also.'

'Ah, you saw it.'

'No, Mustapha. I was just making an educated guess.'

Now the English had stopped chatting about the weather, too. The hot spell had gone on for so long it was a dead subject. Even northerners had become so blasé they had begun planning barbecues a week in advance.

In Sedgefield there were weddings. The pretty central square was lined with ribboned limousines, confetti swirled in the wake of passing vehicles and the broad-brimmed hats of the female guests formed such a solid roof above the pavements that several mice went home with the impression they'd just witnessed a total eclipse.

I walked past the knots of nuptial groupies (was that the woman from the Carlisle train telling the pensioner to her right the exact length of the organza in the bride's train? Quite possibly) hovering round the Catholic church and up to the showground that lay behind a 1960s executive development. Sedgefield is Tony Blair's constituency. Mr Blair wasn't about, but I did see a council house with a conservatory, which I think sort of represented him.

The dry weather had left the showfield the colour of Weetabix. Along the northern edge were pens of Holstein Friesian cattle, an efficient but dull dairy breed, the bovine equivalent of Volvos. In the main ring the judges were examining the Shetland ponies. Tiny, shaggy-maned creatures with bodies the shape of stoves, Shetlands are said to be of Celtic origin, though their nearest relatives are the Irish Connemara and Icelandic and Norwegian Fjord ponies, which suggests some Viking influence, too. Originally, Shetlands were used to haul peat and seaweed; later, like the Dales pony and the Welsh cob, their strength and stature earned them the dubious honour of employment in the coal mines. The pit ponies, from which many of the smaller equine breeds on show at Sedgefield were probably descended, were used from the nineteenth century onwards. At first they turned the windlass on the pithead hoist, then, when drift-mining and lifts came in, they made their way down into the darkness. Most pit ponies spent their entire lives underground. When not working they were housed in subterranean stables. By and large, we read, the Victorian pit ponies were well looked after by the mine owners. Their accommodation was dry and kept in good repair, and they were regularly fed. Pity the same couldn't be said for the miners, really.

The Shetland pony is the smallest British native breed. This will come as no surprise to anybody who knows anything about animals. All creatures that come from the Shetlands are minuscule. The Shetland sheepdog, for example, looks like Lassie after a boil wash. This is just as well, as any normal-sized collie would undoubtedly trample the tiny, flat-tailed Shetland sheep to death. Shetland cattle, meanwhile, are black and white and probably resulted in Shetland dairymaids inventing a special milking cushion. The indigenous Shetland pig is now sadly extinct, but is said to have been no bigger than a terrier and was known to the local populace as a 'grice mite'. Shetland crofters are just about the only farmers who have ever been seriously worried about the threat of livestock being carried off by moths.

I wandered off to find some shade. Outside the industrial tent was a table devoted to farm produce. There were categories for the best field potatoes (kidney), the top stone of hay and for heads of oats, barley and wheat. These categories had once been commonplace at agricultural shows, for the growing of quality crops was just as important to British farming as the production of high-class livestock. Nowadays, though, you rarely see them. Growing show vegetables is left to amateurs. It is a pity, but you could see why the farmers would take more interest in breeding prize-winning cattle or sheep: no matter how many rosettes a turnip collects, it was unlikely to bring in any stud fees.

In the industrial tent I gazed awhile at Sedgefield's own unique baking category: Yogurt Cakes (Confined to Members of Sedgefield WI) and Coconut Haystacks (Egg-cup-Sized). I was particularly keen on the bracketed message attached to the latter. It suggested that at some point an over-literal competitor had entered a plate of fifteen-foot cakes, possibly with sugar-work pitchforks jabbed into the side of them. Over by the jams was a woman in a blue frock so voluminous that if she'd laid out on the grass flights of ducks would have tried to land on her. She was plainly a judge, and was pointing some jams out to her rather nervous companion. 'These,' she said imperiously, 'are no good. They aren't even filled to the top. And those next to them aren't much better. Look at the shrinkage.'

'You don't actually taste them, then?' her friend asked, not unreasonably, you might think.

The woman in blue looked at her as if she had just suggested a three-in-a-bed romp with Hastings Banda. 'Of course not!' she retorted.

In the poultry tent the pigeon men were gathered in a corner. They wore football shirts. Fags balanced precariously on their lower lips and their eyelids formed narrow slits through which you caught occasional glimpses of whites and pupils moving about furtively like soldiers in a bunker. A polite man in a short-sleeved beige shirt and a pair of those slacks that come complete with a matching belt was asking them about the birds. One of the pigeon men was answering in a West Riding accent as flat as a cowpat.

'See these 'uns,' he said, 'they're Blue Cocks, them.' He walked along the line with the man pointing out White Flights, Mealies and Chequer Pieds. 'Judges are looking for a bold and noble head, right? You can take this 'un here as an example. Good, rounded shape, look; no flattening of the crown, but then the wattle's gone over big for a cock that age. That just happens sometimes. You know how it is.'

The beige man nodded dutifully, though he plainly didn't how it was at all. Men, however, are genetically programmed to agree when any other man says, 'You know how it is.' In the pub someone will say, 'So I got back home, and guess what? Suddenly I'm leaped on by five beautiful Balinese temple dancers demanding sexual favours. You know how it is.' And every other bloke in the pub will be wagging his head vigorously and pulling a bloody-hell-not-those-boring-Balinese-birds-again-you-can't-beat-them-off-with-a-stick-can-you kind of face. It's all to do with survival of the fittest. Most male animals fight to establish social position, but more developed species have subtler methods. Mountain gorillas, for example, play Trivial Pursuit, and any one of them who doesn't win at least two slices of pie never gets to mate with anybody, ever. As a result men are instinctively reluctant to appear ignorant of any experience, no matter how outlandish. Because, as Francis Bacon pointed out (or was it the Princess of Wales?), knowledge is power. Which is why Bamber Gascoigne gets such low electricity bills.

'I'm actually,' the nodding man said after sufficient time had elapsed to leave him confident that his bluff on the enlarged-wattle issue was not about to be called, 'more interested in these ones over here.' He gestured towards some exhibition varieties. A brown and white Norwich cropper pigeon responded by inflating its crop so that it bulged out like the jowls of the late Dizzy Gillespie. Its red-ringed eyes gave the impression that the effort of the performance was about to give it a hernia. The pigeon-fancier glanced at the pouting bird. He was a homing-pigeon man. He plainly regarded the more fancy exhibition types as frivolous, workshy and probably of doubtful sexual character. 'Oh,' he said gruffly. 'I don't know owt about them.'

Pigeon-racing is big in County Durham. It is popular practically wherever there is or was mining. Most pit villages had, somewhere on their outskirts, a little shanty town of pigeon lofts outside which you would often see groups of men staring up into the sky like extras from *Close Encounters of the Third Kind.* An old chap I know can remember as a boy in the 1920s sitting with his father and the other pit men around the pigeon lofts of his village near Bishop Auckland on a Sunday morning, watching for the pigeons coming home: 'My dad would be looking up into this clear sky and suddenly he'd shout "Looker! There's a one!" And I'd follow his finger and I'd see ... nowt. Then a tiny black speck would appear and he'd say, "Aye, it's a mixed colour." And I'd be staring up at this titchy thing wondering how he could even tell it was a bird. I was a youngster and here was my father, who spent most of his life underground, and he could see better than me. My dad would watch on as the speck got gradually bigger. "Here she comes. She's a Red Chequer, and here she comes, lad." Then when it was as big as a pinhead he'd spit and say, "Buggeration! She's one of Frank Robson's."'

As a sport, pigeon-racing really began with the foundation of the National Homing Union in 1897, but the homing instincts of pigeons have been used to relay messages since Roman times. The use of the carrier pigeon reached its height during the nineteenth century. Paul Reuter made his fortune by establishing a pigeon-post system which relayed stock-market information around Europe. In the Franco-Prussian and First World wars, pigeons became an integral part of army communication networks, and even in the Second World War their use was so vital that thirty-two military birds, including a pale fellow named Beachcomber who, in photographs, appears to be wearing a monocle, were awarded the Dickin Medal for Gallantry.

No one is quite sure how homing pigeons navigate. It used to be thought it had something to do with the earth's magnetic field, but then a Dr Matthews from Cambridge disproved this theory by mounting powerful lightweight magnets on the wings of a pigeon so as to disturb the magnetic field surrounding it. The bird still found its way home – despite carrying the additional burden of several nails, two tin cans and an artificial leg belonging to a retired sea captain from Clacton.

Nowadays most pigeon-fanciers believe the sun is the main factor, even though birds seem to find their way back quickest in cloudy conditions. However the pigeon orientates itself, one thing is certain: these days more and more birds are failing to make it home. Some of the fanciers have put this down to a rise in the peregrine falcon population (decimated during the last war to allow Beachcomber and his comrades to go about their patriotic duties in relative safety); others to the increased use of mobile phones. It is suggested by the latter faction that the signals from mobile phones somehow scramble the pigeons' sense of direction. But can pigeons really pick up signals from phones? Are they flying along with some sort of third-party directional monologue running in their heads that is prone to interruption? 'Now two points north, flying speed 40mph with no appreciable headwind, we are now cruising at 300ft and in a short while we will be turning east along the *pssssk Hi can I order two deep-pan pepperoni pizzas to take away, please pssssk* miles and then altering course to the *aaarsk Bob? It's me. The Cleethorpes ornamental tap deal – it's in the bag! aaarsk.*' If so perhaps it was some nosy bird who picked up the Princess of Wales's 'Squidgy' conversation and passed it on to the tabloids rather than MI5 or a retired suburban bank manager.

Certainly it is known that during spells of thundery weather more pigeons fail to make it home. Thunder tends to interfere with radio signals, as anyone who has ever flown radio-controlled aircraft will tell you. So perhaps there is something in this after all. Except that in order to use radio signals to get home, the coop or loft from which the pigeon comes would have to be acting as some kind of transmitter or relay station. And the pigeon doesn't leave anything in the coop that could transmit signals. The only things the pigeon leaves behind are feathers and guano. And anyone who suggests that pigeon shit is sending out radio signals is plainly several mealy hens short of a full loft.

A man I know who races pigeons has a more down-to-earth explanation for the recent bout of disappearances. 'Homing used to be a poor man's sport,' he says. 'If you were a pit man you might keep a dozen or so birds. If you had one that had stopped winning or had never won in the first place you wouldn't be able to afford to go on feeding it. If you had a bird that was no good in those days, you ate it. Nowadays people have hundreds of birds and they can keep them no matter what. There's no natural selection any more, which means more poor birds and more disappearances.'

Durham is a big place for pigeon-racing but the real Mecca of homing is Belgium, where the Fédération Colombophile Internationale has its headquarters in a Brussels suburb. The FCI organises the Pigeon Olympiad, held every two years. In Belgium they show pigeon-racing live on TV (and people say the Belgians are boring, I ask you). And they know how to doctor their birds over there, too. The big problem for pigeon-racers is moulting. Racing takes place in the summer, when most birds shed their feathers, and birds that are shedding feathers don't fly as fast. The classic way of getting over this problem is to keep the pigeons in a semi-darkened loft so that they go on thinking it's winter. The most effective and modern way, though, is to use cortisone. Cortisone stops moulting but its repeated use can have side-effects. Stunted growth is one; the other is delusional paranoia. So if a pigeon you've never seen before flies up and says, 'Who told you to follow me everywhere?' you'll know the reason why.

The racing-pigeon man wandered off back to his mates and left his former companion to walk among the cages of the foppish fancy breeds alone. I followed him. The homers were nice enough and they all wore kindly expressions, but, to look at at least, they were the tiniest bit dull. This was certainly not something you could say about the exhibition birds. Apart from the inflationary throat of the Norwich and English croppers, there is much else to be admired. The first breed of pigeon ever to be named, by Shakespeare in *As You Like It*, is one. The Barb has dark feathers shot through with purple and green and such an over-developed wattle it looks as if it has just stuck its beak through a walnut. Then there is the receding chin of the Short-faced Tumbler, which gives it the appearance of a Habsburg emperor; the big-eyed German Shield Owl, which seems to have just swallowed its own beak; the shiny, black-etched feathers of the white Satinette; the apparently tonsured heads of the Monks and Double-crested Priests and the way the Fantail arches its neck so far backwards while displaying its tail feathers that its head seems to disappear up its bottom. Best of all are the Jacobins, fanciful creations with an immense, fluffy ruff around the neck, stern white face and tail feathers that swish along the ground so that each bird looks like Gloria Swanson on her way to a film premiere.

Domesticated pigeons have long been an integral part of country and town life. Before the days of frozen or imported meat and the extensive farming of poultry, the winter months saw most people living on a diet of salted meat. Pigeons offered a tasty alternative. Indeed, they became so popular that at one point during the English Civil War there were estimated to be over 25,000 dovecotes in England, and the poet Milton expressed concern at the damage their occupants were doing to the countryside. Not that the dove and pigeon owners were bothered: one of the beauties of keeping the birds was that it was cheap, largely because they fed off other people's land. Everywhere is common grazing as far as pigeons are concerned.

The showing of pigeons began for certain in the 1720s, though some exhibition breeds such as the Barb and Holle cropper predate this by as much as a century. The birds exhibited were carriers, pouters or croppers and tumblers. Loosely speaking, the non-racing varieties of pigeon can be divided into two categories: high fliers and exhibition. High fliers were once kept for a kind of circuit-racing competition, but now it is their stunt capabilities that attract breeders. The most popular high flier is the Birmingham Roller, which does victory rolls at a rate of five a second during the downward phase of its undulating flight pattern. Birds such as the Polish Danzig and the Orlik fulfil their high-flying role more literally by soaring up into the air until practically invisible.

The poultry section was next to the pigeons. By the old English game cocks two lively-looking bantamweights with bleached jeans, cropped heads and tattooed necks were bounding up and down on the balls of their feet and inspecting the exhibits. 'These are the fighters, Kev,' one of them was saying, jerking his thumb at the cages. 'These are the fighters these, man.' The English game cocks glared out at them. They had reddish eyes, long, wiry legs and the compact muscular frames of bare-knuckle boxers. Their feathers were hard and drawn tightly over them. Their heads were small and smooth and shiny as coshes. They didn't look like chickens at all. They looked like psychopathic pheasants.

I walked off and glanced at the Wyandottes and Leghorns and the Polish cocks whose head feathers were arranged in a fanciful albino Afro; then, when the skinheads had departed in search of other macho livestock, I walked over and took another peek at the game birds. They were the original domesticated chicken, descended from jungle fowl. Alexander the Great is often credited with first bringing chickens to Europe from India, in the days before he himself was brought back from India in a barrel of honey. Rejecting this 'great man' view of animal history, I prefer to think it was more likely to have been some less high-born Celts.

The Celts came to Europe from northern India and in all probability brought fighting cocks with them. It was one of the Celtic tribes, the Belgae, who first introduced them to Britain (the Belgians' interest in birds is clearly long-standing and not just confined to pigeons). The Celts kept the birds purely for sport. The meat from them was meagre, tough and stringy, and the small eggs were seldom eaten. If the Celts wanted a meal they went hunting, not to the chicken coop. The Romans were the ones who first started to think about the chicken as a possible source of food. But as they also ate dormice and lark's tongues, perhaps that's not surprising. The Romans began a selective breeding programme. Instead of picking birds to breed from that were brave and strong, they chose those which were large and docile. The result was chicken similar in size and colouring to the British Red Dorking. Cock-fighting still went on, of course, in practically every country in the world except

Russia. In Russia, when it came to barbaric poultry sports, they preferred to use geese.

Less bloody forms of hen-related contest arrived shortly after the industrial revolution with the institution of chicken shows, usually held in pubs. These were particularly popular with mill and other textile workers and were not the sedate affair they have now become. Opposing breeders faced one another in a one-to-one knock-out competition in which each handler was expected to argue the case for his bird while his rival loudly pointed out its defects. Derbyshire Redcaps, Moonies, Bolton Greys, Bays and Creoles were plumped down in pairs upon the judging table and alternately flattered and insulted. Eventually, after an afternoon of fierce bragging and invective, the field was whittled down to a single winner. This was clearly less brutal than cock-fighting, though the damage done to the personal confidence of the losing hens can only be guessed at.

Beyond the flaps of the poultry tent a woman in a halter-neck top and white shorts staggered past carrying two pints of beer and wrestling with a pair of Dalmatians. In the main ring the horse-borne fancy dress was being judged. I had once seen one of these at a show in the Yorkshire dales where three Milky Bar Kids turned up and it ended in a gunfight. Thankfully, things were a little more restrained in County Durham.

I took a stroll round the showground, past the craft stalls, the Punch and Judy and the prize-winning Suffolk tup, with his black face, yellowing wool, dim-witted, belligerent eyes and his prize assets swinging between his back legs like a pair of coconuts in a satchel. Despite his look of brooding arrogance, I couldn't help feeling a bit sorry for him. It can't be much fun when every time you try to run anywhere you end up tripping over your testicles.

13

· Wrestling ·

Grasmere Sports

There had been no rain for months. Tankers were ferrying water around Yorkshire, hosepipes had long since been banned and rumour had it that the police would soon declare an amnesty for the handing-in of watering-cans. The lawn was so dry at night we could hear it croaking through the window. Rivers had shrivelled to trickles; lakes to mud pans and salmon seeking spawning grounds were being put on a three-year waiting list. All across the north, leaves were curling, plants were wilting and the allotments were full of fanatical and desperate men exchanging blows over the water butts. The situation was critical. There was only one thing for it: in the interests of my fellow men, I would do something drastic. I would commit an act so brazen and provocative that the weather gods would be forced to respond. I would go to Cumbria *without taking a raincoat.*

Actually, this decision wasn't so much a sacrifice as a necessity. I had only one waterproof coat, and I couldn't take that anywhere. It was a Barbour jacket I'd had for about five years, and it was now so ripped and battered it looked like the kind of thing that Ben Gunn would give to the church jumble sale. Worse than that, though, it smelled. Not all the time – during dry spells its odour remained dormant, but the moment it was wet it began to fume. It gave off a fetid, biscuity stench such as you might imagine hovering above a slurry pit in which someone had just dumped two tons of stale digestives. When I wore my Barbour in the damp, dogs ran towards me, then recoiled as if they had hit an invisible forcefield; I was wolf-whistled at by drooling nanny goats and badgers emerged from sets holding their noses and spraying air-freshener. Catherine kept telling me to take my Barbour to the dry-cleaner's but it was too far gone for that. The jacket didn't need a laundry, it needed disposal in a safe and environmentally friendly manner. The binmen wouldn't touch it, the council wouldn't come near it and the man from Sellafield took one sniff at it and went away wheezing and shaking his head. I thought about burying it in the garden, but worried that the poisonous gas might build up over the years and result in a volcanic eruption. While negotiations continue with the Army Chemical Warfare Research Unit I have it hanging up in the garden shed. We no longer have any problems with mice nibbling our tulip bulbs.

By the time I got to Oxenholme it was plain that my dramatic action had born fruit. Dark clouds had budded at Carlisle, blossomed while passing through Penrith and now, at Windermere, millions of little rain hips, aqua-haws and waterberries were scattering themselves across the tan carpet of parched England. As I walked down from the station to catch the Grasmere bus, in gardens all along the route plants and shrubs broke into spontaneous applause, trees cheered and marigolds mouthed their plaintive thank-yous.

The flora weren't the only ones pleased by the downpour. On the bus some Ghanaian women were looking happily out at the fine, swirling rain. When an elderly woman apologised to them for it, they smiled shyly and reassured her: 'Oh no, no,' they said in their breathy accents, 'this is what we had expected.' They were English Literature students come to the Lake District to see the numinous green land of Wordsworth. Instead they had found a place that looked like the savannah with dry-stone walls and

Herdwick sheep instead of antelope. 'But now,' they said, grinning at the misted windows of the bus, 'it has lived up to all our hopes.'

The sports ground stands on the southern edge of Grasmere village. It was easy enough to spot. A giant lightbulb balloon with the name 'NORWEB' printed on it was floating above the craft marquee on the end of a dark wire, looking disconcertingly like a gigantic sperm. In the sports ground the rain was pattering out polysyllabic rhythms on canvas and golf brolly. Cumbria is famous for rain. One of the sponsors of the sports was a shop in Ambleside with the advertising slogan 'Anoraks in Profusion'. The same description might have been applied to the scene at Grasmere sports field. All along the stepped wooden benches that circled the running tracks sat huddles of people looking, in their brightly coloured, hooded garb, like a congregation of funky monks undertaking a penitent soaking. They were undaunted. Downpours such as this one had less effect on old lakeland hands than they would on a shoal of halibut. On one of the benches an elderly man in a blue cagoule sat slowly and deliberately licking a '99' ice cream, twirling it in his hand so that it formed a neat, symmetrical mound while the water dripping from his nose fell straight into the shaft left by the already-eaten chocolate flake.

By the way, why is an ice-cream cornet with a flake in it called a '99'? Is there an answer, or is this just another unfathomable mystery like the Bermuda Triangle, the Yeti and the reason the word abbreviation is so long? If you have the definitive explanation, please write to me via the publisher. And remember to mark your letter 'I am a desperately sad individual with nothing better to do with my time than to send information to authors on the etymology of ice-cream names.' Thank you.

In the pavilion the adult wrestlers were weighing in, while out in the main arena the juniors engaged in bouts of grappling whenever the rain eased sufficiently. The tannoy announcer was standing nearby, commentating on the action and keeping up a stream of whimsical asides. 'It's that damp out here,' he said, after a swift turn and cross-buttock had sent a young wrestler from Millom sprawling on the greasy turf, 'that there's mushrooms springing up all round me. So when you lads leave the ring, now, be careful where you step. Because I'm after some for my tea.'

Wrestling was once a popular sport at the fairs, and Cumberland-and-Westmorland-style wrestling goes back a long way. The deeds of the early champions are detailed in books such as *Wrestliana*, written during the Regency. These volumes tell of men such as Robert Atkinson, the 'Sleagill Giant' who, judging by his cart-lifting exploits, seems to have been the Georgian equivalent of the Incredible Hulk, and my personal favourite among the old-timers, 'Miller Robin' Dodd of Brough, who, it is said, could lift a 160lb sack of wheat and toss it over his shoulder *with his teeth*. Which must have come in handy when both hands were busy with crochet work.

Since then there have been many great wrestlers. Grasmere Sports has been playing host to them since the 1840s, just as Grasmere Fair did before that. In the main the competitors come from Cumbria, but the sport is also popular in Northumberland and the lowlands of Scotland (Milngavie, a suburb of Glasgow, is a fertile breeding ground for grapplers), while more than one world champion has come from across the Pennines in County Durham. Today at Grasmere there are wrestlers from north and south of the border as well as an American and an Icelander ('Larus Kar-ya erm ... Kyart ... Ooh 'eck, I think you'd better come up and announce yourself, Larus').

The wrestlers still compete in the traditional dress of embroidered silk vest, long johns, velvet trunks and dark socks. Coming out on to the field at Grasmere to be judged for the best costume, they look like a troupe of strong men at a Victorian circus.

When fighting, the wrestlers face one another, legs apart, back bent, place their chins on each others' shoulders and clasp their hands behind their adversary. A good deal of jockeying for position then goes on as each man tries to slide his arms as far down his opponent's back as he can, while simultaneously attempting to shift his opposite number's arms back upwards. It is a bit like watching a polite young lady attempting to fend off the wandering hands of a drunk during the last waltz. Eventually, when the two judges signal that they are happy with the position of the wrestlers, the referee calls 'Hods!' and the bout begins. The first person to touch the ground with any part of his body other than his feet is the loser; best of three falls decides the bout.

Tom Harrington is one of the best wrestlers of the modern era. He has dedicated his life to the sport, training youngsters and fighting and refereeing bouts all over the north. He's getting on a bit these days: he has grey hair and wire-rimmed spectacles, and when he takes off his glasses to wrestle they leave little pink marks on the bridge of his nose that give his face a vulnerable aspect. Below the neck, though, he still looks formidable: the muscles on his pale arms bulge like knots in steel cables and he is as slim as a foxhound. In bouts at a small show in Allendale I had watched Harrington as he took on younger opponents and noted the gentle way he threw them, setting them down on the grass carefully, as if they were well-stuffed picnic hampers. Wrestling is a test of strength, speed and skill rather than brutality.

At Grasmere the competition was of a keener and more serious kind. In the 11-stone division, Harrington took on a fierce-looking Scot from Partick named Clark who had dark hair and the short powerful build of a Galloway stirk. In the first fall Harrington hit the ground with a sickening thump, the Partick man coming down heavily on top of him. The Scot got up; Harrington stayed down. A St John ambulanceman ran out to attend him. 'First fall to Clark,' the announcer said, as a concerned group of officials surrounded the wrestler, now rising groggily to his feet.

'That's a bloody understatement,' the man standing next to me laughed.

Wrestling remains to a great extent the combat sport of the countryside (its only serious challenger, free-for-all clog-fighting, was banned from northern fairs in the 1850s after a series of deaths and maimings). Boxing – faster, more flamboyantly skilful and infinitely bloodier – is its urban equivalent. Boxing once played an important part in the fairground. Early prize fighters such as James Figg, who toughened his knuckles by soaking them in vinegar and, judging by contemporary prints, undertook some similar pickling activity with his proboscis, appeared in exhibition bouts at the fairs of the eighteenth century. These staged performances soon developed into the boxing booths, which gradually progressed, just as professional boxing did, from bare fists to mufflers and on to gloves. In the boxing booth, the audience would pay to see staged exhibition bouts, unsavoury punch-ups between schoolboys and dwarfs, or men and kangaroos. Most famously of all, the ringmaster would call for volunteers from the audience, offering a sum of money to any man who could last a round with one of the booth's boxers. The popularity of such contests reached its height in the inter-war years.

Shortly after Eric Cantona made his famous leap into the crowd at Selhurst Park, I was on a phone-in programme on local radio in the north-east. Public reaction to the incident was illuminating. Young and middle-aged callers, while having some sympathy with the Frenchman, found his actions horrifying and condemned them accordingly; older people, by and large, couldn't see what all the fuss was about. One old dear from Hebburn who announced herself to be eighty-five said, 'I cannot see why everyone's getting that excited. When I was a lass, if two strapping young fellas wanted to have a bit of a set-to in the street, you just let them get on with it, and may the best man win. You didn't think that was hooliganism, you thought it was manly.'

With such attitudes prevalent, with money scarce and beer cheap, when the ringmaster offered his sovereign there was no shortage of takers. In Duncan Dallas's book about the fairgrounds, *The Travelling People*, one old booth boxer, Billy Wood of Dumfries, recalls setting up the ring at Durham Miners' Gala in 1919. The booth opened at 7 a.m. and closed at one o'clock the following morning. During that time, Wood fought eighteen colliers, knocking out fifteen of them. It was a living.

As Wood's story indicates, few of the volunteers who got into the ring left it on their feet. The boxing booths were the workplace of men as tough as tortoise sandwiches, whose scarred eyelids drooped over their sockets like Austrian blinds. They were the training ground of many great British fighters, among them men like welterweight champion Jake Kilrain and the Welsh heavyweight Tommy Farr, later to take the lethal Joe Louis the distance. Added to their undoubted abilities, the booth fighters were also handed advantages by the management, and while these never quite amounted to the old horseshoe-in-the-glove trick, they were important 'equalisers' nonetheless. The booth boxer's hands were properly taped; sometimes they wore lighter gloves than their opponents and often the time-keeping had a certain degree of flexibility to allow them to dispatch a more durable foe. As a place to learn your trade, however, this was definitely part of the Faculty of Hard Knocks at the University of Life (formerly Mortal Coil Polytechnic).

After their heyday between the wars, boxing booths gradually disappeared from the fairgrounds. Greater prosperity and a different attitude to violence made volunteers for a hiding more difficult to find. Booth managers were forced to resort to plants in the audience – old women who claimed their sons had been badly mauled the night before and begging someone to avenge them – in a bid to drum up trade. Fighters, too, could make a better living in the professional ring than had ever been possible before and were unwilling to risk their health and their future taking on unknown drunken lunatics in unsupervised bouts. By the 1960s, only a handful of booths were still on the go. Now there are none.

By contrast, Cumberland and Westmorland wrestling is in good shape. The sport hit a dip about the same time as the boxing booths were at their peak, but after the Second World War the establishment of wrestling academies at Carlisle, Gilsland,

Gosforth, Bootle and Kendal rekindled interest in the sport. By the 1950s, indoor bouts in Carlisle Drill Hall were drawing crowds of over a thousand people, and even contests in small lakeland villages would attract hundreds of spectators. The sport no longer pulls in people in the same numbers, but it remains one of the highlights of shows across Cumbria and Northumberland, and there is always a thick circle of knowledgeable fans around the ring.

The rain kept on pouring down. I was now reaching saturation point. My jacket felt as if it were made out of moss and the seat of my trousers was beginning to sag so that from the rear I must have looked as if I were carrying a concealed hanging basket. The rain no longer fell straight on to me, it circled around first, searching for a dry place to land. Luckily, my ability to manipulate precipitation works both ways. I went and bought a red and white umbrella from a stall to the rear of the bookmaker's arena. It cost £5. The minute I handed over the money, the blanket of cloud which had previously concealed the crooked heads of the Cumbrian peaks parted. 'The mist on the hills is clearing now,' the tannoy man said. 'Which means ... it's going to rain even harder.' He clearly hadn't see me laying out cash for a brolly. The rain stopped as soon as I opened it.

On the main field, the runners were lining up for the 90m handicap. These were professional sprinters. The handicapping system ensured that they were a disparate lot, ranging from young striplings bouncing nervously on their toes, through powerful men in their mid-twenties with thighs like boiling fowls, right up to grey-haired veterans who looked as if their bending into the starting crouch would be accompanied by a glissando of pinging rupture appliances, but then sprang off at the sound of the gun and belted down the track as if they were late for the post office on pension day. The tannoy man read through the field, listing names, home towns and the number of yards' advantage the runner had been awarded. 'Hedley, Bedlington, half a metre; Stewart, Hawick, three metres; Malloy, Newcastle, twenty-three metres ... By lad, you'll have time to boil the kettle and have a coffee ...'

Professional running, with the possible exception of Edinburgh's Powder Hall Sprint, is something you never read or hear much about. Yet at one time many of the fastest sprinters in the world were professionals, and big meetings such as the Morpeth Olympics drew huge crowds right up until the end of the 1950s. The Scottish borders and north-east England were the sport's strongholds and remain so to this day. Nearly three-quarters of the runners at Grasmere came either from the textile towns of the borders (Kelso, Hawick and Jedburgh) or the Northumbrian coalfields. The top prizes were not massive, but £120 still isn't a bad return for eleven seconds' work. Running for prizes had been part of the entertainment at fairs for centuries. However, the Olympic movement and the move towards an amateurism in athletics which, however high-minded its ideals, remained vindictively punitive towards anyone it suspected of being tainted with the poison of professionalism soon killed it off in all but a few places. Cumbria was one of them. But then, the Cumbrians seem to take a particular pleasure in preserving activities everyone else has discarded. Wrestling was one, professional running another, and on the other side of the Cumbrian Hills from Grasmere, at Egremont, they maintained a whole range of strange competitions which had once been popular nationwide.

Egremont Crab Fair is held in September. It dates back to 1267, when the tenants organised a feast to celebrate having paid their rents to the lord of the manor, Lord de Lucy, and he responded magnanimously by sending the revellers a few barrels of crabapples for the buffet. As you are no doubt aware, except when made into jelly, crabapples are totally inedible. Obviously, then, they weren't the generous De Lucy's first choice as a gift of party nibbles. It was just that his pigs had already scoffed all the conkers. The De Lucys' benevolent rule was ended a few centuries later when they backed the wrong candidate in a Tudor leadership contest. Nowadays, their former castle is a ruin and the apples at the crab fair are supplied by the town's

Gateway supermarket, and can be eaten without first having to be boiled with a hundredweight of sugar, then strained through an old sock. At the crab fair you can still see many once-popular old entertainments such as climbing the greasy pole to win a leg of mutton, street-racing and, most famously, gurning, or face-pulling.

Gurning was once a feature of many of Britain's horse fairs, particular those in the Midlands. Nowadays, though, you have to go to Egremont to see it. If you're the sort of person who fancies the idea of watching someone remove his or her false teeth and then endeavour to swallow his own nose while simultaneously rolling his eyes up inside his skull, then it is a trip well worth making. I am, and it was. In the Market Hall on the night of the fair, a crowd already whipped up to fever pitch by a junior talent contest and a pipe-smoking race in which a line of men sucked their way through wads of thick-twist tobacco in the time it takes most ordinary pipe-smokers to get the thing lit, went ballistic as young and old, male and female, stuck their heads through the 'braffin', or horse collar, and did medieval things with their faces. 'Breughelian' is perhaps the adjective that best describes the scene, though 'barmy' runs it a close second.

At the Grasmere sports field the handicappers had done their jobs well, and the sprinters powered across the line in a clutch. 'It'll go to a photo finish, will this,' the tannoy man said. 'Trouble is, we've only got a Box Brownie and t'film takes a week to develop.'

I wandered off into the craft tent in search of shelter. The rain was back again, and it had brought a friend – the wind. Whenever I opened my new and vast golfing brolly and was caught by a gust, I felt myself lifting off the ground and a vision of myself as a tatty and irascible Mary Poppins ('No you can't have any sugar. It causes tooth decay. Just swallow the bloody medicine and shut up! And stop that terrible singing. I'm trying to watch the football') floating over the russet lakeland hills, until brought down by a myopic grouse-shooter, flashed before my eyes. Even being sur-rounded by stalls selling appliqué pictures of butterflies, barge-ware and beeswax was preferable to that.

Inside the craft marquee there was a second-hand-book stall. I am irresistibly drawn to second-hand books. I collect books on conspiracy theories. There are absolutely hundreds of them. It's a recent phenomenon many people ascribe to man's determination always to create pattern and reason out of series of chance incidents. I don't agree. I think it's some kind of plot.

The hounds had been set away further north, but now the announcement came that they were on the way to the finish in the centre of the arena. Up on the craggy outcrops of the fells, judges were signalling down. When trailing, hounds have to be gone for a certain length of time and they have to be watched. These precautions are necessary because hounds are quite a lot like small boys. There is a certain percentage who, when sent off on a cross-country, will go a couple of miles then nip behind a wall for a fag, a Mars bar and a quick flick through *Health and Efficiency* before smearing their legs with mud and returning to base, panting and calling out, 'Oh, wow! How absolutely knackering', in loud voices whenever they think the PE teacher is within earshot. Too much pride and money is being gambled on the hounds for that to be allowed to happen. Now they rounded the flag post at the top of the hill and came leaping down the slope, a bobbing canine stream of liver and white and chocolate, pink tongues lolling, heads held low across the scent of the aniseed and paraffin trail. As soon as they appeared, their handlers in the showring unleashed a volley of whistles and calls, yelps, howls and yippees.

'Ooh 'eck,' the commentator remarked wearily. 'What a bloomin' racket.'

Waiting for the bus opposite the showground, two tanned young blokes were attempting unsuccessfully to hitch a lift. Eventually one came over to me. 'Hi,' he said. He had an American accent. 'Can you tell me, is this, like, the right sign we're making?' He made a thumbing gesture. I said it was. 'I don't know,' he said, shaking his head. 'The way they're not stopping, I figured maybe it was an obscene gesture here or something.' I said, no, it was just that the drivers thought maybe he and his friend were psychopaths who would murder them, defile their bodies in some fetishistic ritual, then bury them in a shallow grave under the floorboards. He nodded. 'It's that obvious, huh?'

The two blokes were Israeli students. Like the Ghanaians, they were pleased with the weather. They loved the Lake District; they loved England. Everything was great. They had been in London until Wednesday, then they had come on here. They were staying in Troutbeck Youth Hostel. Today they had gone to Grasmere, spent all their money and not realised that English banks closed so early. That was why they were hitch-hiking. They were getting around by train, mainly. The chattier of the two, the one who had asked me about the thumbing sign, said they were amazed at the number of lines there were. 'British Rail,' he said, shaking his head. 'Wow, I gotta say it's awesome.' I was so delighted with this verdict that I offered to pay their bus fares back to Troutbeck for them.

We chugged along the congested lakeland roads. I couldn't understand why everyone insisted on using their cars to get around these narrow lanes. Couldn't they see that their incredible selfishness was ruining this beautiful place? Why didn't they show some consideration for the environment and the local inhabitants and get the train and bus, as I had done? Then I remembered that the reason I got the train and bus was not through any sense of magnanimity towards the planet, but because I am too incompetent to drive. For me to lecture the world on the benefits of public transport is a bit like a beetroot-hootered octogenarian with halitosis banging on about the righteousness of celibacy. I was making a virtue from a necessity. Besides which, it was quite impossible to feel peevish in the company of the two Israelis. The two Israelis were keen fans of English football, English girls, English beer – in fact, they got such a great belt out of all things English that I found myself basking in a kind of reflected glory all the way to their stop. 'Thanks,' the quiet one said as they got up to go. 'We'll pay you back some time.'

'Yeah,' his friend said, smiling. 'We ever see you hitch-hiking on the road from Haifa to Tel Aviv, man' - he slid the palm of one hand swiftly across the other and laughed - 'we'll just shoot on by.'

14

· Pigs ·

The Bellingham Show

I was walking the dog along the riverbank. The remnants of the rainclouds from my trip to the Lake District prowled the murky skies, glowering, frustrated and unspent. A sullen breeze muttered through the crinkly leaves of the sycamore trees, and downstream an inelegant heron stood knee-deep, staring glumly into the water like a teenage Narcissus after the first onset of acne.

I was watching a hook-beaked tree creeper free-climbing a lime tree when my fellow dog-walker Tommy suddenly exploded through a tangle of elder saplings, Chappie straining at the leash, rasping. 'Hey, would you believe it?' Tommy said as the terrier paused momentarily to sniff a likely-looking tussock. 'What about this for summer?'

It's amazing how quickly the English forget the weather. We suffer from an acute form of meteorological amnesia. Five days before it had been so hot gardeners had been rubbing sunblock on to their cabbages and putting beanie hats on the broccoli; basking lizards had exploded and the only birdsong was the pitiful SOS calls of helpless swallows being swept up into the stratosphere by treacherous thermal currents. Now people were shaking their heads, shivering and saying, 'Well, I suppose we'll just have to keep our fingers crossed for an Indian summer.'

Not that Tommy had the chance to say that. Chappie was too eager to get off. 'Champing for a bit of breakfast,' Tommy said, pointing at the dog as he disappeared through a sloe bush. My dog watched him go. 'So,' he said in his best Colditz kommandant accent. 'It seems that for you, Tommy, the walk is over.' He chortled all the way to the paper shop.

At one of the tiny north Tyne villages a party of school-children got on the bus. A girl of about seven, with blonde hair and a missing front tooth, clumped down in the seat in front of mine. As the bus set off she turned round and stared intently at me. 'I'm called Gemma,' she announced. I began to feel uneasy. It was a residual thing left from a decade of living in London. Unaccompanied children made me nervous. They were a prob-lem. Or rather, reacting to their behaviour was a problem. How did you respond if small boys swore at you? What was a reasonable show of force if a playgroup pupil jumped you with a machete? If you stumbled across an incident in the corner shop would a sharp, 'Put that flame-thrower down and untie Mr Constantides this instant!' be acceptable? Or would it lead to a visit from a social worker and a programme of psychological evaluation? I wrestled with these conundrums every time I saw children in the street until I had developed such a neurosis about them that I would willingly cross six lanes of speeding traffic and walk through a gang of drunken Nazi skinheads out prom-enading their pitbulls rather than pass a bus queue containing a single five-year-old. In the rural communities of the north I began to unwind. Here a hearty cry of 'Hello, mister!' was enough to earn a boy a reputation as a fearless daredevil among his peers. In London lone children encountered while out walking eyed you with a mixture of loathing and suspicion. Here they fell in step with you and began chatting cheerily about their par-ents' marital problems. The youngsters of the north really were no trouble at all.

'Do you have any children?' the little blonde girl suddenly asked me.

'No.'

'Are you trying, then? Why have you gone red? Looker! Heather, Emma, Gary, man! He's gone all red!'

Well, not much trouble, anyway.

After Wark the road through the North Tyne Valley rises gradually, then just before Bellingham you crest a hill and suddenly the countryside is laid out before you, the glistening slate roofs and smoking chimneys of the village, the tree-furred banks of the Tyne and the Rede and the ash-and-hazel, sheep-speckled hills stretching off in all directions. Whenever I come across that brow I always find myself instinctively humming the theme from *The Big Country* (at least, that is what *I* think I'm humming. Anyone else listening would probably imagine I had got my teeth stuck together with toffee and was mumbling for help). Which is not so far-fetched as it may seem - Belling-ham, after all, was once the centre of the British equivalent of the Wild West. During the reiver times the north Tyne was one of the most notoriously lawless areas in England. The reputation of the area for criminality persisted for centuries afterwards. Up until the 1860s it was illegal for companies in Newcastle to take on apprentices from the North Tyne Valley for fear that they would bring crime into the city. It had somehow managed to worm its way in anyway, but Bellingham at least was blameless.

At the entrance to the showground a pair of tethered racing camels stood chewing hay and haughtily surveying the crowd around them as if it was something brown and squishy they had narrowly avoided stepping in. The camels were one of the show's star attractions and their expressions suggested they had 'abso-lutely no idea why we have been booked to appear in this ghastly little place, darling'. In fact the camels' undisguised contempt was no reflection at all on Bellingham - it is perennial. The Arabs say that the camel's sense of superiority stems from its secret knowledge. Apparently, Muhammad knew the hundred names of God, but told only ninety-nine of them to the faithful. The last he whispered only into the ear of his camel. It is this that makes the ship of the desert look so smug. Personally, I don't doubt the veracity of this story for a minute. After all, it would take something extraordinary to make you look that pompous when you spend your entire life dressed in beige. It's hardly the colour of arrogant majesty, is it? No football team has ever cruised to victory in the European Cup inspired by the chants of 'Come on you Beiges'; kings never appear all bedecked in jewels and regal fawn; and I doubt Rhett Butler would ever have been moved not to give a damn by Taupe O'Hara. Legendary fire-fighter Mushroom Adair? I think not.

In the main ring, the Country Fair Special Dog Show was about to begin. There were classes for Labradors and a terrier section, but mainly it was just for fun. There was a prize for The Dog Who Loves The Most (an inspiring title for the next Colleen McCullough blockbuster, surely), for The Dog The Judge Most Wanted To Kidnap and for The Dog And Handler Most Alike (In Looks). Once again, the show organisers' parentheses seemed to hint at an untold story. Had some mad and bewildered pet owner entered this category in a previous, pre-bracketed, era and created a stir by cocking his leg on a tree, biting the postman, then clutching the judge's leg in an amorous embrace? Finally, there was a prize for The Dog Who Had Not Yet Won A Prize. This latter category said something about the egalitarian nature of the smaller shows. Away from the serious judging, there was reward for effort on the broadest scale. The children's sections in particular seemed designed so that no entrant should go home empty-handed. Sometimes, looking through the programme, it was a surprise not to find: Class 342 – Under-Tens Prettiest Little Blonde Girl Named Gemma (With One Tooth Missing). At a show earlier in the year a boy, faced flushed with triumph, had come running out of a tent in front of me, yelling to his parents, 'Mam! Dad! My pizza got second! It nearly won!' When I went to inspect his effort, it turned out to be one of only a pair of entries, a fact which didn't bother him in the slightest. And why should it? He had come second, and he had a certificate and 25p to prove it.

The husband of a friend of ours insisted that she enter their

King Charles spaniel in the pet show at their local village fête. She found herself lined up against a bowl of goldfish, a vivarium of stick insects and a cardboard box filled with shredded J-cloth which allegedly housed a very shy mouse. The woman doing the judging took it all quite seriously. When she came to our friend, she inspected the dog, then said, 'Does he do any tricks?' Our friend had not been able to hear if the judge had asked the boy with the stick insects the same question. I rather hoped she had.

'Do they do tricks?'

'Yes. They do impressions.'

'Really? What do they do impressions of?'

'Er, sticks.'

'Anything else?'

'Well, if you dip them in Marmite, they do Twiglets.'

Everybody got a rosette, including the reclusive mouse.

The smaller shows no longer seriously function as a showcase for new farming methods, or as an encouragement to selective stock-rearing. Instead they have become a focus for increasingly diverse communities. In rural areas, where the old patterns of life, of local industry and shopping, have been gradually eroded by economics and the efficiency of the motor car, the shows bring people together. They have lost their original educational role and taken on a social one.

The sheep were up on the highest part of the showground, where the grass was as fine as fusewire and explosions of bob cotton jitterbugged in the wind. The largest entry was for Blackfaces. In deference to the 'bound-on' principle, these were divided into two distinct categories: Open and Confined. The Blackface has a reputation for dourness. As it originates from just across the border in Ettrick, this seems more than likely. The border between Northumberland and Roxburghshire marks more than delineation between two countries; it is also a divide between two extremes of loquacity. Northumbrians are the most chatty people on earth. I used to think I talked a lot. After moving to Northumberland, I consider myself laconic. While I was writing this chapter the phone rang. A woman with a

Northumbrian accent said, 'Mr Pearso...' then began coughing. I said it sounded like she had a cold. She said, didn't she, though? The worst one she'd ever had. Couldn't shift it. Had I seen the documentary the other night? Apparently, the germs are getting immune to modern antibiotics. She could believe it. Been to the doctor twice. She was thinking of trying aromatherapy as an alternative. She'd bought some lavender oil last year. They'd been on a coach trip to Norfolk Lavender. Had I ever been? I should go. Wonderful. The scent! But then, Norfolk's lovely all round. Oh, I'd been at Wells. They'd been at Wells, two years before. The kippers weren't as good as at Craster, mind. And so it went on. Then, after twenty minutes, the woman said. 'Eee, here's me going on! Any road, what can I do for you, pet?'

'I don't know. You phoned me.'

She said: 'Hey, what am I thinking of, eh?' then she cleared her throat. 'Mr Pearson, this is a courtesy call on behalf of Himalaya Window Fitments. Have you ever considered the savings double-glazing could make to your heating bills...'

The border Scots were of a completely different stamp. The American president Calvin Coolidge was famous for not saying very much. Once at a dinner party a woman sitting next to him said: 'Mr Coolidge, I bet I can get you to say more than two words during the course of this meal.'

Coolidge replied: 'You lose.'

I suspect that Calvin Coolidge was of border Scots extraction. The Blackfaces looked similarly tight-lipped. And well they might. The beastly English usually get the blame for the High-land Clearances, but these were the real culprits. When it became clear that the efforts of the likes of the Culley brothers had succeeded in producing a large, well-fleeced sheep tough enough to survive on open moorland, the Highland landlords attempted to force the crofters to take the Blackface and the Cheviot as economically more viable replacements for their tiny, dun-faced sheep. As far as the Highlanders were concerned, this was just what the doctor ordered. But only if the doctor was called Crippen. The crofters resisted, the landlords turned nasty,

America got a new influx of immigrants and the Highlands got a new and more easily controlled population. There are now over two million Blackface sheep in Scotland.

Across from the sheep pens stood the rare breeds tent. Inside there were a pair of sheep closely related to the original Highland sheep, Portlands. A cross between a Soay-type native breed and the heavier sheep imported by the Romans, the Portland is small, sandy-coloured and bears a strong facial resemblance to Benny the Ball, the tubby, gruff-voiced moggy from *Top Cat*. The Portland has strangely flattened horns that droop down the side of its head to form a kind of Elizabethan ruff. Think of any other animal with horns – the rhinoceros perhaps, or the reindeer, the buffalo or the bison. Notice any similarity? Yes, when they charge the points of the horns face the target. Now examine the sheep. Any breed will do. Spot the difference? That's right, the horns curl so that the points can never make contact with an enemy. The sheep's horns are like those arrows with suckers on the end – good for practice, but useless for drastic offensive action. The sheep is a pacifist dressed as a commando.

From the entrance to the upper livestock area you could look down to the main showring where the mounted fancy-dress parade was in full swing. The tannoy announcer, who had an accent so plummy you could have made jam out of it and scooped a prize in the industrial section, was chortling gleefully as a garden gnome, King Solomon and the Queen of Sheba, a policeman, a posse of cowboys and what seemed to be the entire cast of *Alice in Wonderland*, including the Mock Turtle, sauntered past the grandstand on a variety of ponies and horses. The noise of clapping and the chuckling announcer mixed with the sound of the Forestry Commission chainsaws and the nearby rocky clunk from the dry-stone walling demonstration. It had been raining off and on all morning, but now the sun had finally chiselled its way through the plaster-grey clouds and emerged, smiling, to the rippling applause of closing umbrellas. The damp grass glistered, the white canvas flashed and dark shadows sculled across distant hillsides. Farmers unzipped their dog-eared Barbours, dogs shook themselves and elderly ladies in see-through macs and rain hoods peeped from the flaps of the craft tent and blinked at the brightness. There was a smell of pine resin and drying straw. And frying onions, naturally.

Bellingham Show was first held in the mid-nineteenth century under the auspices of the North Tyne and Redesdale Agricultural Society, a body which was led by the now wealthy and respectable descendants of the reiver clans, among them the Charltons of Hesleyside. Over the years, the show has attracted its share of famous visitors, including an old shepherd who, according to a popular song, got drunk, lost all his money and ended up in jail, and the poet Philip Larkin who, to the best of my knowledge, did none of these things. Larkin came to the show every year with a girlfriend who owned a house at Haydon Bridge. In his literary output, at least, Larkin is not noted for his jollity, but he wrote a cheery poem, 'Show Saturday', about Bellingham. Whatever else it has done, or will do in the future, putting a smile on the face of Philip Larkin will surely rank as one of Bellingham Show's most singular achievements.

In the refreshment marquee the steel legs of the service counter buckled beneath the weight of delicious home-made cakes, pies and pasties. The pile of beef baps looked like a sculpture by David Mack. You could have built a 1:32 scale model of the Great Wall of China from the flapjack slices. As I sat down, the tent suddenly began to empty. It wasn't a problem even my best friends couldn't tell me about, it was just that the pig-racing was about to start. Pig-racing is one of the great attractions of Bellingham Show and the star runner, Lester Piglet, was something of a local celebrity. Pigs are intelligent creatures and through history have been trained to undertake many tasks, from pulling buggies to pointing at partridges; from truffle-hunting to fairground fortune-telling. Racing them goes back a long way. The farming community of Yorkshire was particularly keen on the grounds of value for money: a pig race took far longer to complete than a horse race. It might seem unlikely that pigs should run, their body shape being about as suited to it as a sumo wrestler's is to the high hurdles. However, not all breeds of pig are fat and lumbering.

In the rare breeds tent there had been one of the speedier breeds, a very fine Tamworth. Tamworths have a slender body covered in bristly ginger fur and lop ears. Their most noted characteristic, however, is a pointed snout. It is said that a good Tamworth can pick a pea out of a pint pot. Though not by anyone with false teeth.

The Tamworth is one of only two purely British pig breeds still in existence. The other is the slow-moving, wearily genial Gloucester Old Spot, which traditionally sustained itself on windfall apples in the cider orchards of the West Country. At one time, practically every part of Britain had its own particular, and often peculiar, pig. In Lincolnshire there was the 'curly coat', a burly, white-skinned pig which appeared to have had bits of kapok stuck on it by naughty children, while Shetland had the tiny 'grice mites'. Irish pigs were gaunt and ungainly and had wattles like turkey cocks; Montgomery boasted a swine which was said to resemble 'an alligator on stilts'. This cornucopia of physical specimens was gradually whittled away by more scientific breeding methods, chief among which was the crossing of native species with imported Chinese and Tonky swine. These oriental pigs, which first appeared in Britain in the 1780s, had rounder bodies than the British breeds and much shorter legs. Indeed, the ratio of inside-leg measurement to waistline was so slanted in favour of the latter that in China pigs were carried from place to place in a kind of hammock rather than forced to walk as they were in Britain.

With its tubular frame and long pins, the Tamworth is the closest thing remaining to the early Celtic pig. It was bred by driving the domesticated Turbary sows out into the forests so that they could mate with indigenous wild boar. The result was a swift-moving, bad-tempered creature which the invading Romans found more dangerous than the wolf.

Early pigs weren't kept just for meat. Man made use of their rooting abilities, too. In conjunction with the devastating defor-

esting goats, pigs could clear woodland quicker and more effi-
ciently than most modern machinery. The herds were also used
to turn over the soil in late winter and then in spring to trample
in the seed corn. When the Saxon sat down to his bread and salt
pork he was effectively eating a rotavator sandwich.

As well as being the most edible of animals (as the saying
goes: you can eat every bit of a pig except his squeak), the large
swine population also opened up a variety of employment
opportunities. The most interesting of these new jobs was
undoubtedly that of the itinerant swine-gelder, who travelled
from farm to farm and, as I have already mentioned, signalled
his arrival with a blast on a horn.

Castrating animals was a full-time occupation during the
Middle Ages, and it is not far off it today. In fact many of the
same organisations which campaigned so vigorously to end the
docking of puppies' tails are now equally tireless in their
attempts to spread the practice of gelding far and wide. In vets'
waiting rooms nowadays you quite often see a poster posing the
bold question: 'What's your excuse for not castrating your dog?'
Once, when on holiday in the West Country, I had to take my dog
to the vet's after he had developed a cyst on his foot and then
insisted on treating it using the old canine folk remedy of licking
it until it went septic. The vet's waiting room there featured the
same pro-castration poster – except that some disillusioned voter
had crossed out the words 'your dog' and put in 'John Major' in
green magic marker. It was hard to resist the temptation to add
'I couldn't be bothered to sew them back on first' to the bottom,
but somehow I managed. I'm sure there are sound arguments as
to why you should oppose tail-docking as cruel, yet advocate
castration as sensible and necessary, but if I were a dog faced
with the choice between losing my tail or my testicles, I know
which I'd rather hang on to.

At parties I often find myself talking to people with whom I
can find no common bond, at which point I ask, 'And what do you
do?' And when they reply, confidently, 'I'm in international
diphthong swaps at Brunson Gilts & Bonds,' I pause for a

moment and then say, 'And is this your busy time of year?' Somehow I know that if I had lived in the Middle Ages and been invited to a party, the person to whom I would have ended up talking would have been the swine-gelder. And I'd have said, 'So do you have your hands full at the moment?'

It was during these pointless musings that I realised the pig races were about to start. The runners were all piglets and the course over which they ran was about thirty yards long and required them to 'jump' over half a dozen poles laid flat on the ground. Each pig wore a bib with his or her number on it. They were little lollopy creatures whose back legs seemed to be operated by a different part of the brain from the front pair. As they scampered down the course, their rear feet skipped and jerked, apparently at random, and their pointed pink ears flapped endearingly. One of their owners ran behind them ringing a bell to encourage them. I couldn't help feeling they'd have gone a lot faster if he'd borrowed a swine-gelder's horn from a folk museum and given a few blasts on that.

After the last race had finished I walked across the bridge and into the village to buy some jam tarts at the little bakery. Granny knots of elderly villagers were standing on the pavements, chatting and flashing waves and smiles at passing cars. The stone of the parapet on the bridge was smooth to the touch and the warbling notes of the Northumbrian pipers playing in the music tent came skipping out across the water and disappeared up the burnished hillsides.

15

· Sheepdogs ·

The Kildale Show

I had been up since just before dawn, in time to see the pink light spreading across the blue-grey sky like the colour pulsing into a newborn baby. Now it was just after seven and I was in the village waiting for the first bus. Swallows were gathering on the telegraph lines in their hundreds, twittering and tumbling. From an upstairs room I could hear children yelling: 'Away, Gary, man. I just shot you.'

'Yeah, but your power supply's run too low for the laser to break through my forcefield.'

'It has not.'

'It has, man.'

A pause long enough for a spaceman to cross the control room of a Mergatron Destroyer. Then a satisfying, hollow clunk. The unmistakable childhood sound of someone being brained with a ray-gun.

It was September. The swallows were going back to Africa and the kids were going back to school. The harvest was home, the watering-cans had been put away and in the early-morning air you could feel the first feinting rush of autumn's offensive.

At Newcastle Station there were groups of veterans in berets and bemedalled blazers setting out for a VJ Day commemoration.

In a melancholy mood brought on by the stabbing wind and overcast sky and the premonition of winter, I wondered what my own generation would have to commemorate. Decimalisation Day, maybe. ('I was just ten years old and suddenly everything I had worked towards was gone in a flash. Who cared now how many shillings in a guinea, or what a farthing was? The rules had changed, and for better or worse we knew our world would never be the same again.') Or the moon landing. ('It was a time when we all had to make sacrifices. They cancelled *Disney Time* and didn't even bother to reschedule it.')

In Kildale it was windier and wetter. Great schools of raindrops, glimmering like guppies, swerved and swayed across the valley. Outside the refreshment stall groups of people in Barbours, caps and waterproof trousers stood around blowing on their tea. One man said: 'T'ferrets are right next to t'beer tent, like. So we can just shuttle between t'two.'

After the hottest, driest summer in history, it seemed cruel that such weather should have been visited on this little show, spread across the village sports field in the lap of the wooded hills. It was easy to imagine the committee members who'd spent their spare time throughout the year planning and organising it waking to the sound of water tap-dancing across the roof and muttering the words: 'Bloody typical.'

On a bank to the south of the main ring, sheepdog trials were in progress. As the bleary plumes of moisture billowed across the valley, gaggles of farmers with plastic mugs of coffee warming their knees watched through the steamy windows of Land Rovers and battered Vauxhalls and shouted out encouragement and comments. They had the accents of the North York Moors, creaky, warm and worn. When they spoke they opened their mouths only fractionally and the noise of the words squeezing out was like the sound of a plump man sinking into a favourite leather armchair. In front of them a shepherd with so much facial hair you could have been forgiven for thinking he was metamorphosing into one of his charges was standing by the command post struggling to keep a grip on things. He had three sheep to direct through a series of gates, but his dog was having problems.

The trio had gone through the first wicket easily enough, but then one of their number, a bunty beast with the jack-rabbit ears and haughty mien of a Border Leicester, had suddenly decided enough was enough. As the collie swung back and forth, hazing them towards the next gate, the maverick sheep turned round and faced him. The dog darted toward it. The sheep stood stock-still and stared back at him defiantly. The collie's confidence was instantly shattered. He darted forward again, this time with all the conviction of a man attempting to beat off a shark attack with an egg whisk. When the sheep failed to budge, he retreated, bamboozled. A confused dog is a pitiful sight. Dogs like to know where they stand. Their wholehearted struggle to comprehend an alien situation is never without pathos. Now the dog hunkered closer to the ground, turning his sad, bemused gaze from sheep to shepherd and back again, trying desperately to grasp what was going on. Emboldened by his success, and displaying excellent timing, the rebel chose this psychologically crucial moment to seize the initiative. He started to advance. The collie panicked totally and began to skip backwards. Gradually the sheep drove him through the first gate and out the other side.

The hirsute shepherd was using a whistle the shape of a lemon-segment squeezer. It produced a high-pitched toot. At first he'd used it to make curt blasts, but now he began to sound like Mother Clanger being chased round the table by the Soup Dragon.

'Contrary sheep, are these,' a man beside me ventured from a crack in his mouth barely wide enough to house a cigarette paper.

'Aye,' a chapped voice answered from the window of a Land Rover. 'That 'un's got a bit cheeky, to say the least.'

The collie was now in full retreat before the revolutionary sheep. The whistle howled, shrieked and tweeted to no effect.

'Do you want a second dog, Bob?' someone shouted helpfully.

'It's not a dog he wants,' commented a man leaning against a red Allegro. 'It's a lion.'

I suspect that taking part in a sheepdog trial is rather like doing one of those get-the-balls-in-the-holes puzzles you have as a child. You tilt and turn the thing with immense patience and get all but the last orb in and then, as it trickles to the very lip of the last vacant orifice, your hand shakes and one of the other balls rolls loose again. Sometimes the tension your patience creates becomes so strong it feels like a great weight pressing down on your head and you just want to smash the glass top, stick the ball-bearings in the relevant slots, shake your fist and snarl. 'There you are, you buggers! That'll teach you!' The shepherd with the mutton-chop whiskers had now reached this point. Abandoning any pretence of command, he bounded up the hill, oilskin flapping and arms waving, like some demented bird man approaching take-off. As he ran towards the recalcitrant sheep and the cowering collie he bellowed in that strange tongue farmers use when directing livestock. 'Half yeti! Half yeti! Why me? Yoohoo, I'm a yak!' It only made the situation worse. All three sheep suddenly turned and fled in separate directions. The dog chased first one then another without any plan other than to look busy.

'It's a weak dog, that 'un,' the man in the Land Rover said.

'Aye, well, he got it from Danby,' someone offered by way of explanation.

The shepherd was now hurtling about the hillside as futilely as his dog, whistling and shouting and whirling, the sheep cavorting hither and thither. In a mercy mission, another farmer released his own dog. It was a small, slim collie with brown markings around its face and it was as bold and decisive as the crisis demanded – a real square-jawed *mensch* of a dog. It hurtled up the field and immediately waded into the agent provocateur, snapping at its flanks. At the first sign of resistance, the flame of revolution was snuffed out and the sheep turned and trotted obediently off to the pen.

The hairy shepherd stomped down the hillside, water streaming from his oil skin, his eyes fixed on the ground. His collie quivered along behind him. When they crossed the rope out of the trial area, everyone looked away and pretended to be suddenly fascinated by the falconry display.

A few minutes later the farmer who had supplied the sheep for the trial came down for a chat with some of the spectators. He was hailed with great jollity and was plainly pleased with the performance of his flock. 'Well,' he said, 'it's got to be a test or what's the point of it?'

Contrary to popular belief, sheep are not always easy animals to herd. Some in particular provide all sorts of problems. The primitive Soay, tiny as it is, does not take kindly to being bossed about by dogs and will stand its ground and stare at them. All dog owners know that if there is one thing a dog does not appreciate it is being stared at. Staring at a dog drives it crazy with baffled embarrassment. The Soay knows this, and will glare at the sheepdog until he is so overcome with self-consciousness he is completely paralysed, then it will spring off like the Alpine chamois it so closely resembles.

Small sheep in generally seem to be more difficult for dogs to deal with than the larger breeds. This is probably because the smaller breeds, less refined by man, still have a vestige of the primitive survival instincts of their wild ancestors. The black four-horned Hebridean sheep is notoriously hard to herd – so much so that in the western isles the dogs were trained not to chivvy the sheep but to chase after them, grab hold of the neck, pull them to the ground and then sit on them until the shepherd ran up and took over. Mind you, the Hebridean sheep had more reason to run than just their Viking blood. Up until the late nineteenth century, no one on the islands had heard of sheep shears. Instead the poor brutes were plucked. Even to this day, Hebridean sheep don't so much bleat as squawk.

The use of trained dogs for herding sheep didn't really begin until the growth of the wool trade in Elizabethan times. The introduction of hill grazing during that period made the use of dogs essential. Initially, the breed most commonly seen trundling across downland and pasture was the large, bumbling bobtail, an ancestor of the old English sheepdog. His supremacy was quickly usurped by the arrival of the quicker, smaller collies, brought down into England by the Scottish drovers. The collies - rough, bearded and border (that's breed types, not a description, by the way) - had another advantage over bobtails: they were more savage. As the actions of the belligerent tough-guy dog on the hillside had just proved, sometimes it is necessary for a sheepdog to apply a bit of ivory to a problem. This was particularly the case with some of the stouter upland sheep, whose wind-blasted lifestyle left them impervious to subtlety. As a result, many early collies had their canine teeth removed and the rest regularly filed to prevent them doing too much damage to their stubborn wards.

To this day farm collies remain a distinct breed, far removed in appearance and temperament from the show varieties you see flouncing about the ring at the NEC. My grandfather's last dog, the aptly named Rebel, was a farm collie. Rebel was obedient, faithful and a stout companion, but there was something primitive and untamed about him. Indoors was not really the place for Rebel. He had a coat the texture of garden twine that emitted a marshy odour, his breath was corrosive, his belches faded the paintwork. When Rebel broke wind, even the roses on the wallpaper wilted. Luckily, my grandad had spent his entire working life in an ICI chemical plant, so he was completely immune.

Near the entrance to Kildale Sports Field was a pack of dogs with which Rebel would have felt at home: working huskies. A little toffee-coloured cocker spaniel bitch kept running up to them, then, the moment they stood up, running away again with an expression of giggling excitement on her face. I imagined that she was thrilled by the proximity of these sturdy Arctic brutes, repelled and yet strangely attracted by their sunken, lupine looks. Huskies live life in the raw; they walk on the wild side. Exuding vibrancy and danger, they are the rock 'n' roll outlaws of the canine world.

The huskies had pale eyes and their faces were white saucers. The first time I ever saw a husky was on a ferry in Norway. A little girl of about three was eating an ice-cream cornet close to him. As the child alternately licked the ice-cream and jiggled it about, the dog's eyes followed it intently. It was obvious that he wanted that ice-cream, but he couldn't take it while the little girl was looking, so he bided his time. The little girl was suddenly seized with the idea that her parents, who were sitting behind her, might have run off. Leaving her hand and the ice-cream where they were, she turned the rest of her body away from the dog. As she swivelled the husky leaned forwards and gently bit the top off the cornet, swallowing it as he rocked back into his original position. The child, satisfied that her parents had not deserted her, swung back to her ice-cream. All that now remained of it was the pink tip, sheared off about a quarter of an inch above the soft, shrimp-like curl of her fist. She looked at the decapitated cornet, then at the floor, then at the dog. The husky was sitting two feet in front of her. He fixed her with a look of innocent and totally disingenuous helpfulness: 'Yes? Can I be of some assistance, miss?' I have been a fan of huskies ever since.

You see them more and more in England nowadays. Dog-sled racing has caught on. The British Championship is held up in Kielder Forest, and thousands of people go up to watch it. Kielder is noted as one of the coldest parts of Britain. Whenever manufacturers want to test the extreme-weather performance of their goods they send them up to Kielder in midwinter. As well as being cold, it is also windy: it is one of the few places where you see horizontal icicles. Oddly, though, it never seems to snow when there is dog-sled racing. Instead they have to fix wheels to the bottoms of the sleds. It is a good working compromise, but it robs the event of some of its romance. You couldn't imagine the Mad Trapper hurtling across the Yukon pursued by Mounties on a glorified shopping trolley.

The rain had at last soaked through my jacket, so I was relieved to see that the judging had finished and that the industrial tent was now open. I walked round the showring, where a soggy gyr falcon was flying in ever-widening loops, past a display of vintage farm machinery. There were little rattling motors which powered gnashing sheep clippers and oscillated winnowing machines; water pumps sloshed, milkers slurped. Beside them was a row of immaculately restored tractors, the original grey Massey–Fergusons and the French blue Fordhams which flooded into Britain from the US in the late 1940s. They were sturdy little things, as tiny in comparison to the modern monsters as is a Neolithic bull to a Simmenthal. All the tractors dated from the immediate post-Second World War years, by which time British farming was already highly mechanised. In fact, by the 1930s Britain had the most heavily mechanised farming industry in the world. Even the Americans and Canadians lagged behind. The reason was simple enough. The White-faced Woodland sheep wasn't the only animal to suffer in the Great War: during that conflict, heavy horses were commandeered to pull artillery and supply wagons. In five years, close to half a million of them were slaughtered – over a third of Britain's entire breeding stock. It was a blow from which the working horse would not, could not, ever recover. The introduction of the tractor, a gradual process in most intensive-farming countries, therefore became a sudden necessity in this one.

In the industrial tent the rain beat hollowly on the canvas. There was a smell of trampled grass, fresh scones and drying rainwear – the authentic scent of British summer. Pasted along one wall were the entrants for the children's handwriting competition, neat battalions of black letters marching stiffly across a white no-man's-land. The writing was immaculate, the contrast between the lines and curves so stark that the letter 'b' looked like a pregnant guardsman. Beneath the writing, arrayed on white tablecloths, were the children's crafts: bouquets for dolls, drawings of a future world, collages made with wallpaper off-cuts and bottle tops, edible necklaces and a seagrass stool.

The seagrass stool recalled a painful incident in my life involving woodwork. I was thirteen and, without going into detail, the making of a seagrass stool taught me that I was not going to grow up to be a craftsman. It's not so much DIY with me, you see, as DI-why-oh-why. A household store designed to cater for my type of manual incompetence would be called Don't-Do-It-At-All. I'm not sure how I ended up like this. My dad was a structural engineer. He could build anything. Give my dad a squeezy bottle, two paperclips and a brick and he'll make a night-storage heater. My dad is good at explaining things, too, and for years he has given me extraordinarily patient advice. I phone him up and say: 'I'm going to put some new steps in the garden.'

My dad says, 'What are you laying the stones on?'

'The ground.'

'No, they'll subside if you do that,' he tells me. 'You've got to lay them on sharp sand. You know what sharp sand is?'

'No.'

'Well, you know what sand is?'

And half an hour later my dad is saying, in the same even tone, '... and then, after the Ice Age, the glaciers retreated, leaving a fine powder of ground quartz...'

I think I get my DIY genes from my grandad. The only thing that made my grandad a handyman was that he lived locally. Once, when there were mice in his house, my grandad set out to catch them using snares made of red wool. He set them out at night and the next day when he came down they had disappeared. My granddad told the family: 'If you see any mice wearing red sweaters, the little buggers are mine.' Later on, my grandad got rid of the mice. He made Rebel sit with his back to a crack in the skirting board and smoked them out.

Over in the corner of the industrial tent were the home-made wines. Alongside the bottles of elderflower, parsnip and damson, one inventive person had entered a full-bodied red made from a combination of beetroot and pineapple. Perhaps it was the soaking I'd endured, or the intoxicating scent of the cactus dahlias, but this wine, with its blending of the homely and the exotic, seemed to me to be a pint-sized summary of what the shows are all about.

16

· The Big Onion ·

The Harrogate Autumn Flower Show

I was on the train to Harrogate, reading a book about farming history. I had just discovered that farmers in the eighteenth century had taken to growing mangelwurzels not as feed, but because they believed that when they were left to rot in the fields, the farty stink they gave off helped to prevent livestock getting lung diseases. I was quite prepared to believe this. When I was a boy and went out with my granny, whenever we passed a dung heap or muck-spreading tractor, she would always tell me. 'Take a deep breath. It'll clear your tubes.' It says something for the increasingly sanitized nature of the world we live in that modern aromatherapy sees fit to ignore such ancient lore. Scan the ranks of essential oils in your local healthfood shop and you'll find only things that smell pleasant. There's wild thyme, lemon balm and lavender, but no one bothers to wring the juices from malodorous root vegetables, no matter how efficacious they might prove to be. And you never hear the inquiry, 'I've got a touch of bronchitis. Is there anything you can recommend?' meet with the response, 'Yes. Here's a pair of rotten swedes. Go home and have a bath with them.' And this despite the fact that many people dream of taking a bath with a couple of swedes, and the rottener the better.

I would like to have held this latter thought for a while longer, but I couldn't concentrate because the man opposite me kept sniffing. It was not just any old sniff, either. It was a massive, mucoid, snarfing noise such as you might imagine emanating from a great blue whale when it emerges with a maw full of krill after hours of deep-water submersion to discover that a plump and short-sighted turbot has got wedged in its blow-hole. *Ssssschnaaaaarph!* And that wasn't all. Because you don't just launch into a sniff like this one from a standing start, you have to limber up a bit first. So the man went through a routine. A couple of light skipping snuffles, like the initial bouncy steps of a long-jumper, then into full stride with a prolonged adenoidal slurp, before finally exploding off the board. *Ssssschnaaaaarph!*

If sniffers kept this up with any kind of sustained rhythm, it might be possible to ignore it. Sniffing, though, is the human equivalent of a dog's barking: there is no pattern to it, no timing. It is completely random. The only thing you can predict about it is that it will always come, *ssssschnaaaaarph!* when you least expect it.

Queen Isabella I of Spain is usually viewed as a ruthless and cunning woman, but I can't help feeling she'd have done greater damage to Protestantism if, instead of arming the Inquisition with racks and thumbscrews, she'd simply given Torquemada a spoonful of horseradish sauce then confiscated his hankie. Sitting near someone who is sniffing is a mind-annihilating torture. After each burst of slimy nasal suction, you count the seconds to the next one. The gap widens and widens. Your nerves stretch ever tighter, the skin on your scalp contracts, your temples throb. Still the awful silence wears on. And on. You start trying to anticipate when it will come. Now! No. Well then, surely … now! No. You catch your breath. You rally; perhaps he's not going to sniff again. Perhaps he's finally finally rounded up all that escaping snot and got it safely away under lock and key in the dank tower of his sinuses. And anyway, isn't this all terribly silly? You ought to relax. Life's too short. What does it matter? For heaven's sake, it's only somebody sniffing. And you smile a wry smile and gaze from the window at the passing countryside, observing afresh the shifting nap of the green winter wheat and the goldfish glint of beech leaves. And you begin to wonder why the art of building scarecrows has fallen into such terrible decline. I mean, nowadays Wurzel Gummidge would be two sticks, a fertiliser sack and a punctured ballcock, and poor old Sally—*ssssschnaaaaarph!*

I sat staring at my book, unsure whether to commit suicide or murder. Thankfully, I was saved from having to make a decision because at that moment the tannoy burst into life: 'This is your senior conductor speaking. I'd like to remind passengers wishing to sniff that sniffing accommodation is provided at the rear of the train. For the convenience of other passengers, please do not sniff anywhere else on the train. I would also invite anyone who requires a prolonged mobile-phone conversation with a man named Charlie about the bathroom fitments situation vis-à-vis Cleethorpes, or wishes to talk non-stop for two hours about the many amusing pronouncements of his or her four-year-old granddaughter, Polly-May, to proceed to the front of the train, where the Irritating Buggers Car is now open.'

Forget Cheltenham, Beverly Hills, Bel-Air and the Forbidden City - Harrogate is easily the poshest place on the planet. When driving in to the town it's a surprise to find that the 'Welcome to Harrogate' sign doesn't include the suffix 'Please wipe your feet.' The smartly dressed sandstone houses that sweep around the immaculate bonsai dale of the Valley Gardens are corseted with intricate iron verandas and underwired filigree balconies. Through the misty windows of the tea rooms you catch glimpses of the residents, handsome middle-aged women with ash-blonde hair and houndstooth jackets, sipping Earl Grey tea and wielding their cigarette with refined savagery. In the neat mewses, between oyster bars and the sort of antique shops that never stock more than six items at one time and whose entire window display is a vase, drawling voices say, 'Oh Rupert, dah-ling, don't be such a terrible bore,' and teenage boys in baggy jumpers have hair so world-weary it just, kind of like, flops. In Harrogate, even the French sound their aitches. I once bought a copy of the *Guardian* in Harrogate and the newsagent put it in a brown paper bag before handing it to me.

I boarded the bus to the Autumn Flower Show in buoyant mood. There was something about the gilded splendour of Harrogate that cheered me. No matter what time of year I came here, it always felt like Christmas.

The Autumn Flower Show is Harrogate's second major horticultural event of the year. The first is, fittingly I think you'll agree, the Spring Flower Show. I had decided not to go to the spring show because it boasted of being 'The largest daffodil show in the north', and I hate daffodils. The smell of them is just *so* strident. If anyone brings so much as a single dwarf narcissus into our house I cry out in anguish, 'Oh, damn, damn that wretched odour! Take it away, pray do!' and then collapse on the chaise-longue clutching a cologne-soaked linen handkerchief to my quivering nostrils. Actually I don't. I just made up that to make myself seem more interesting. It wasn't because of the daffodils that I didn't go to the Spring Flower Show, it was because the tickets were too bloody expensive.

The Spring Flower Show is held in the Valley Gardens. The autumn version had recently moved to the Great Yorkshire Showground, site, as you may have guessed, of the north's biggest agricultural show and the second-largest in the country, the Great Yorkshire Show. I had been to the Great Yorkshire once as a boy, and with a childish acquisitiveness had dashed about the place collecting enough free leaflets about grain hoppers, silage towers and milking machines to paper the inside of Durham Cathedral. We had to hire a team of mules to carry them back to the car park. When we loaded them in the boot of our Morris Oxford the axle snapped. The show attracts thousands of such children every year. Scientists have calculated that if all the glossy sheaves of paper they amassed were laid end to end, they'd all blow away in the first stiff breeze.

The Great Yorkshire was first held in 1838 under the auspices of the Yorkshire Agricultural Society, whose chairman, Earl Spencer, was another of the aristocratic farming progressives and one of the founders of the Royal Agricultural Society. Earl Spencer believed that the annual show would help improve farming standards throughout the county. Not everyone agreed. At the first meeting, a member expressed the view that the whole principle of a show was to mislead farmers and betray their best interests. For farmers, a healthy distrust of all authority, occasionally edging towards paranoia, is a prerequisite of the job.

For the first hundred years and more the show moved from place to place, visiting most of the larger Yorkshire towns and occasionally even nipping across the border into Durham to pay a call on Darlington or Stockton. By the 1940s, however, it had become so large and was attracting such huge crowds that many places could no longer cope with it. A fierce battle ensued between York and Harrogate for the right to host the event permanently, and Harrogate won. The first show on the new site was held in 1951, and that, some will tell you, was when the rot set in.

The Great Yorkshire had preserved its agricultural purity for much longer than many of its counterparts in other counties. Show-jumping, for example, was not introduced until after the Second World War. Before that, anyone craving sporting excitement had to make do with the butter-churning contests. After the move to Harrogate, though, commercialisation did not so much creep into the Great Yorkshire Show as leap, slavering, into its arms crying, 'I love you, I love you, and I want to have your babies.' As a consequence, the show's harshest critics have said, it is now nothing more than a gigantic car-boot sale with a few animals attached. Unperturbed, the crowds continue to come in vast numbers. It is this, rather than the threat of row after row of stalls selling dried flowers, hand-made fudge and dolls with heads made from walnuts, that has put me off the Great

Yorkshire Show. The site covers around 200 acres but the milling throng makes it practically impossible to stop and look at anything. One minute you're admiring the ginger dreadlocks of a Highland cow, the next you've been swept away by a flood of schoolkids and washed up in front of a trade stand for pig nuts.

The main hall of the flower show vibrated to the happy hum of contented gardeners. The air was filled with the acerbic, florist's-shop smell of concentrated chlorophyll. A great flouncing sweep of furbellowed gladioli, all bright reds, oranges and yellows, gave one wall the appearance of the washing line outside a Wild West bordello. In the rose section, miniature blooms were arranged on pallets like dabs of paint. Among the pinks, serious men in cavalry twills crouched to study the lacy crinolines of the carnations, while across the way a bloke with a pipe in the top pocket of his sports coat tucked in his chin and nodded approvingly at a plate of rich purple-skinned potatoes.

The dahlia and chrysanthemum men were out in force. They were gathered in knots among their respective exhibits, arms folded and eyes watchful. They were talking, but only half listening – men on the verge of action. I was relieved to see that the organisers had created a buffer zone in the form of a wide public thoroughfare between the two groups. Dahlia and chrysanthemum exhibitors are implacable enemies. Their dislike for one another is palpable. 'Nowt but mops on sticks,' the dahlia-growers say of chrysanths. 'What's the matter with dahlias, exactly?' you ask a 'mum man. 'Nothing,' he replies, 'if you're a ponce.'

Such contempt seems even odder when you consider that to the untrained eye (if you hear a loud explosion in the next few seconds, don't panic – it's just committed dahlia and chrysanthemum men exploding), the two flowers often appear very similar. Then again, the theological difference between Catholicism and Protestantism isn't that great, but look at all the deaths it's resulted in. Sometimes it's the narrowest of differences that lead to the bitterest argument. Enmity over flowers is not confined to the dahlia- and chrysanth-growers, of course; nor is it a peculiarly British thing. The worst-ever outbreaks of floral violence have occurred in the Netherlands. In seventeenth-century Holland it wasn't uncommon for men to kill one another over a tulip. Bulbs had a huge monetary significance for the Dutch, and they formed the basis of some of the first-ever commodity speculation. The big trouble arose, however, when gentlemen began wagering huge sums of cash on the colour of bloom a randomly selected bulb would produce. The Dutch are a liberal and laid-back people: the tulip competition wasn't as quick as a horse race, but its slow, remorseless unwinding perhaps suited the national temperament better. As the winter snows melted and the first rays of sunshine began to coax the flowers from their earthen eiderdown, betting men and bookmakers licked their lips, dried their sweating palms and fixed their eyes on the soil. By March the tension was unbearable. With fortunes riding on the pigment of the gradually unfurling petals, tempers frayed, accusations of match-rigging and bulb-tampering flew, and daggers were drawn.

As yet nobody has been murdered over dahlias and chrysanthemums. The growers of these plants may not get on, but they prefer to work out their aggression on insects. Sometimes you will pass a garden and see, bobbing in the breeze, a strange, spectral ectoplasm. On closer inspection this turns out to be cheesecloth, draped over exhibition flowers. The cloth is designed to keep insects out, but, frustratingly for the growers, it is simply not protection enough against the most dangerous foe of prize dahlia and chrysanthemum blooms, the earwig.

'They get right inside,' a chrysanth-grower at Harrogate told me. 'They chew up the petals and then…' He paused, overcome by the awfulness of it all. 'They defecate.' The prospect of one of his show flowers being decorated with earwig turds is more than any self-respecting grower can stand. The man had many ways of dealing with the problem. He scattered Dipterex round the bases of the plants and he fashioned straw-filled traps out of hollow beanstalks and concealed them among the leaves. Mainly, though, he liked to go into one-to-one combat with the enemy. Before he went to bed at night he would sneak out into the garden with a torch and a pair of tweezers. 'It's the only way,' he said, and his eyes took on the mad glint of a character in *Apocalypse Now* talking about the Vietcong, 'that you can make sure.'

I was pleased to meet someone with such an intimate knowledge of earwigs, because there is something about them that has puzzled me since childhood. Why do they have pincers on their backside? It seems to me that the pincers are badly placed. If they were designed to help the earwig cut up food, they are at the wrong end; and if they were for defence - well, most creatures' natural response to attack is to protect their heads and necks, not their arses. It's no coincidence that when someone has been particularly ruthless we say, 'He really went for the jugular,' and not, 'Wow, she certainly bit the buttocks on that one.' So what is the earwig's game, exactly? Does he plan to reverse into combat like a skunk or an Italian tank? Or is his grasp of basic hygiene so rudimentary that he thinks it all good and healthy to cut up his dinner with his bottom hanging over the plate? I put all this to the chrysanthemum man. I didn't get much of an answer out of him, though. He just smiled nervously and shuffled off to look for a security guard.

I wandered away through rows of pastel blooms which looked like the kind of thing Audrey Hepburn might have worn as a hat in *Breakfast at Tiffany's*, past pelargoniums, interpretive flower arrangements, giant cacti and racks stacked with Wellingtons. Gardening is like this. It is a world where beauty and mundanity mingle in a way that would shock Bohemia. Camellias and cabbages co-habit unashamedly. Over in the corner, a correspondent from *Garden News* was jauntily answering questions about compost. At a stall selling bizarre, spidery plants from the Brazilian rainforest, a worried customer from Bradford was saying: 'I've given it a regular soaking, but it still just droops.' One minute it's pink-lipped, pornographic orchids, the next it's compacted cow manure. At times visiting a horticultural show can be a disarming experience. It's as if you've walked into a village post office to find Kate Moss and Johnny Depp working behind the counter and Frank the retired plumber queuing up to pay his paper bill in an electric blue lurex body-stocking.

I restored some equilibrium by eating a massive ice-cream while studying the Royal Horticultural Society's fruit display. There was a fine selection of English apples. I have never been a great one for apples, but there is something about the sight, the idea of them, that is strangely cheering. It's the same with kippers. Whenever I think of kippers it brings a smile to my face. There's something cosy and Edwardian and 221b Baker Street about kippers. Arbroath Smokies, bloaters, the smacks and cobbles a-bob on the foaming sea; the smell of the smoke houses at Craster, Seahouses and Whitby; breakfast, brown bread and butter, a roaring fire, willow-pattern plates and a mist-wreathed winter's morning. Yes, all the associations of kippers are great. The trouble starts after you cook them. Or at least, it used to. Because I can now reveal the classic method for getting the best out of kippers. Place them on a tinfoil-lined tray under a hot grill. Cook until the outer skin is beginning to bubble and blister and the entire house is filled with that wonderful aroma. Then remove the kippers from the grill, throw them in the bin and make yourself a bacon sandwich.

English apples aren't as unblemished as those from France or as Adonis-like as their Californian cousins, but there is something distinctly plucky about them. Arranged in groups on white paper plates, the little nobbly platoons of rosy-cheeked pippins and copper-skinned russets looked as if they were prepared to do their damnedest. They had a John Mills-ish quality. They had poetic names too: Barnack Beauty, Ashmeads Kernel, Michaelmas Red. My favourite was the Darcy Spice, a cider apple which really ought to sport a waxed moustache and a caddish expression. Like swine husbandry, apple-growing has its own specialist wooden implement, the panking pole. This is used to shake recalcitrant pippins from the bough, and as the foundation of 95 per cent of all orchard-related *double entendres*. In fact, if it wasn't for the comment, 'I'm off out for a quick pank,' there would be no jokes in Shropshire whatsoever. The panking pole also serves to emphasise the importance of hand-held lengths of timber in country life. Practically every aspect of rural exist-ence includes one. The shepherd has his crook, the fisherman his rod and the village shopkeeper has a sour old stick who helps out behind the counter on Saturday mornings.

Over in the vegetable section, the main business of the day was being concluded. The vegetables were one of the wonders of the show. Walking among them you felt that you had either shrunk or wandered on to the set of the '60s TV show *Land of the Giants*. The leeks were the length of broadswords. You could have rigged a schooner with the string beans and played carpet bowls with the peas. The carrots and parsnips were endless. I couldn't understand how you could grow anything that long in a vegetable bed, or get it out in one piece if you did. Later, I found out that you don't: show carrots and parsnips aren't grown in the garden, but in 45-gallon oildrums filled with sand, or a mix of sawdust and compost. Ordinary soil has too much grit in it. Root crops tend to weave their way around even the smallest stone, and nobody wants kinky carrots.

The prize vegetable-grower spends on average five hours a day in his garden. As the show season approaches this may increase to as many as fifteen. On the day of the event he will be up early, raising and picking his prize specimens and washing them down with soapy water. It is fashionable to mock people who devote themselves so wholeheartedly to a hobby. This seems to me unfair. After all, which is more stupid: devoting hours to DIY just to save a couple of quid, or growing a marrow that could win you a new TV and video?

All the vegetables at Harrogate were impressive, but pride of place went to the onions. The autumn show played host to the National Onion Championship, and the winner had just collected his cheque for £1,000 and was posing for photographs. He was holding the winning onion shot-putter-style on the palm of his hand up next to his face. It weighted over 13lb. The grower was smiling broadly. I couldn't help feeling a little uneasy for him, though. Onions originated in the Middle East, and I was sure that somewhere in the Old Testament there was a law prohibiting growing one that was bigger than your head.

I took the bus back into Harrogate and went to Betty's Tea Room. I was sitting wrestling with a fat rascal and imagining myself to be in a Merchant-Ivory film when one of a pair of elegant women sitting at the next table pronounced: 'So the policeman said to me, "Your son's name, Mrs Tressle - Wentworth. It's a bit odd, isn't it?' I said, "Perhaps so, sergeant. But it has been in my family for 500 years and I see no reason to lose it now. And by the way, *sergeant* - it's Lady Tressle."'

Nobody sniffed.

17

· Fluffy Things ·

The North-Eastern Rabbit and Cavy Championship Show

Catherine and I were coming down the A68 between Corbridge and Crook. It's a narrow, contorted road, dotted with the sort of blind summits and swooping dips that have your stomach leaping out of your mouth then bouncing back down it again off the car ceiling. We had been moving along at a steady clip and then we'd turned a corner and got stuck behind a couple in a Volvo who were travelling so slowly I kept expecting a man with a red flag to emerge from behind a wall, fastening his flies, and jog back in front of them again.

But the A68 is always like this. It has been given the Route of the Century Award by *Hold-Up!*, the official magazine of the International Traffic-Jam-Makers Society. Members of this august yet secretive body come from all over the world to use it nowadays. You can see them in merry groups outside pubs and cafés along the way – Sundays and Bank Holidays are a particularly busy time. They are easily recognisable by their tell-tale accessories: driving gloves, caravan, sky-blue trilby, white-haired companion who points at things and makes sure all maps are kept upside-down and the road atlas is permanently open at the wrong page. If you moved among them you would hear the swapping of tales and tips: 'Notice anything different about this old jalopy? That's right! Just sawed straight down the middle and widened her by two feet using fibreglass wadding. Now with a bit of skilful placement, I can occupy a lane and a half of any dual carriageway here or on mainland Europe… Borrowed the brother-in-law's tractor, spiked a bail on the front and set off. By Honiton I had a quarter-mile tailback behind me! I had to laugh. You could see them all thinking, "He's got to be turning off soon. He's got to be turning off soon!" He bloomin' well didn't, though! He went all the way to Salcombe… Yes, you get more wind-sway with these '50s models. Nothing like the sight of a sixteen-foot mobile home swinging about a bit to keep the blighters behind you, eh?'

The A68 is the ultimate hobby workshop for the ITJMS. It is busy, it is bumpy and it is virtually impossible to overtake on it. A few miles south of Stagshaw Roundabout there is a police warning notice about the perils ahead. It concludes, '87 accidents in the last three years'. The figure 87 is on a separate bit of sign, and every so often they come along and screw on an updated one. When you have been past it a few times you begin to wish they would replace it with something just a bit less scary. Like a skull and crossbones and the legend, *abandon hope all ye who pass.*

The Volvo slipped out of sight just before Tow Law. It was a little too early for other ITJMS members – they do their best work around lunchtime – but even this little delay made me impatient. All through the summer I had been seeing rabbits at shows and I had become frighteningly obsessed with them. To help in my research, I had got a couple of books about rabbits out of the library (one by the aptly named Brian Leveret). A cursory flick through these little coloured volumes on the bus home and I was in the grip of a feverish consumer-lust of a type I had not experienced since the day in my childhood when the new Matchbox car catalogue arrived in the mail.

I used to pore over those pictures of toys for hours, trying to figure out which one I liked best. This was no easy task, as I had three top automotive model judgement criteria, all of which were more or less incompatible. The vehicle I wanted had to have a realistic internal feature, a working part and a flashy name. It had to be American, too, because to my mind American things were always more exciting than their British counterparts – they produced Champion the Wonder Horse; we produced Muffin the Mule. In fact, my ideal toy car would have been a Ford Mustang fire engine with removable ladders, a flip-up bonnet and caterpillar tracks. Matchbox didn't make one. So instead I assiduously studied the pictures and read the description and whittled it down to a top three, and from that, agonisingly, to the final car, the one I wanted above all others. Then I'd count up my money and prepare to set off for the shop. Just before I went out of the door, I'd think, maybe I'd better just have another look at the catalogue to make really, really sure. And I'd get it out and leaf through it and suddenly – wham! right out of the blue I'd spot some other car I'd previously dismissed without a second look, but now saw was the most brilliant ever. Definitely! Certainly! But then again, maybe ... And the whole thing would start all over again.

This was the problem I was now experiencing with rabbits. Only with the rabbits it was worse. With the Matchbox cars the reason I had to pick a favourite was that one was all I could afford. With the rabbits, the problem was that I didn't really need to pick a favourite, because rabbits breed rapidly and as a result even the most glorious show specimens rarely sell for more than £10, and I was a grown-up now, and that meant that if I took a fancy to I could buy *all the rabbits I wanted*.

Except, of course, I couldn't, because that would have been ridiculous. One rabbit is enough for anybody. And in moments of remission from my rabbit fever, I knew that even one rabbit was really more than was strictly necessary. And part of that cold logic always remained tucked away in a corner of my subconscious, even when I was at my most vulnerable, and *Lagamorphia lunititis* struck with such force that the bunny-buying pressure built up in me to a level where I felt that if I didn't purchase a rabbit *this instant* I would explode with sufficient force to flatten everything within a thirty-mile radius. This usually occurred in the fur and feather tent at agricultural shows, when I'd walked around for a bit and found myself, as if guided by an unseen hand, right in front of the 'for sale' cages, trying to determine which was the most charming, the tall, butterscotch-coated and alert-looking Belgian Hare, or the ale-and-stout-coloured black and tan – or did, perhaps, the white-coat and piratical black eye-patch of the Blanc de Hotot edge it over both of them? But then, of course, the black stripe and chain spots of the Blue English Butterfly were also striking, while the breed's lively nature made it a captivating pet. And then again … Hey, why was I worrying anyway? I could get the whole lot for under thirty quid! Big cardboard box, 3:30 train, no problem. At this point logic would leap from its hiding place and drag me into a Portaloo, slap me hard and hiss: 'You do not *need*, or even, if you think about it clearly, *want* a rabbit.'

And I would quiver and yelp, 'Yes, I do! Please, just one. Or two. Because they need a companion or they get lonely. In fact half a dozen would be best, because they're herd animals, really, I think, and …'

And logic would deliver another backhander and snarl: 'You are not having a rabbit!'

'I must! I must!'

'You must not!'

'Must!'

'Must not!'

Then I'd be interrupted by a banging on the door and a stern voice would say, 'This is the police. What's going on in there?'

So now I was going to the big rabbit show. I wasn't going to buy anything: this was a desperate measure to cure myself. It was the workers-at-the-chocolate-factory principle. I told myself that if I saw enough rabbits I would become totally sickened by them and that would be an end to it.

The North-Eastern Championship Show was in the Newton Aycliffe Leisure Centre, a large, unprepossessing concrete block at one end of a windswept shopping precinct. Inside there was a smell of chlorine, the echoing yells and splashes of kids, the bang and squeak of trainers and vending machines selling cheese-sandwich biscuits in the stairwells. The rabbits and cavies were in the main hall, two flights of stairs above the din. Here there were rows and rows of wire cages criss-crossed by lines of white-covered judging tables; men and women in lab coats with embroidered badges ('English Silver Fox', 'North-East Rex Circle', 'National Otter Rex Rabbit Club') sewn down the fronts putting the finishing touches to their charges, brushing or rubbing their pelts with silk cloths; spectators wandering up and down the aisles between cages, stern-faced, glancing every once in a while at their chunky show catalogues, while up in the gallery others sat with styrofoam cups of tea and took an aerial view of proceedings. There was a busy hush of concentration. This was a serious show. Competitors had travelled from as far away as Bognor Regis. Not only were championship cups and shields up for grabs, there was also a bewildering range of intermediate, club and specialist prizes for which to battle.

The tension was palpable. The Rabbit Fancy were known to be a competitive bunch. A few months before, a senior show judge from Yorkshire had resigned after decades of service, disgusted by the sharp practice and tampering that went on. In the hall at Newton Aycliffe, groups of stewards stood chewing their lower lips, eyes sliding about the hall as if anticipating a riot; judges stared into space collecting themselves; the Fancy blinked, minds running over checklists, lips moving silently and rapidly. I suffered a sudden self-conscious pang, as if I had entered the holy place of some arcane religion and was now expected to act correctly when I didn't have a clue what exactly that involved. I decided to follow the man in front of me and mimic his actions – that way I would just blend in. I walked down an aisle between cages of French Lop rabbits, big beasts that could weigh as much as a King Charles spaniel, had long, drooping ears with the Dumboesque span of two feet, and sprawled, indolent and debauched-looking, across their cages, legs outstretched, heads resting on forepaws, as if they were odalisques posing for a French impressionist. Every few yards I looked at my catalogue, narrowed my eyes and nodded sagely, as if to say, '"Meis. Lop. AA. NLP – No Entries." Well, that figures.'

Rabbits were first introduced into Britain by the Normans. For the next eight centuries the rabbit population, for some unfathomable reason, remained relatively small and their meat was a luxury commodity which commanded a high price. So much so that farmers actively encouraged rabbits to set up home on their land. Warrens were considered a valuable addition to any property: George Culley tells of one near Pickering in the North Riding which, in 1788, was being let for the sum of £300 a year. As a consequence of the systematic management of these warrens, rabbits came to be regarded as farm livestock and attempts were made to breed specifically for size and weight. The result was hefty creatures such as the French Lop and its English and German (known as Meissner) counterparts, the mighty Flemish Giant from Ghent and the now extinct Angevin, which was recorded as long ago as the 1500s and is said to have been 5ft long and well over 200lb in weight. The extinction of a breed is normally a sad event, but I can't help feeling relieved that the Angevin is no longer with us. Having seen the damage a tiny wild rabbit can do overnight in the garden, the thought of one the size of a Shetland pony rampaging through the radishes doesn't bear contemplating. And then there'd be the burrows. They'd have to be the size of drift mines. During the years of Richelieu, whole French villages must have collapsed as a result of Angevin subsidence.

Rabbits were not only bred for their meat. As I walked along (consulting my catalogue and mumbling expertly, 'Mmm, pleasing to see the ISRRA Area Show Agouti/AOC Challenge Ad. has drawn a large field of entries'), I came across a cage that appeared to contain some mutant strain of albino candyfloss. This great puff of fluff filled half the cage. I studied it from various angles. It appeared to have no head or feet. Just as I was beginning to suspect that this was some trap to winkle out unwary novices such as myself ('Hey, Jack, look at that. We've got another of the beggars. Staring at that extruded glass wool as if it's an exhibit. Wait till I tell our Maureen, she'll blow a gasket') a man in a lab coat came along, opened the cage and placed a saucer of seeds and grain on the floor. As he shut the door again a dark head topped by tufted ears suddenly shot out from the cloud of hair and began chomping the food. It was an Angora rabbit. Angoras were bred for their fine wool. You get $1\frac{1}{2}$lb per year of it off a fully grown adult, so you'll need quite a few if you're planning on knitting a twin-set.

Rabbits were also valued for their pelts, and many, such as the chinchillas, were bred in imitation of more expensive animal furs. As the number of varieties increased, so too did the interest in keeping them as show animals. This was boosted by the sudden boom in the wild rabbit population which, for no reason anyone can fathom, occurred in the 1870s and depressed the price of rabbit meat accordingly. An added impetus came from an important change in the life of the human population. For most of history man had lived in close proximity to animals, whether they were the sheep or goats that were brought indoors in winter, or the cow he kept in a byre next to his house. Even when the industrial revolution came and people moved into the cities, they still did not give up their livestock. Pigs were kept in sties in the back yards of the majority of terraced houses in British cities, and the sight of thousands of swine running about the streets on a Saturday afternoon while their lodgings were cleared and fresh straw was laid in was a common one until well into the nineteenth century (and seems to have been revived in some shopping centres lately). The Large White, one of the most popular modern varieties of pig, was first bred by a Keighley weaver, Joseph Tulley, who used to wash his beasts every Saturday night with the soapy water left from his own bath. Goats and small cows such as the Dexter were also kept by the working-class urban population, primarily for milk and meat, of course, but there was more to it than that. Over the centuries, man's constant close proximity to animals had given him a kind of emotional dependence on them. He liked having them around. In his book *The Land First*, Ralph Whitlock tells how he once paid a visit on an elderly smallholder to check his accounts. A few calculations showed that buying and fattening a pig was hardly turning a profit for the old man. When Whitlock pointed this out to him, the smallholder nodded in agreement, then said, 'Still, I had his company for six months.'

By the late 1800s, the days when a town- or city-dweller could keep a pig for company were gone. Outbreaks of disease caused by the huge numbers of inner-city pigs had led to them being banned. If urban man wanted to continue to live near animals, he would have to choose something smaller and more manageable. It is no surprise, therefore, that it was around this period that the practice of rabbit- and pigeon-keeping in Britain rapidly expanded. Like pigeon-racing, showing rabbits had another side to it. It was a hobby with a product you could eat. When times were tough, the rabbit and pigeon men still sat down to a decent dinner, while across the road, the man at Number 22 looked at his matchstick model of York Minster and listened to his stomach rumbling.

I wandered down the final aisle of rabbits. Rabbit shows are, broadly speaking, divided into two main sections, 'Fancy', which includes older breeds such as Angoras and Lops, and 'Fur', which features more modern varieties such as the New Zealand Red and the Beveran Blue. I was in the fur section now, tracking down an Orange Rex. As its name implies, this is a rich marmalade colour and, like all Rex rabbits, it has fur that is as thick and velvety as a mink stole. The Orange Rex was definitely my all-time favourite. If I ever do buy a rabbit, it will certainly be an Orange Rex. But only if it comes with a free Dwarf Lop chinchilla, obviously. And maybe an Argente de Champagne as a reserve in case anything happened to the other two. I decided it was time to go and look at the cavies.

Cavies, or guinea pigs, arrived in Europe from South America in the 1500s. They became popular as a pet about the same time rabbits did, though nobody ever ate their surplus stock. Not in this country, anyway. A friend of mine was once staying in a house up in the mountains in Peru. After the meal was finished his host simply swept the crumbs on to the floor. Seconds later, there was a chorus of whistling and a large herd of guinea pigs came trundling across the floor from the kitchen and began nibbling the crumbs. 'Aha,' my friend exclaimed, gesturing to them, 'they clean up for you.' The host smiled, then rubbed his stomach, smacked his lips and pointed at the remains of dinner in the pot on the table. My friend had just eaten the Peruvian equivalent of fricasseed vacuum cleaner. He said they tasted of pork. Which, along with the fact some species live in Guyana, is how they came to be called guinea pigs. Nowadays they are usually known as cavies, which is a corruption of their generic name *Cavia* and has no unpleasant crackling-and-apple-sauce connotations.

Cavies are sweet creatures. They have fat bottoms, protruding lower lips and bright, round eyes. They emit a slightly startled high-pitched cry. 'Ooooh!' they go, 'Oooh-oooh!' In combination these characteristics give them the appearance of the type of kindly yet silly old spinsters who populate the novels of Charles Dickens.

When I was at infant school my class was bought a guinea pig. He was a curly-coated character, brindle in colour, with ears that had the shape of potato crisps and the texture of felt. As proud recipients of this fine and fascinating fellow, it fell to us to christen him. The teacher decided we would draw up a list of names and then vote for our favourites. She stood by the blackboard, chalk in hand, and we called out suggestions. Being six or seven years old, we had not yet formulated any fixed ideas about the suitability of certain names for different types of animals, or indeed any ideas at all. In our world, there were just names we liked and those we didn't, and that was that. My classmates and I would have found nothing odd in a gerbil called Bambi or a Siamese cat named T. Rex. So we shouted out the best names we could think of and the teacher wrote them on the board, a look of despair spreading gradually across her face as the chalk squeaked up Dougal, Donny, Babar and Sooty. Eventually the votes were called in and counted and the little brindle cavy was officially christened Skippy.

I was pleased to have a guinea pig as classmate, especially one who shared a name with the famous TV bush kangaroo. I fondly imagined that our own Skippy would play a similar part in the many exciting adventures that were sure to come our way. We would find him slightly singed around the whiskers on the doorstep when we arrived at school. 'What's up, Skip?' we would ask anxiously, gathering around him. 'Oooh! Ooooooh! Oooh!'

We would listen attentively and then one of our number, a boy more dashing and intelligent than the rest (i.e., me) would say, 'I think he's trying to tell us that Mrs Tidman's helicopter has crashed into Burton's shirt factory and ... Look! He's signalling for us to follow him!'

Strangely, nothing even remotely like this ever happened. Skippy didn't find any mysterious treasure at the bottom of disused jet mines, capture any escaped prisoners or uncover any evil property developers who were dressing up as ghostly monks to scare people away from the ruined twelfth-century priory so that they could buy it cheaply and turn it into a car park. No swarthy gang was handcuffed by the local bobby as I fed Skippy a carrot and outlined their cunning plot to defraud the local sweet shop, or responded when I had finished by sneering, 'And we'd have gotten away with it, too, if it hadn't been for these meddlesome kids and that pesky guinea pig of theirs.' In fact, Skippy didn't do anything much at all except sit and whistle a bit when he heard his dinner coming.

Years later, my mother, who was an infant-school teacher herself, told me of the perils of class pet-naming sessions. She had once had to cunningly rig an entire election to avoid ending up with a white rabbit called Flipper.

In front of me on a table, flanked by lab-coated competitors, was what looked to be a collection of half a dozen rather badly made toupees. They were black and silky and had a noticeable lump in the middle. Without warning, one of the wigs suddenly scuttled towards the edge of the table. A competitor picked it up gently and popped it back in the line. These were Peruvian cavies. Some of them had hair twenty inches long. Back in their cages they had it wrapped up in special rollers made from paper and balsa wood and held in place with rubber bands. If you stared too long at the Peruvians when they were in this state, they pouted their lips out and looked embarrassed. Nobody likes to be seen in their curlers.

On the table next to the Peruvians some cavy-fanciers were sorting out their Abyssinians. These were the variety to which Skippy belonged. The Abyssinians' hair was medium length, formed into a series of rosettes and ridges that gave them a wild and disgruntled appearance, as if they'd had a shampoo and then gone out straight afterwards and got caught in a hurricane. The Abyssinians' owners were combing them with toothbrushes. They used only ones with natural hair – nylon bristles create static which makes the cavy's hair stand on end and the judges yelp.

Apart from the Abyssinians and Peruvians, there was a huge variety of smooth-haired cavies on display, some of a single colour (or 'self', as it is known) and some of two or more ('non-self'). Among the latter were some crested varieties which had a forehead that was a contrasting colour to the rest of their bodies. I couldn't help noticing that several of them bore a startling facial resemblance to Sir Peter Ustinov. This discovery made me smile broadly. I looked around absentmindedly. A man a few yards away saw me grinning and fired a hostile look in my direction. It ricocheted off my forehead and buried itself in the ceiling. I had given myself away; I had forgotten that this was no place for merriment. I decided to skedaddle before they raised a posse.

Later that morning we drove south to a restaurant to which I'd been promising to take Catherine for over ten years. The day was cloudy and the oncoming traffic was heavy with caravans and crawling cars heading towards the A68. The food in the restaurant was very good, but I couldn't really concentrate on it. I was too busy trying to decide which was better, a chocolate-crested Himalayan or a tortie-and-white Abyssinian.

18

· Sheep ·

Masham Sheep Fair

Catherine and I were riding along the edge of the north Pennines. Heavy late-summer rain had revivified the woods and pastures, green creeping through dun like watery ink across sugar paper. Now the sky had cleared, the air was fresh, dark-eyed Rudbeckias swayed lithely in gardens, yarrow heads nodded rhythmically and the dawn chorus was a doo-wop version of 'Zippadee Doo-Dah'. We were bounding along the undulating road in a friend's pick-up truck and I was fighting a mounting urge to yell 'Yee-hah', listen to ZZ Top and buy a gun rack and a couple of Confederate-flag bumper stickers.

The reason we were in the pick-up was that a few weeks before, in Newcastle, our car had been stolen. The following Saturday we got a call from the police. Tynesiders are remorselessly cheerful. The average Geordie is so upbeat and optimistic that if you put him in a pot and boiled him down to his very essence, the substance left would be Prozac.

'It's about your car,' the WPC said. 'I'm afraid we've some good news and some bad news.'

I am from Teesside. Teessiders are by nature pessimists. If you put a Teessider in a pot and boiled him down to his very essence, he wouldn't be a bit surprised. 'Bad news first, please,' I said.

'We've found your car ablaze in Benwell.'

'So what's the good news?'

'The fire brigade is on its way.'

Coming through a village south-east of Darlington I saw a pub sign that reminded me of something I meant to tell you about ages ago. It showed a massive, spotted beast with a great lumpy body, a brisket that practically scraped the ground and a head so disproportionately small it looked like a satsuma on a blanket chest. This strange creature was the famous Ketton or Durham Ox. The Ketton Ox was one of the first great marvels of the new farming age. He was a celebrity. Just how famous the Ketton Ox was can be gauged by the fact that there are at least two pubs named after him, whereas there's only one named after Charles Dickens and none at all called The Gazza.

The Ketton Ox wasn't the first male bovine to be so celebrated. That honour fell to Apis, the sacred black bull of ancient Egypt. Apis was said to be the son of the god Ptah, who fell in love with and later impregnated a beautiful heifer (Victorian show judges clearly weren't the first people to notice the attractiveness of the bovine female form, nor even the second – Zeus coupled with Parsiphae when she had cunningly disguised herself as comely cow, though admittedly he was masquerading as a bull himself at the time, so no charges were ever brought). Apis and his male offspring were thought to have the gift of seeing into the future. The ancient Egyptians kept them in special luxury houses and supplied them with harems of exotic cows. Of course, the bulls couldn't communicate their prophetic visions themselves, so a specially trained group of priests was employed to interpret their actions. In many ways this is similar to today, when our government employ specially trained people to interpret statistics. Statistics are the sacred bull of the twentieth century, but you don't get to make hamburgers out of them afterwards.

The Ketton Ox didn't predict the future. His celebrity stemmed from the fact that he was massive. Increasingly good grazing and management had seen cattle double in size between the sixteenth and eighteenth centuries, but even so the Ketton Ox, born in 1796, was remarkable. He was bred by Charles Colling of Teesdale, who had applied Robert Bakewell's breeding methods to shorthorn cattle. By the time he was five years old the Ketton Ox weighed over 3,000lbs – at least four times the size of an average ox of the day and about 25 per cent more than a modern Simmenthal bull. Colling sold the ox to a Mr Bulmer of Harmby in Yorkshire for £140 (as a result of the fame accrued to him by the Ketton Ox, Colling was later able to sell a herd of forty-seven shorthorns, including the bull called Comet, for the then staggering sum of £7,115. The ox might therefore be viewed as the first ever example of the loss-leader principle). Bulmer made a special carriage for his acquisition and five weeks later sold both for £250 to a man named John Day. Day exhibited the ox at showgrounds throughout that summer and by the end of it was being offered £2,000 for his beefy ward. He preferred instead to go on raking in the cash from guest appearances. For six summers the Ketton Ox was the star of shows all over Britain.

As the reaction to the BSE scare demonstrated, there is something about the importance of beef to the British which goes way beyond its mere food value. It is a national symbol. This was even more true in the nineteenth century, when eating meat in general and beef in particular was seen as the patriotic duty of every loyal English gentleman. Such was the volume of meat consumed that there was usually very little space left in the English stomach for anything else. Beau Brummel, the Regency dandy, was once asked if he had ever eaten any vegetables. He considered for a moment before disdainfully replying, 'I think I once ate a pea.'

In such a *viande*-worshipping climate the success of the Ketton Ox seemed assured for years to come, but in 1807 he dislocated a hip when alighting from his carriage and had to be shot. It was a sad end, but at least it spared him retirement followed by a series of ill-advised comeback tours.

At Masham it was warm and humid, the small, dark clouds rolling across the sky like a smoke signal warning of a coming ambush of patchy rain. We parked the pick-up down by the river and walked up the steep steps into the town. In the centre of the market square, against a backdrop of three-storey stone-built pubs and houses, were rows of wooden pens filled with sheep. This was pretty much what a livestock market must have been like in the days before purpose-built marts: a throng of people, the busy buzz of wrangling and chatter merging with the high bleating of gimmers and ewes, the bar-room odour of tobacco and beer and the astringent whiff of sheep, whose natural hair oil is lanolin, and who consequently smell like old gents freshly shaven.

In the aisles between the pens, judging was going on. Men in tweeds and official badges leaned on walking sticks, closed one eye, rolled their lips in, gripped their chins and nodded enigmatically; handlers wrestled with massive, purled Teeswater tups with macramé fringes smeared across their snouts, tugged at the halters of Oxford Down lambs with bodies as bulky as laundry baskets, or took brushes to the shagpile fleeces of curly-horned Dalesbreds.

Masham Sheep Fair had been started ten years before to raise money for famine relief, and has continued as a charitable event ever since. It runs for the whole weekend, with the second day devoted to continental and rare breeds, a fleece competition and a stock auction. Sheep fairs themselves are an old tradition. The one held at Penistone in South Yorkshire, home town of my old favourite, the Whitefaced Woodland, dates back to 1699. Sheep farming and shepherding were lonely occupations, and those engaged in them welcomed the chance to get together with others for a chat.

A friend of mine went on a walking holiday in the mountains of Sicily. He has a stressful job in London and just wanted to be on his own. His whole holiday was ruined by shepherds. He'd be striding along through some wondrous scenery, alone with his thoughts, when suddenly he'd hear from the hillside above him a croaking cry, and some old codger would come hurtling down the incline, jabbering wildly and waving his crook in the air. At first my friend was alarmed, fearing attempted murder, kidnap or some Mafia vendetta against him for a crime of which he was unaware. It turned out to be something far worse than any of these. Stuck out in the hills for months on end, the shepherds were desperate to talk to someone. They approached him with bounding steps, their mouths already running. My friend spoke little Italian and no Sicilian dialect at all. He tried to explain this to the shepherds, but they were indifferent to it. Night after lonely night, day after solitary day, the shepherds had been turning things over in their minds, working things out, making up jokes, coming to conclusions, and nothing as minor as complete incomprehension was going to prevent them from unburdening themselves. This ambush by shepherd blather happened to my friend at least three times a day. He tried hiding when he heard them coming, but they knew the landscape too well and always found him huddled behind a rock or bush. He tried running, but their big, spike-collared dogs rounded him up. As a last desperate measure he got out his Italian phrasebook and wrote the words I AM DEAF on a sheet of paper in large letters and hung it round his neck. It changed nothing. Many of the shepherds were illiterate, and those who could read simply shouted until he got a migraine. Eventually he gave up on the mountains and retreated to Palermo. Here, among the roar of engines, the beeping of scooters and the sporadic outbreaks of gunfire, he at last got some peace and quiet.

It was partly to prevent a similar situation developing in England that the fairs and markets were instituted. In Cumbria they have an added safety valve, the shepherds' meets. These are held in pubs at pre-arranged dates and times so that the sheep-farming community can get together for a guaranteed social evening. It must have been pretty dispiriting before the meets were invented, when you might walk all the way down from your isolated hill farm for your twice-yearly night out only to find the pub deserted and the whole village gone off to Blackpool for the illuminations.

The markets and shows remain a place for farmers to get together to exchange news and information and, although they will deny this vehemently, gossip. Despite their protests farmers are brilliant for gossip. The national press could save itself a fortune in wage bills by employing one Pennine farmer, who could do the job of ten investigative reporters and still have time left over to raise a flock of Herdwicks. Whenever you meet a farmer and ask him about some other farm you have driven past, giving him a location and a description, you can watch him as he thinks, sliding mentally across the countryside to locate it (farmers know farms like a librarian knows books). When he finds it he'll say, 'Aye, Bonnetscleugh, belongs to a feller named Parker.' Then, nine times out of ten, he'll add something like, 'Well, of course, his father was the one that carried on with the whipper-in's missus. Then one night when he was walking back from the pub, he was set upon by a mystery assailant, given a right hiding. They never fathomed who it was did it, but them as saw the wounds on his head say they were the shape of a hunting horn.' Then he'll pause for a moment and say, 'Not that you can believe everything you hear, like,' just to show you that he is above such tittle-tattle.

There was a large crowd of people in the square watching proceedings. Every once in a while a small child could be seen nervously approaching a pen and tentatively shoving fingers into the soft, spongy fleeces of the long-wool breeds. The sheep seemed oblivious to it all. Even the big-nostrilled Texel fat lambs, who had taken first prize, having been adjudged 'most suitable for the butcher' seemed unconcerned by the implications of their victory. But then sheep always do. They are the least expressive of animals. A tortoise is Marcel Marceau compared to a sheep. Maybe that's because sheep haven't got much to express.

Sheep graze for around ten hours a day. What they do the rest of the time is a mystery, though it is a safe bet that it doesn't encompass witty conversation or nuclear physics. The sheep's wild relatives are resourceful, cunning and brave, more than capable of living in the most hostile environment and beating off attacks by wolves. The domestic sheep, by contrast, is a nervous ninny with a death wish and what might politely be described as depressed mental capabilities. It is hard not to feel sorry for it. Bred first for its fleece and then for meat, the sheep has gradually grown bigger and hairier and whiter. And somewhere along the way it has lost its spirit and most of its brain. That, at least, is the usual theory.

Recently there has been a lot of discussion about the effects of sheep dip on farmers. Apparently, the formula of some sheep dip is similar to that of nerve gas and can cause short-term memory loss in those exposed to it. Most farmworkers drive as if they have forgotten there is a speed limit because they have. This information is particularly worrying for me as I live about fifty yards away from where the sheep are dipped, and apparently the formula of some sheep dip is similar to that of nerve gas and can cause short-term memory loss in those exposed to it, because apparently it has a formula similar to nerve gas. The old jokes are the best, aren't they? Anyway, if sheep dip has that effect on the farmers using it, what must it do to the sheep who are submerged in it? The possibility is that sheep are actually very intelligent and spend the fourteen hours a day they are not eating learning all kinds of things – the dates of battles, elementary book-keeping, the principles and practice of sewage-management – but the minute they hit that dip, bang! It's all gone. The law relating to sheep-dipping has recently changed and it is no longer compulsory. In the near future a sheep may well win *Mastermind* with a record score and no paaaah-ah-ses.

In the pens at the far side of the square were some Jacob's tups, heavy-shouldered, four-horned with distinctive goat-like eyes that looked suspiciously as if they might glow in the dark. There was once one of these in a field near our house. One day when I was walking the dog, who is insatiably nosy as all dogs are, he insisted on going and taking a closer look at the ram, which was standing next to the gate. When we got within a couple of yards of him, the Jacob's tup rocked back slightly on his heels then catapulted forward and butted the gate. It vibrated with a noise like a Jew's harp. The dog suddenly noticed a particularly interesting smell on the other side of the road and I insisted on accompanying him to investigate it. The ram shook his head slightly as if a gnat had just landed in his ear and went back to munching grass.

Jacob's sheep were brought to England as an ornamental parkland breed in the late 1800s. They came from Spain and Portugal, but as their name implies they have some tenuous link to ancient Israel. In the Bible Jacob tended the flock of Laban for seven years to win the hand of Rachel. During that time he got to spend many nights in the hills, alone except for the flock, and used these solitary hours to dream up some fairly strange ideas about sheep breeding. The Israelites were anxious to breed white sheep, because white wool was easier to dye than the dark brown wool which came from most early sheep (the brindle-coloured Soay is a modern equivalent). Jacob looked around and saw that the sheep were the same colour as the earth. Making a sideways mental leap, he decided that the way to create a white flock was to ensure that when the lambs were conceived their mother was looking, not at the brown ground, but at something white. So he ordered that the mating pens be hung around with bedsheets when the tup was put to the ewes. Either Jacob's theory was wrong, or the Israelite laundry service was somewhat lackadaisical: Jacob's sheep are white with dark spots.

The Israelites were very keen on animal husbandry. The Song of Solomon, the great love poem of the Old Testament, is full of livestock similes. The mistress has teeth as white as 'sheep that are even shorn, which came up from the washing'; her hair is compared to a flock of goats and her breasts to a pair of roe deer. I find this latter comparison a bit disquieting. Every time I think of it I imagine Solomon being taken aside by one of his mates: 'Aye, she's a canny enough lass, Your Majesty, but just watch you don't take an eye out on them antlers.'

Sheep continued to be an integral part of farming throughout the next few thousand years. They were brought to Britain by

Neolithic man, improved by the Celts and the Romans and added to by the Vikings, but it was during the Middle Ages that they established themselves as arguably the most important animal in English history.

At Bellingham there were some Ryeland sheep. Impossibly chunky with a heavy, curled fleece, they looked as if they had been invented by Walt Disney. They had fleece on practically every part of their bodies. You could have knitted a matinee jacket out of the wool from one ear. Each cheek would have yielded a balaclava. The Ryeland was the foundation of the Cotswold wool industry. The fleece was known as Leominster ore, one of the fluffy cornerstones on which the modern British economy was built. Another came from the back and sides of an ancestor of the rope-coated Teeswaters and Wensleydales that were now being lugged before the judges in the marketplace at Masham. The Longwool was the specialist breed farmed by Cistercian monks at nearby Jervaulx and Fountains Abbey. It was a huge sheep with a fleece of tightly wound cream-coloured dreadlocks, the hair swishing across its eyes, giving it the stoic, blinded look of Oliver Hardy after a custard pie has hit him in the mug. The Longwool and the Ryeland were bred strictly for their fleeces. They produced little if any edible meat and were never milked because that would have affected the quality of the wool. Between them this unlikely pair sparked a financial revolution far greater than any produced by politicians or radical economists.

In the fourteenth century a combination of depopulation caused by the Black Death, the reduced labour needed for ranch-style sheep farming and the rising price of wool throughout Europe resulted in the English countryside being overrun by sheep. The fifteen Cistercian monasteries in Yorkshire alone produced 200,000 fleeces annually, while a 1341 Act of Parliament granting the monarch a levy of 30,000 sacks of wool a year would take roughly seven million sheep to fulfil, indicating that the ovine population of England at this time must have been huge, perhaps greater than the human population is today. The financial benefits for the nation were enormous, too. The burgeoning wool trade almost single-handedly created a modern market economy, swelled the nobility, founded the middle class and transformed subsistence farmers into wealthy gentlemen. It is no coincidence that to this day the Lord Chancellor sits on a woolsack.

After lunch Catherine said she wanted to go and see the exhibition of weaving. I wasn't so keen. I had seen a lot of weaving that summer and it had rather lost its thrill for me. At practically every show you went to there was a weaver, and they were dedicated evangelists for their trade. Quite often they seemed to turn up more or less unannounced and just set up alongside their cars as a kind of busking crafts-person. Nothing put them off. You would see them cheerfully carding and spinning even when the rain was splatting across their heads with a noise like bursting bladder-wrack. At one show, the weaver was an old man with a shiny pink pate and flowing white whiskers. He sat hunched over, busily twirling his wheel, so that from a distance it looked as if he were spinning his own beard. I thought at first it must be something he had sent away for from the back pages of a Sunday newspaper ('Turn unwanted facial hair into instant cash! Those unfashionable sideburns could soon be an attractive pair of socks with Spin-o-Stubble. It's fun for all the family!') but it turned out just to be an optical illusion.

Outside the building housing the weaving exhibition I stood and listened to the brass band playing. A man came up and started talking to me about my dog. He said he had a Jack Russell himself, and he was having a bit of trouble with it. 'We used to live out here, you see. Well, he would have a dart at any dog he met. Now, out here that wasn't such a problem, because we didn't meet that many dogs. Then me and our lass moved to Leeds. Now I'm out walking him in the park every day and there's masses of other dogs. I thought he'd calm down when he got into the swing of it, but he's carried on just the same. Last week I sat him down. I said, "Listen, pal, this is a big city. There's thousands of other dogs here. You've got to calm down. Go on the way you're doing, and you'll wear yourself to a stump." Did he listen? Did he buggery. First thing next morning he's wading into a shi-tzu. He'll have a heart attack before he's five the rate he's going. What can you do, though, eh? You can warn them, but if they won't take any notice, well…'

Later on we drove over to the Smallholders Show at the Great Yorkshire Showground in Harrogate. Smallholders were making something of a comeback in the English countryside. There was more interest now in how food was produced; specialist old breeds, bred for flavour rather than size, and leanness were starting to become popular again. British cheese-making had finally recovered from the crushing effects of wartime central-isation and a series of scares and exposés had led many to the conclusion that traditional farming methods were healthy and humane rather than merely backward.

The smallholders were business people, but there was also something of the hobbyist about them. Diversification was their buzzword. Inside the main hall there were ostrich chicks, mules, handbooks about llama farming and water-buffalo rearing, cages filled with what looked like clockwork powder puffs, but which turned out to be quail; there were society stands for Icelandic sheep and Boer goats, the latter extolling the virtue of goat meat in a country where it had once been disparagingly nicknamed 'Welsh venison', and in a pen lodged between some tiny North Ronaldsay sheep (the only breed in the world that can survive on a diet of seaweed – now doesn't that make you proud to be British?) and a couple of Aberdeen Angus were a pair of Oxfordshire sandy and black pigs. This is a controversial breed. At first they were designated as a rare breed by the Rare Breeds Survival Trust, but later it was decided that actually, they weren't a breed at all but the mongrel offspring of Tam-worths and Saddle-backs, so now they had been taken off the list and downgraded. I thought they looked rather fine. They had the Tamworth's ginger coat, but were spotted with dark flesh patches and tottered on stiletto-heeled trotters.

The pig is one of those animals that seems to divide society. You either like pigs or you hate them. Dr Johnson was very fond of pigs. He believed they could attain higher educational and moral standards if only mankind would let them live for a while longer and paid better attention to their upbringing. Johnson may well have been right, though it has to be said that some of his other ideas on animal life were less sound. He once explained the disappearance of swallows during the winter by saying that in autumn flocks of them formed themselves into a tight ball and then hibernated in the mud at the bottom of rivers. Even the cleverest people get it wrong sometimes.

Charles Lamb, on the other hand, was a feverish opponent of pigs. He advocated eating them as young as possible. If you didn't, he ranted, they would only grow to gross adulthood and spend their days in gluttony while 'wallowing in all filthy conversation'. The image of pigs lounging around cracking dirty jokes is indeed an unappealing one, but the sad fact of Lamb's argument is that it could equally have been advanced as a justification for cannibalism – and probably was in Papua New Guinea.

The pig used to be one of the key animals at agricultural shows. The only animal ever to challenge seriously the status of the Ketton Ox as Victorian England's farm animal superstar supreme was a pig, the illustrious Yorkshire Hog. Captured on canvas by Pollard in 1809, this mighty lop-eared and piebald juggernaut weighed 1,344lbs, was almost 10ft long and measured 12½ hands at the shoulder. It's little wonder that the man in the top hat standing beside the hog looks so tiny – and so nervous. The Yorkshire Hog was exhibited all over the country. Posters advertised his appearance at inn yards and auction marts with all the gusto reserved for a visiting celebrity: 'Positively the last week! Great novelty!! Which may be see ALIVE!! A wonderful large pig. Admission 2d. Children and schools 1d.'

The success of the Yorkshire Hog ensured that the sight of the pig handlers manoeuvring jowly sows about the ring by tapping their forelegs with brightly painted pig bats became a favourite with the crowds at early shows. Those who liked their entertainment more lively preferred to wait for the boars. Boars are more headstrong than sows, and prone to making sudden bursts for freedom. Furthermore, the glimpse or whiff of another boar is likely to produce a fit of uncontrollable rage. In their wild state pigs operate in a strict hierarchy. The lead boar is the only one who serves the females. You get to be lead boar by battering the current incumbent into submission. Like the Beastie Boys, the porcine male has to fight for his right to party. As the boar weighs the same as a fully laden security van it is really not a good idea to have him charging about the place in a jealous fury. Thankfully, pig handlers have a secret weapon at their disposal – the boar board. The boar board is a length of plywood, about six inches wide by three feet long. It is not very thick. This may not seem like the ideal implement with which to halt the rush of the farmyard equivalent of a runaway steamroller, but that is to misread the psychology of the boar. Originally a woodland animal, the pig has a fixed sense of the nature of objects (and how to react to them): if you can see through it, it must be a bush (smash through it); if you can't see through it, it must be a tree (go round it). By placing the boar board in front of the pig's eyes, you convince him that he is facing an impenetrable line of tree trunks and stop him dead in his tracks. A reliable source has told me that a sheet of black sugar paper will stop a boar more certainly than an electric fence, though it should be noted that when called on to give a practical demonstration he pleaded a prior engagement.

We bought a couple of delicious rump steaks from a farmer who raised the black, short-legged Dexter cattle, and some great sheep's milk ice-cream from a company who kept bulbous-uddered Frieslands. There was more to see, but it was half-past four and Betty's Tea Room wouldn't be open for that much longer.

19

• The Final Curtain •

The Alwinton Border Shepherds' Show

In the Tyne Valley you could hear the west wind coming. On Friday night, as I lay in bed in the dark, a first insistent whisper of distant treetops announced its impending arrival. It built in a rush, scuttling across slates, crashing through undergrowth, picking off the bin lids and spinning them across the driveway, kicking over milk bottles and rattling the doors of the sheds. It keened and wailed around the house to the accompaniment of the humming aerial cables for an hour, then it left eastwards, the clatter and whirr growing ever fainter like a departing train, until, at last, it was gone.

Next morning the sky was clear, the day bright, but the wind's chilly trail still lay in the valley. We drove up over the high, white grasslands through Otterburn and Elsdon and down into copsed and brackened Coquetdale. The sun was out, but, as if exhausted by his summer's work, could hardly raise himself above the blanketfolds of the hills. The rowans were heavy with fruit and the digital leaves of the horse chestnuts, now turned pale and translucent, hung as limply as the hand of a dying romantic poet, the conkers scattered across the floor like discarded vials of laudanum. Autumn was here, and the air seemed heavier; viscous with decay. Lumpy groups of sheep stood stern-faced as if they had caught a first whiff of the hardships to come; among the hawthorn hedges blackbirds gorged themselves like friars before a fast, while in the back of the car the dog yawned and wound himself into a shaggy ball.

A steady stream of traffic was heading up the winding road to Alwinton. The Border Shepherds' Show is a small event, but it is held in one of the most beautiful places in the north, on the springy watermeadows of the Coquet and the Alwin, flanked by the Cheviot Hills. And it is the final show of the season, a last chance to breathe in the smells of summer.

On the showground the Highland hoover-gargle of the Rothbury Pipe Band blended with the thumping music of a small fair and the occasional clink of clashing quoits. Border terriers were fizzing at one another so that the dog showring sounded like a glass of Alka-Seltzer and trail hounds in their pick-up trucks wowled and yelped. Away in one corner, a porky-jowled Cheviot tup loftily surveyed the scene, proud and statesmanlike: a monarch watching his people at play. Coquetdale and the Cheviot Hills are sheep country. It was near here that the Culley brothers had put into practice the selective-breeding techniques they had learned from Robert Bakewell and produced the Border Leicester, with its Roman nose and jack-rabbit ears and, later, the heavy-faced and aristocratic Cheviot.

These new breeds, hardy yet productive, transformed the hill country of the north, just as they would later, and more painfully, transform the Scottish Highlands. But they were not the only livestock that lived in the uplands of Northumberland. In the Cheviots there were also feral herds of the descendants of the hill livestock the new sheep had replaced, sabre-horned goats. These goats had for hundreds of years been the only domesticated livestock tough and resourceful enough to survive the winter climate. They had been kept for meat and milk and their hides had been sent down to London to be made into parchment and the so-called 'Spanish' leather. Discarded by their owners, the goats didn't panic – they simply went back to nature. Given what we know about goats, it probably actually came as a bit of a relief. Certainly it caused them no problems. Some domestic animals are like that: dogs, for instance, can go back to fending for themselves quite easily, despite thousands of years of breeding and Bonios. You could put a pack of Yorkshire terriers down in the Alaskan tundra and within a week they'd be living contentedly in caves and bringing down elderly caribou. A herd of cows couldn't hack it, though. And you're more likely to find a feral accountant than a feral sheep.

In the horticulture tent there were leeks. Leeks are big in the north-east, in all senses of the word. They fall into two categories: blanch and pot. Blanch are judged on length, pot on girth, but both lose 'inches' for physical imperfections. They are entered individually or in 'stands' of three. The fanatical leek-grower's season starts in midwinter, when every other gardener is indoors putting his feet up and flicking through seed catalogues. His prize specimens are in special beds, raised with planking, drip-fed with brown ale, dried blood and whatever other nutritious concoction his imagination can come up with. He is ever vigilant against the cruel whim of Mother Nature, who might at any moment send an eel worm boring through a pale and fleshy barrel, or dispatch an early frost to bleach the dangling pennants of the leaves. By September he is in a frenzy, worried by the weather, insects and the dire threat of nobbling by his rivals. Leek-growing in the north-east is steeped in legends about men who camp out at night to protect their leeks from attack, of devious and cunning adversaries who overcome all obstacles placed in their path to fatally damage an opponent's prize pot with a well-aimed pellet from a high-powered air rifle.

Not everyone takes it quite so seriously. The last leek show I had been to was a fortnight before, in a prefabricated concrete garage behind a pub. A member of the local leek club was sitting in a vinyl chair at the door, collecting the 20p entrance fee and sipping a pint. Inside there were flowers, carrots, beans, cabbages. The animal-made-from-vegetables competition had been won by a Loch Ness monster made from bananas which undulated above a tinfoil lake. The main business was down one side, where there were leeks as thick as a thigh, with tops curling like a cockerel's tail feathers and albino beards of roots. An old man wandered in and began inspecting the leeks. 'Are these here yours, Bob?' he asked the man at the entrance, and turned to Catherine and me and winked. He wore a flat cap. Beneath it a face crazy-paved with wrinkles, skin as tough as crows' knees.

'Aye, why?' Bob said, rising from his chair as if anticipating trouble.

'They're very good,' the old man said. 'Very impressive. A nice display.'

'Thanks,' said Bob, suspicious rather than grateful.

'Aye, fine indeed,' the old man went on. 'Mind, if I'd known there was a class for spring onions, I'd have entered some of mine.'

Bob smiled resignedly and shook his head. 'They're not spring onions, they're leeks.'

'Leeks?' the old man squawked. 'Wey, these aren't leeks, Bob.' He winked at us again. 'They're drips.'

'Oh, aye,' Bob said, smiling now, enjoying the double act, the crack, 'and what would a Mackem like you know about it, anyway?'

A Mackem is someone from County Durham. The old man feigned disgruntlement. 'A Mackem like me? I'll tell you something, lad. Mackems like me were growing prize leeks when you lot were still wandering round in checkered skirts with handbags dangling off the front of them.' He turned to Catherine and me. 'Geordies. They're just Scotsmen with their brains bashed out, you know.' He returned his attention to Bob. 'The greatest leek-growers in the world come from Durham.'

Bob nodded. 'Aye, that's true, right enough. And you know why, don't you?'

'Why?'

'Because they've got their own inexhaustible supply of horseshit – you!'

He spun round and went back to his chair. Every once in a

while you'd hear a strange hiss-hissing noise and see his shoulders bouncing up and down.

I walked along the tables of exhibits at Alwinton: parsnips, celery, shallots (French pear-shaped), carrots (stump), onion sets (flat). One of the good things about the shows being held in summer and autumn was that it meant I didn't have to look at any Brussels sprouts. I hate Brussels sprouts. Brussels sprouts were the bane of my childhood.

My dad was different; he loved Brussels sprouts. He is from a generation who remember the days when vegetables were still seasonal. You couldn't just go out and buy strawberries in December in those days. If it wasn't the season you couldn't get them, so the most unlikely things had novelty value. The season for Brussels sprouts was very short and it came around Christmas, so to my dad I think they took on a sort of yuletide glamour. He associated them with tangerines and model aeroplanes and chestnuts roasting on an open fire. In his mind the Brussels sprout was linked with festivities and holidays and presents. In mine it was synonomous with misery and Subbuteo table football.

My dad still loved Brussels sprouts when the seasonal element had long gone. Now you could get them frozen and have them seven days a week if you wanted. And he did. For a couple of years when I was at primary school, we seemed to have Brussels sprouts with every meal. If I'd come down in the morning and found my dad tucking into a bowl of them with with milk and sugar I wouldn't have been at all surprised.

My parents were very indulgent of my faddish childhood eating habits. They didn't demur when I insisted on having pancakes with grated cheese for breakfast, or demanded that they surround any meat that was placed on the table with cereal boxes so that I couldn't see it. They didn't mind that I refused to eat mashed potato or custard because it might have lumps in it; they never complained when I made them dissect my sausages and inspect them for gristle before bringing them to the table. Brussels sprouts were different, though. Brussels sprouts were good for me. 'They'll put colour in your cheeks!' my mum would say. And I'd say, 'Who wants green cheeks?' It did no good.

Eventually an unspoken compromise on the consumption of Brussels sprouts was reached. It was agreed that I should only ever be made to eat four at any one sitting. This would have been fine, except that I could not manage even that many. Three was my maximum. Yes, three were all right. Three went down with no problem. The fourth one was a different matter. It always made me gag. There was something weird about it. It was just an ordinary Brussels sprout like the other three until I put it in my mouth. Then it swelled up like some sort of irate, slimy, pulsating toad. It was suddenly the size of a cannonball. There was just no way it would go down my throat. I'd have swallowed an anaconda more easily.

I tried telling my parents about this bizarre phenomenon, but they were unimpressed. They thought I was making it up. They said: 'Don't be silly. It's good for you. It's got iron in it.' And I said, 'So has a magnet. You don't make me eat that.' But argument was futile.

Instead I found another way round the problem. I'd wait till my parents weren't looking and then I'd sneak the fourth Brussels sprout off my plate and into my pocket. After tea I'd go upstairs and stuff it under the chest of drawers in my bedroom. I did this for quite a while. I was a child, you see – I had no sense of consequence. The smell in my room after a few weeks of this must have been horrendous. I don't know what my mum and dad made of it. Perhaps they just thought I'd reached adolescence early or something.

After I stuck the Brussels sprouts under my chest of drawers I forgot about them. Then a friend would come round and we'd be playing Subbuteo on the floor and some player, probably Emlyn Hughes, would blast the ball miles wide of the post and it would bounce off and disappear beneath the chest of drawers. I'd put the side of my head down on the carpet and look into the darkness and I'd see the ball, way over in a distant corner. I'd roll up my sleeve to make my arm skinnier and reach in for it, stretching. I'd stretch as far as I could and eventually I'd get my fingers over the ball and grab it. And a furry, rotten Brussels sprout would explode green slime all over my hand. I've never been able to look at one since without feeling queasy. Even the sight of Emlyn Hughes makes me feel slightly sick, but that's probably more understandable.

I wandered about the show for a bit, noting how the skin bunches round a basset hound's ankles as if it is wearing a pair of too-tight shoes, trying to take an interest in the dressed walking sticks, wondering briefly what the difference was between a sportman's stick, half-head and a natural-grown thumb stick, and standing watching the tug-of-war. But I was listless and my heart wasn't really in it. A feeling of melancholy hung over me.

For the previous six months I had wandered about the north, eating blueberry frozen yoghurts, buying raffle tickets and home-made rhubarb jam and ginger biscuits; sitting in marquees and pavilions with cups of tea and plates piled high with floury baps and raspberry buns; I had smirked at sooty fawn Lops, wrinkled my nose at Sheltie guinea pigs, patted Dexter cattle who were no bigger than Newfoundlands, sniffed Angora goats, smelled ferrets and sneered at sheep. This was the last outing. All told, I had been to twenty-five shows and fairs and numerous other fêtes and field days, and in all that time and all that travelling I hadn't managed to work out a way to fit in the information that the counterweights in grandfather clocks were once hung from cord made from the insides of a bull's testicles. No wonder I felt sad.

We drove over to Holystone and walked the dog in the woods. The day was fading as we drove home and I began to feel more cheerful. Every season brings advantages. Along the road through Bellingham the lights were going on in the houses and curtains were being drawn. The heavy feast of summer was over, and now it was time for a nap.

· Index ·